Health Education Ideas and Activities

24 Dimensions of Wellness for Adolescents

ROGER F. PUZA

Human Kinetics

ISBN-10: 0-7360-5982-2
ISBN-13: 978-0-7360-5982-4

The Web addresses cited in this text were current as of August 10, 2007, unless otherwise noted.

Credits for photos used on the CD-ROM correspond to the interior photo credits found in the book.

Acquisitions Editor: Bonnie Pettifor-Vreeman; **Developmental Editor:** Ragen E. Sanner; **Assistant Editor:** Anne Rumery; **Special Projects Editors:** Jeff King and Anne Cole; **Copyeditor:** Bob Replinger; **Proofreader:** Kathy Bennett; **Permission Manager:** Carly Breeding; **Graphic Designer:** Robert Reuther; **Graphic Artist:** Kathleen Boudreau-Fuoss; **Photo Manager:** Laura Fitch; **Photo Office Assistant:** Jason Allen; **Cover Designer:** Keith Blomberg; **Photographer (cover):** © Photodisc; **Photographer (interior):** © Getty Images (page 167), © Human Kinetics (pages 43, 55, 69, 85, 127, and 157), © Image Source (pages 7 and 135), and © Photodisc pages 1, 23, 33, 61, 75, 95, 103, 111, 115, 149, 177, 193, 203, 217, and 227); **Art Manager:** Kelly Hendren; **Associate Art Manager:** Alan L. Wilborn; **Illustrator:** Art on handouts 2.3, 2.7 (activities 1 and 2), 2.18, 2.20, 3.8, 5.6, 5.12, 5.13, 16.6, 16.9, and 19.11 by Keri Evans; **Printer:** Sheridan Books

Printed in the United States of America 10 9 8 7 6 5 4 3 2 1

Human Kinetics
Web site: www.HumanKinetics.com

United States: Human Kinetics
P.O. Box 5076, Champaign, IL 61825-5076
800-747-4457
e-mail: humank@hkusa.com

Canada: Human Kinetics
475 Devonshire Road Unit 100, Windsor, ON N8Y 2L5
800-465-7301 (in Canada only)
e-mail: orders@hkcanada.com

Europe: Human Kinetics
107 Bradford Road, Stanningley, Leeds LS28 6AT, United Kingdom
+44 (0) 113 255 5665
e-mail: hk@hkeurope.com

Australia: Human Kinetics
57A Price Avenue, Lower Mitcham, South Australia 5062
08 8372 0999
e-mail: info@hkaustralia.com

New Zealand: Human Kinetics
Division of Sports Distributors NZ Ltd.
P.O. Box 300 226 Albany, North Shore City, Auckland
0064 9 448 1207
e-mail: info@humankinetics.co.nz

Contents

Lesson Finder

(continued)

(continued)

(continued)

(continued)

How to Use This Book and CD-ROM

The purpose of *Health Education Ideas and Activities: 24 Dimensions of Wellness for Adolescents* and the accompanying CD-ROM is to act as a companion to be used alongside health education programs that are already in place. It provides instructors with ideas that can help spark in-class conversation, as well as student self-awareness, about a wide range of health topics. The forms on the CD-ROM will help the teacher and students to do this, as well as review and test students on information learned in class.

The book's chapters are divided into lessons, though the forms can be used in any way that works best for the instructors. The lessons of this book are broken into the following sections:

- Objective—What will be accomplished by using this lesson idea and the accompanying handouts from the CD-ROM.
- National Standards—A list of the potential NASPE standards that the lesson allows you to address.
- Introduction—A quick way to start the conversation flowing and get students thinking about the topic at hand.
- Handouts—A list of answers for the handouts, as well as some discussion on more open-ended topics or instruction on certain games and activities. Also, this is a place to find explanations for true and false answers that are "false."
- Closure—A way to help students synthesize what they discussed and learned while completing the handouts for that lesson.

The CD-ROM that accompanies this book is where you should go to get all of the handouts. Follow the instructions found in the back of the book to best access the files. Once you have them open, you can print them out on 8.5 x 11 paper to use in your class. You will notice in each lesson in the book that the handout section has little thumbnails next to each handout's answers and discussions. This is so that you can get a look at what the handouts are before you go to find them on the CD-ROM. There is also a list of each lesson's available handouts in the Lesson Finder, on page iv.

It is not necessary to follow the lesson order or even the order of the book. What is necessary is to help students learn about these important mental, physical, emotional, and social health issues so that they are able to make healthy choices throughout their lives. Hopefully, the handouts and ideas presented in this book will get the s tudents thinking about their lives and how they can better maintain a healthy lifestyle.

1

Happiness

YOU ARE ABOUT AS HAPPY AS YOU MAKE UP YOUR MIND TO BE.

Abraham Lincoln

Lesson Finder

The Science of Happiness

OBJECTIVE

Students will be able to list some key factors related to happiness from a general discussion on the science and chemistry of pleasure hormones.

NATIONAL STANDARDS

- #1 Health Promotion
- #7 Healthy Behaviors
- #4 Communication

INTRODUCTION

One of the most interesting questions in life is, What does a person need to be happy and blissful in life? By the end of this unit you will be better able to answer this question after analyzing all the current data concerning happiness. What is more important than being happy? Maybe nothing!

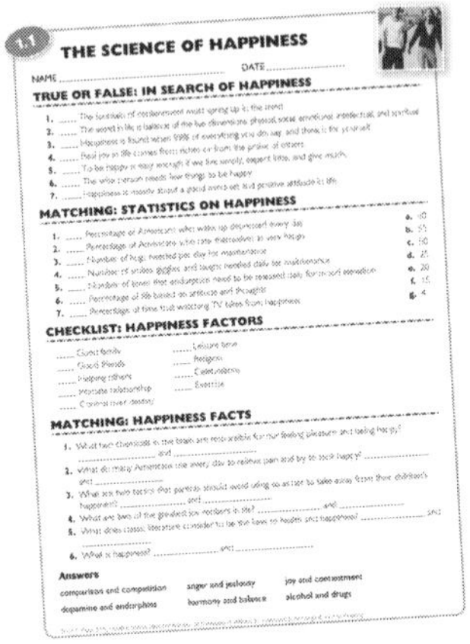
THE SCIENCE OF HAPPINESS

TRUE OR FALSE: IN SEARCH OF HAPPINESS

MATCHING: STATISTICS ON HAPPINESS

CHECKLIST: HAPPINESS FACTORS

MATCHING: HAPPINESS FACTS

Answers

comparison and competition — anger and jealousy — joy and contentment

dopamine and endorphins — harmony and balance — alcohol and drugs

1.1

HANDOUT 1.1

True or False: In Search of Happiness

1. true
2. true
3. false—Happiness is most often found when you spend time helping others.
4. false—Real joy doesn't come from things; it comes from within and helping others.
5. true
6. true
7. true

Matching: Statistics on Happiness

1. c
2. b
3. g
4. e
5. f
6. a
7. d

Happiness Factors Discussion

Have a discussion about the nine major factors that contribute to happiness as described in the American psychology report found in the *Time* cover article of 2005.

Matching: Happiness Facts

1. dopamine and endorphins
2. alcohol and drugs
3. comparison and competition
4. anger and jealousy
5. harmony and balance
6. joy and contentment

HANDOUT 1.2

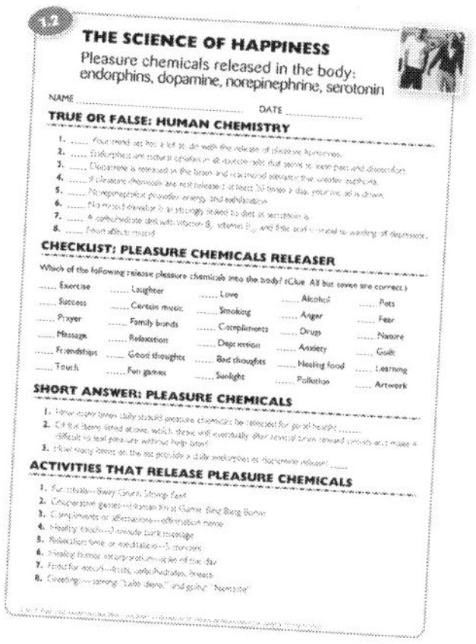
THE SCIENCE OF HAPPINESS
Pleasure chemicals released in the body: endorphins, dopamine, norepinephrine, serotonin
NAME DATE
TRUE OR FALSE: HUMAN CHEMISTRY
CHECKLIST: PLEASURE CHEMICALS RELEASER
SHORT ANSWER: PLEASURE CHEMICALS
ACTIVITIES THAT RELEASE PLEASURE CHEMICALS

1.2

True or False: Human Chemistry

All true! These are interesting facts about brain chemistry and happiness.

Checklist: Pleasure Chemicals Releasers

All but seven are beneficial. Those that do not release pleasure chemicals are fear, anxiety, guilt, bad thoughts, pollution, anger, and depression.

Short Answer: Pleasure Chemicals

1. 20 times
2. tobacco, alcohol, and drugs
3. poll of students' opinions

Activities That Release Pleasure Chemicals

1. Fun rituals
    - Sway-Grunt—From your cadence, students sway right with their bodies and arms, then sway left, then sway right again, and finally bring their arms down with a grunt.
    - Stomp Feet—On key word, students stomp feet with excitement
2. Cooperative games—Activities vary according to age.
    - Human Knot Game—Six to nine participants get in a circle and reach across to grab the hand of any person who is not next to them. They then unravel the knot into a big circle.
    - Bing Bang Boom—This cooperative quick-thinking activity works with groups of three doing imitations of animals. The game produces plenty of laughs. A group of 10 to 15 students forms a circle. One person is in the middle. The teacher starts there. The middle person points with an arm out straight at a specific person and says an animal name. The person targeted and each person beside him or her depict the animal as quickly as possible while the middle person says, "Bing bang boom . . . bing bang boom!" very fast. The group of three have to depict the animal correctly before the middle person completes the bing bang boom statements. If the group of three makes an error or isn't fast enough, one of them goes to the middle. Continue playing until everyone has been part of the action or until the students seem bored. Base the number of animals on the makeup of your students. Here are a few examples:
        - Cow—The targeted person puts his hands out with his thumbs down (udders), and the partners grab his thumbs and milk them by pulling down.
        - Lobster—The targeted person puts her arms up like the feelers of the lobster, and the partners clap their straight arms out like the claws, close to the body to look like a lobster.
        - Elephant—The targeted person puts his two arms out from his nose to be the trunk of the elephant. The two partners each form a huge ear by holding their arms in a circle formation by the elephant's head.
        - Frog—The targeted person crouches down halfway with her hands on her knees (frog look). The two partners put their closer arms on the frog's shoulder and kick out their outside legs to resemble a frog's kick.
3. Compliments or affirmations
    - Affirmation name—Each student picks a positive adjective and introduces him- or herself to other students by saying, "I am . . . honest," or awesome, or funny, or

positive, or some other affirmation. Each students meets several other students by using the new affirmation.

4. Healthy touch—3-minute back massage—Students who are uneasy about touching other students or about being touched by other students can perform a series of shoulder rolls and shrugs, and stretch their arms to the ceiling. Handheld massagers are another option.
5. Relaxation time or meditation—Students sit or lie comfortably for 3 to 5 minutes with their eyes closed in a quiet atmosphere, focusing on a pleasant mental thought.
6. Healing humor incorporation—Tell a joke of the day. See *Encyclopedia of Good Clean Jokes* for reference.
7. Food for mood—Fruits, carbohydrates, breads (nutritional snacks brought in by students for extra credit).
8. Greetings—Find your own to use at the beginning of class. I use "laba diena," a Lithuanian term that means "good day." I say it first, and the students say it back. At the end of class I say, "Namaste," which means "I am at peace with myself and you." The students then say it back to me.

CLOSURE

This information will help you understand the current data on happiness according to psychologists in the United States and may help you decide what you need to be happy in life. Happiness seems to be based on mind-set and the release of pleasure hormones from activities that make you feel good inside.

Happiness Is an Inside Job

OBJECTIVE

Students will evaluate their personal happiness from two separate checklists on happiness factors.

NATIONAL STANDARDS

- #7 Healthy Behaviors
- #5 Decision Making

INTRODUCTION

The book *Happiness Is an Inside Job* by John Powell describes 10 practices that improve overall happiness. The two checklists in this handout summarize the book. The first checklist is to get you to realize how you are doing on the 10 key happiness principles. The second checklist helps you examine how many boosters you practice on a daily basis. Both are interesting and thought-provoking.

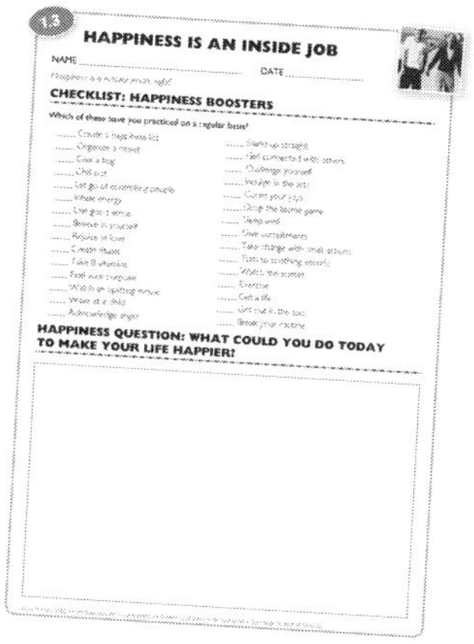

1.3

HANDOUT 1.3

Checklist: Happiness Boosters

This self-evaluation has no right or wrong answers. The more passions and desires that a person has, the more ways he or she has of being happy.

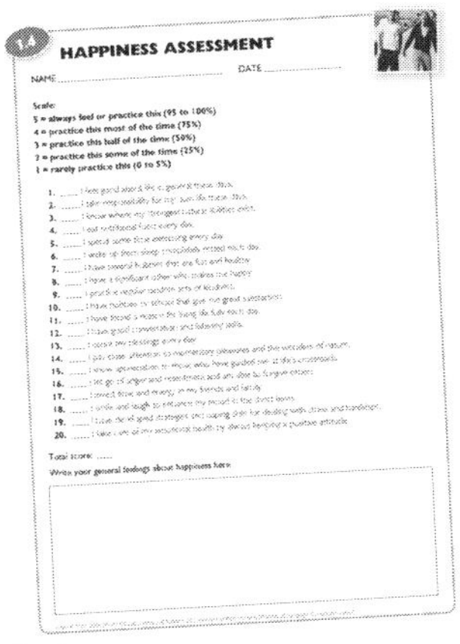

1.4

HANDOUT 1.4

Happiness Assessment

The total score indicates the student's general level of happiness—the higher the score, the greater the student's chance for happiness.

CLOSURE

The theory behind any checklist activity is to stimulate you to make positive changes that may lead to overall happiness.

Guidelines to Happiness

OBJECTIVE

Students will be able to list the seven top guidelines that would help ensure their personal happiness.

NATIONAL STANDARDS

- #3 Information and Services
- #5 Decision Making

INTRODUCTION

This sheet is an assignment to be handed in today. After spending the last few days studying what researchers say are the factors most related to happiness, you are now to write down which guidelines you think would be most beneficial in making you happy most of the time.

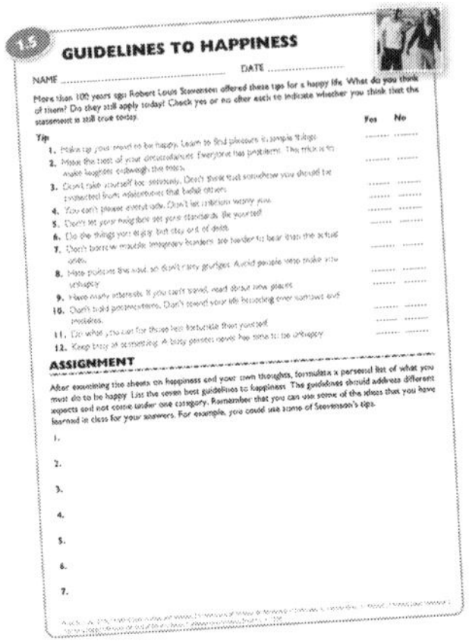

1.5

HANDOUT 1.5

CLOSURE

If it is true that most people ultimately seek the goal of happiness in life, you should have had a meaningful week of self-examination. Many factors contribute to finding daily happiness. This study may cause you to change some aspect of your life to boost your level of happiness.

2

Brain Power

> GREAT SPIRITS HAVE ALWAYS ENCOUNTERED VIOLENT OPPOSITION FROM MEDIOCRE MINDS.
>
> **Albert Einstein**

Lesson Finder

The Brain and Learning

OBJECTIVE

Students will learn how to make their brains work better through a classroom discussion about the brain and neurotransmission boosters.

NATIONAL STANDARDS

- #1 Health Promotion
- #4 Communication

INTRODUCTION

You will be able to answer these questions after analyzing the facts on learning and the brain.

- How much do you know about the brain and learning?
- How would you like to learn faster and more easily?
- How would you like to learn a technique that results in almost perfect recall after learning something just once?
- What are some neurotransmission boosters and some inhibitors?

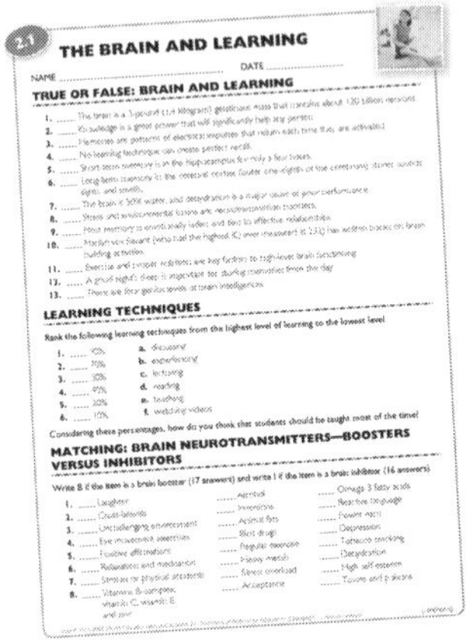
THE BRAIN AND LEARNING

TRUE OR FALSE: BRAIN AND LEARNING

LEARNING TECHNIQUES

MATCHING: BRAIN NEUROTRANSMITTERS—BOOSTERS VERSUS INHIBITORS

2.1

HANDOUT 2.1

True or False: Brain and Learning

1. true
2. true
3. true
4. false—A seven-step memory technique permits almost perfect recall.
5. false—Short-term memory persists for only a few minutes.
6. true
7. false—The brain is 80% water.
8. false—Stress and toxins are neurotransmitter inhibitors.
9. true
10. true
11. true
12. true
13. false—The research of Howard Gardner says that there are eight brain intelligences.

Learning Techniques

1. e	**4.** f
2. b	**5.** c
3. a	**6.** d

Matching: Neurotransmitters—Boosters Versus Inhibitors

1. B-I-B
2. B-B-I
3. I-I-B
4. B-I-I
5. B-B-I
6. B-I-I
7. I-I-B
8. B-B-I
9. B-I-B
10. B-B-B
11. I-I-I

CLOSURE

Remember that the brain has great potential. People can develop many skills to improve memory, increase recall, and enhance creativity. On the other hand, some personal habits hinder learning and cause frustration and disappointment. People need to realize that by incorporating brain boosters, they can increase brain performance.

Brain Facts

OBJECTIVE

Students will learn many facts about the human brain from class discussion.

NATIONAL STANDARDS

- #1 Health Promotion
- #4 Communication

INTRODUCTION

With this handout, you will learn some facts about the brain that will help you understand its power. You will also be able to match the 10 parts of the brain to their functions.

BRAIN FACTS
MATCHING: BRAIN FACTS
MATCHING: BRAIN VOCABULARY

2.2

HANDOUT 2.2

Matching: Brain Facts

1. m	**11.** l
2. f	**12.** o
3. h	**13.** d
4. c	**14.** g
5. q	**15.** j
6. e	**16.** r
7. b	**17.** a
8. k	**18.** n
9. i	**19.** p
10. s	**20.** t

Matching: Brain Vocabulary

1. g	**6.** d
2. j	**7.** e
3. f	**8.** h
4. a	**9.** c
5. b	**10.** i

CLOSURE

We can benefit from understanding how the brain works and what we can do to make it work better for us.

Brain Anatomy: Perfect Recall Lesson

OBJECTIVE

Students will practice the seven-step perfect recall format while learning the 10 major parts of the brain and their functions: spinal cord, medulla oblongata, pons, cerebellum, thalamus, hypothalamus, amygdala, hippocampus, corpus callosum, and cerebrum.

NATIONAL STANDARDS

- #7 Healthy Behaviors
- #6 Goal Setting
- #4 Communication

INTRODUCTION

Today we are going to learn about the most complex organ in the human body. We will learn at least 10 parts of the brain, their location, and their general function.

Here is the seven-step recall format that we will use to learn about the brain:

1. Locate the area of the brain on the diagram.
2. Say the word aloud a couple of times.
3. Write down the word.
4. Write down a function of the brain part in one or two words.
5. Act out the function of the brain part.
6. Color the brain part with a color that describes its function to you.
7. Do some visual tracking exercises for brain integration into locked memory.

We will all appreciate the potential of the brain and improve our retention if we use this technique.

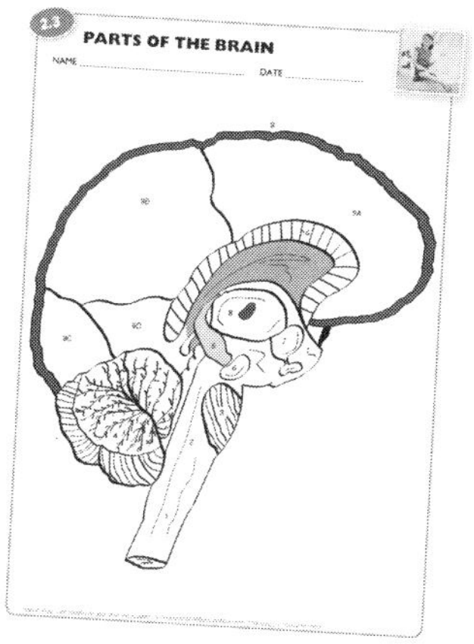

2.3

HANDOUT 2.3

1. spinal cord
2. medulla oblongata
3. pons
4. cerebellum
5. hippocampus
6. amygdala
7. hypothalamus
8. thalamus
9. cerebral cortex (outer one-eighth of all lobes in the cerebrum)

9a. frontal lobe of cerebrum
9b. parietal lobe of cerebrum
9c. occipital lobe of cerebrum
9d. temporal lobe of cerebrum
10. corpus callosum

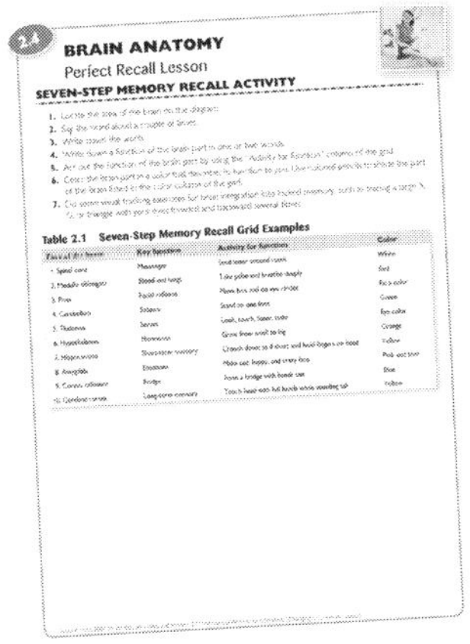

2.4

HANDOUT 2.4

Provide a handout picture of the brain and colored pencils for students to use for the activity.

CLOSURE

The brain is complex and records information in many different lobes. The best way to learn material is to use as many senses as possible. You can greatly enhance memory and recall by using the correct procedure. Practice this technique in other areas of learning to increase your memory and recall. Develop a photographic memory by using specific brain-building techniques.

OBJECTIVE

Students will be able to determine which of the eight brain intelligences is their natural talent by taking a multiple intelligences test.

NATIONAL STANDARD

#7 Healthy Behaviors

INTRODUCTION

Howard Gardner has done considerable research on the eight types of intelligences. This assessment is derived from the materials in his book *Multiple Intelligences.* This exercise will give you insight into your natural genius levels. We all have some areas of outstanding talent that will help lead us toward a career. Recognize that there could be some genius levels that you may not access well. You should challenge these areas to develop better total balance.

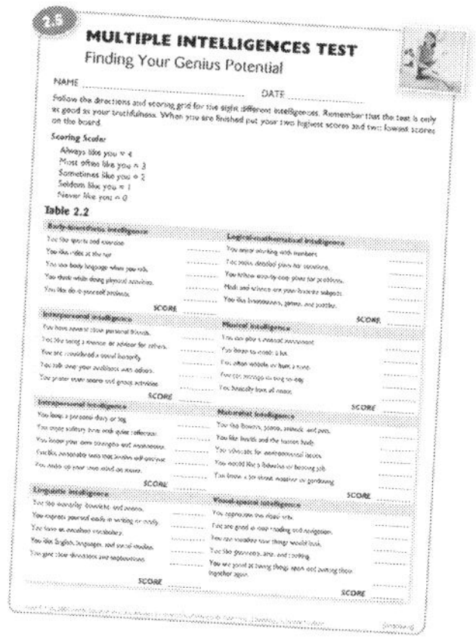
MULTIPLE INTELLIGENCES TEST
Finding Your Genius Potential

2.5

HANDOUT 2.5

After students have finished the test, you can talk about the class as a whole and what each of the eight intelligences means to them as their brain dominance or strength. All intelligences are useful, and students benefit by knowing where their natural strengths lie.

CLOSURE

We are all intelligent in different ways. You should focus on your natural intelligences and work to be more balanced in all eight areas.

Brain-Building Games

OBJECTIVE

Students will be able to learn at least eight games based on thinking and strategy.

NATIONAL STANDARDS

- #7 Healthy Behaviors
- #4 Communication

INTRODUCTION

Research has shown that some games can build thinking and strategy skills while at the same time being fun. We are going to learn eight of these games and develop some strategies for success. These games keep the mind alert and can help you develop terrific thinking skills useful in other aspects of life.

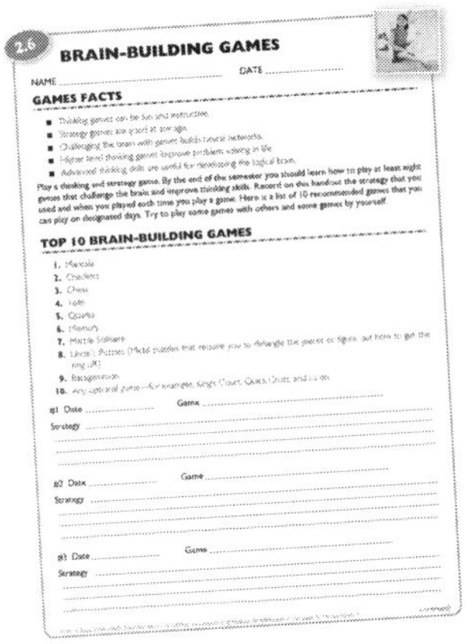

2.6

HANDOUT 2.6

Designate certain days for playing games so that students have time to work on learning the games.

CLOSURE

I hope that you learned at least one new game today. Be prepared to learn some others before the semester ends. Games are good for thinking and logic!

OBJECTIVE

Students will practice four brain-training actives that will assess and challenge them in perception, visual spatial sense, memory, and general IQ.

NATIONAL STANDARD

#6 Goal Setting

INTRODUCTION

Today we are going to practice fun and challenging activities that build neural transmission. These brain-training activities last only a couple of minutes each. Do not work ahead on the sheet. Just as your heart becomes stronger as the demand on it increases, so does the brain. Any activity that gets you to think and analyze is beneficial for mental awareness. You can raise your IQ and become a better problem solver by challenging yourself mentally with these kinds of activities.

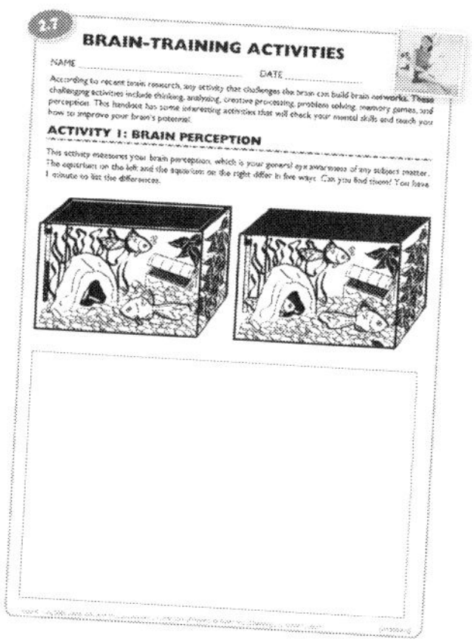

2.7

HANDOUT 2.7

Activity 1: Brain Perception Answers

- The left tank has a line of white around its rim while the right tank does not.
- In the left tank, there is a fish inside the cave, but there is not one in the right tank.
- The temperature in the left tank is warm, while that in the right tank is cool.
- The bottom fish is swimming to the left in the left tank, but to the right in the right tank.
- All of the stones are white in the left tank, but there is a black stone beneath the bottom fish in the right tank.

Activity 2: Visual Spatial Sense Answers

1. b
2. d
3. a
4. c
5. e

Activity 3: Short-Term Memory Discussion

Ask how many students got all 15 items in 1 minute. Ask how many got 14, 13, 12, 11, and 10. Anyone who got 10 or more has great short-term memory. Ask whether anyone used any special technique to help remember the items quickly. Would the student be willing to share that method with the class? Association is a good way to remember random items like this for short-term and long-term memory.

Activity 4: Test Your IQ

1. c—33 (double previous number and subtract 1)
2. d—north east west south
3. c—129 (each increment multiplied by 3 plus the subsequent number)
4. c
5. c

CLOSURE

I hope that these activities were a healthy challenge for you. Remember that when you do activities like these, your brain will remember how you did them. Taking a test like this will then be easier next time. Train your brain so that it will work better for you in the future with all kinds of real problems.

Brain-Training Activities: Albert Einstein Puzzle

OBJECTIVE

Students will be able to earn extra credit by trying to figure out the Albert Einstein puzzle.

NATIONAL STANDARD

#7 Healthy Behaviors

INTRODUCTION

This test of logic and reasoning skills was supposedly done by Albert Einstein. At the time, Einstein figured that you would be in top 5% of the world population in logical deduction skills if you could figure it out.

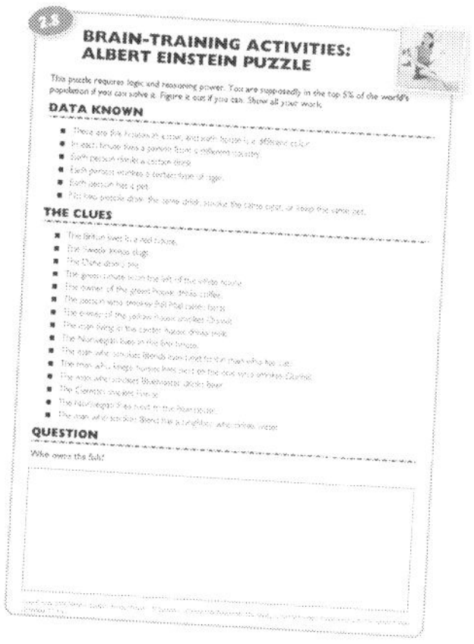
BRAIN-TRAINING ACTIVITIES: ALBERT EINSTEIN PUZZLE
DATA KNOWN
THE CLUES
QUESTION

2.8

HANDOUT 2.8

The German owns the fish.

Logic Puzzle Answers

House 1	House 2	House 3	House 4	House 5
Yellow	Blue	Red	Green	White
Norwegian	Dane	Briton	German	Swede
Dunhill	Blend	Pall Mall	Prince	Bluemaster
Water	Tea	Milk	Coffee	Beer
Cats	Horses	Birds	**Fish**	Dogs

Adapted from *Life (International Edition)*, March 25, 1963.

CLOSURE

Stretching your mind to new dimensions is always beneficial. Taking on these puzzles challenges you mentally. Continue to train your mind so that it will be better able to help you with real-life problems.

Food for the Brain

OBJECTIVE

Students will be able to determine which foods are best for brain functioning by participating in a class discussion on food and neural transmission.

NATIONAL STANDARDS

- #1 Health Promotion
- #4 Communication

INTRODUCTION

Everything written about the brain mentions the importance of food for brain functioning. The foods that you eat influence the type and number of neurotransmitters in the brain. Eating the right food is vital for all body functions and peak performances. Let us examine the latest information on food for the brain.

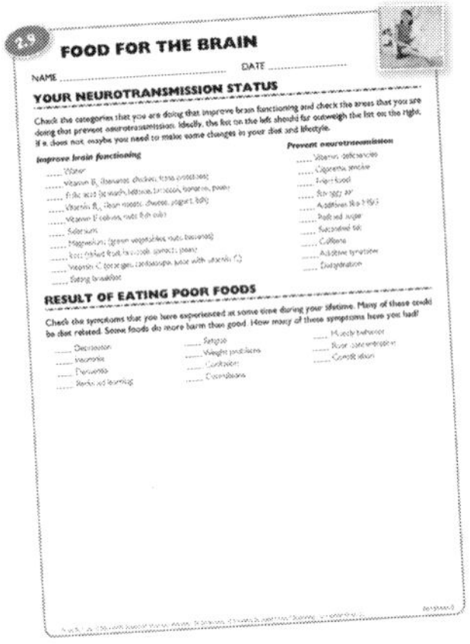

2.9

HANDOUT 2.9

Matching

1. f	**6.** a
2. g	**7.** b
3. h	**8.** c
4. i	**9.** d
5. j	**10.** e

Brain Food Brainstorm Answers

- lean meats
- spinach
- skim milk
- beans
- peanuts
- oranges
- peas
- fish, turkey, and chicken
- whole-grain bread
- dried fruit

CLOSURE

This week we will be eating in class, and your grade will be determined by the nutritional value of the food samples that you bring to class for our nutrition delight. Use this sheet as a guideline to what foods to bring. (If the classroom is not adaptable for eating, then just have students bring nutritional food for extra credit.)

Brain Booster Project

OBJECTIVE

Cooperative groups of students will teach a brain booster activity to the class each day for a week.

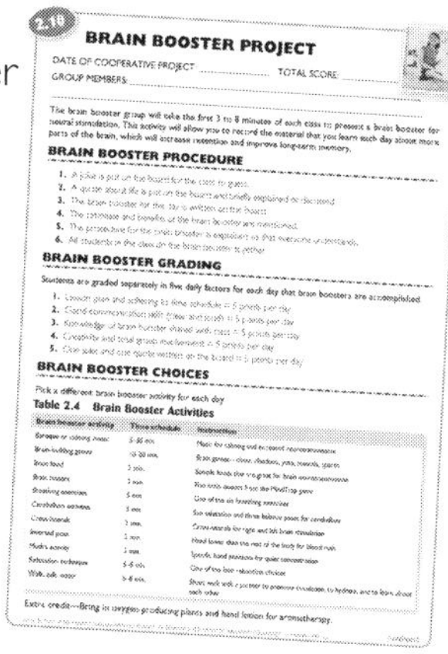

BRAIN BOOSTER PROJECT

BRAIN BOOSTER PROCEDURE

BRAIN BOOSTER GRADING

BRAIN BOOSTER CHOICES

Table 2.4 Brain Booster Activities

2.10

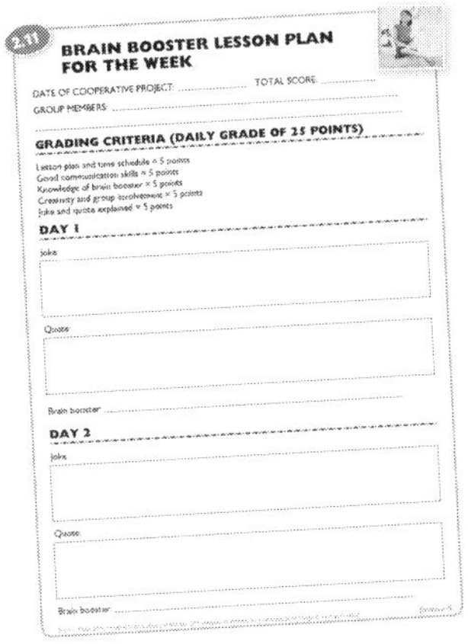

BRAIN BOOSTER LESSON PLAN FOR THE WEEK

GRADING CRITERIA (DAILY GRADE OF 25 POINTS)

DAY 1

DAY 2

2.11

NATIONAL STANDARDS

- #1 Health Promotion
- #7 Healthy Behaviors
- #5 Decision Making
- #4 Communication
- #8 Advocacy

INTRODUCTION

If you understand how the brain works, it makes sense to get it charged up to boost memory and retention to the highest levels. We are all going to learn 10 brain booster activities that you will teach in the weeks to come. My job as a teacher is to teach these to you so that you will understand their rationale and logic. Then each day at the beginning of class you will choose one of these brain boosters and explain its benefits to brain functioning. Afterward you will demonstrate how to perform the activity, and we will all do it together. Learning any sort of material is much easier when the brain is ready to receive it. These brain boosters will stimulate your brain so that you will remember the material better.

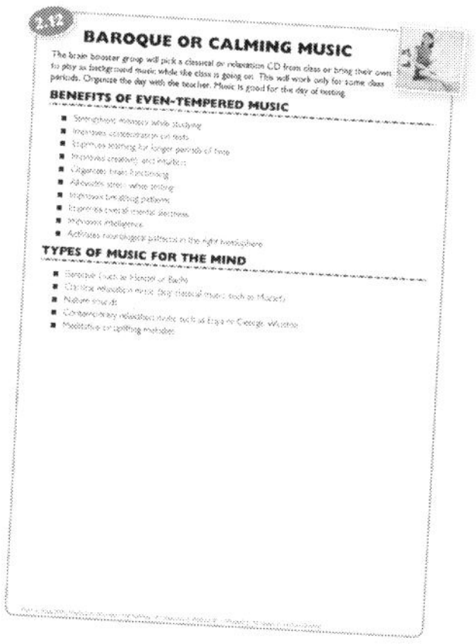

BAROQUE OR CALMING MUSIC

BENEFITS OF EVEN-TEMPERED MUSIC

TYPES OF MUSIC FOR THE MIND

2.12

HANDOUT 2.10

Randomly select students and put them into groups of two or three. Have each group hand in a brain booster project sheet with a tentative schedule for teacher grading purposes.

HANDOUT 2.11
HANDOUT 2.12
HANDOUT 2.13
HANDOUT 2.14
HANDOUT 2.15

The students will choose three to five brain teasers from the game MindTrap. These mind puzzles and brain teasers are meant to challenge the way that people think. If the students cannot come up with the answers, the presenting group will provide the answer (it is on the back of the card). If you would like to order MindTrap, contact

Mindtrap Games Inc.
Pressman Toy Corporation
New York, NY 10010
www.pressmantoy.com

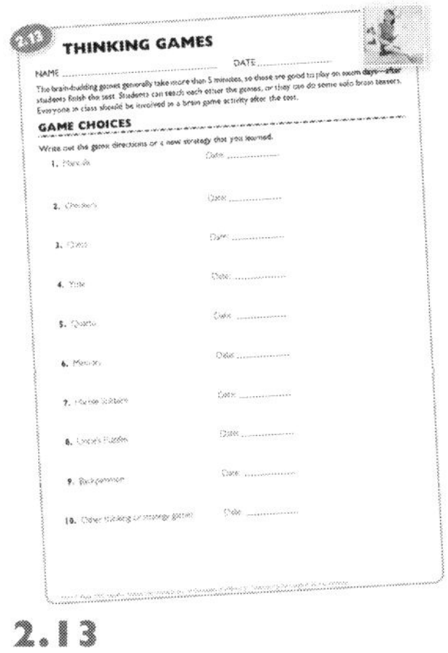

THINKING GAMES

GAME CHOICES

2.13

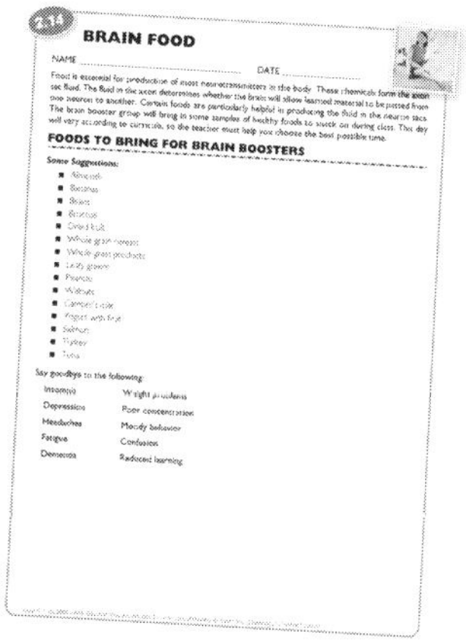

BRAIN FOOD

FOODS TO BRING FOR BRAIN BOOSTERS

2.14

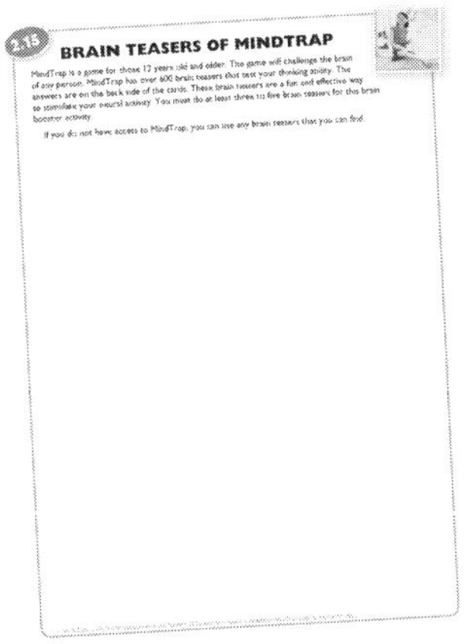

BRAIN TEASERS OF MINDTRAP

2.15

HANDOUT 2.16
HANDOUT 2.17
HANDOUT 2.18
HANDOUT 2.19
HANDOUT 2.20
HANDOUT 2.21
HANDOUT 2.22

CLOSURE

Teaching is the highest level of learning. Getting your brain stimulated before teaching is necessary for learning and retention. I hope that you enjoy the brain boosters and choose the ones that you think are most effective in stimulating neural transmission. We will start next week, so each of you should be ready in case someone is absent. You will lose points if you are absent, and you will have to make up the brain booster activity later.

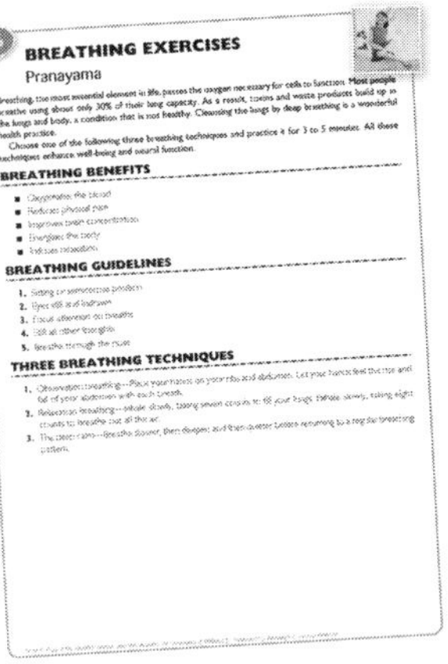
2.16 BREATHING EXERCISES
Pranayama
BREATHING BENEFITS
BREATHING GUIDELINES
THREE BREATHING TECHNIQUES

2.16

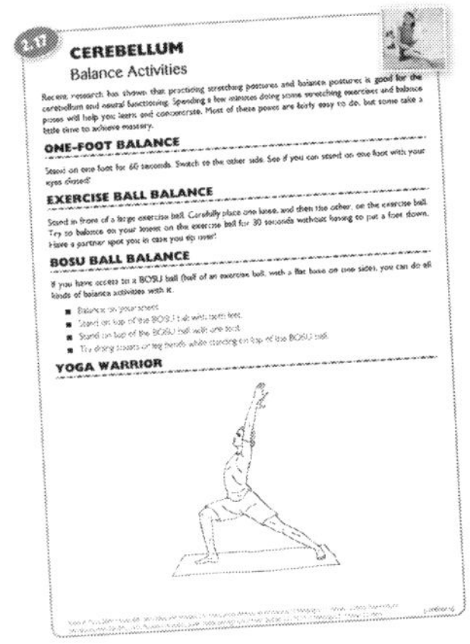
2.17 CEREBELLUM
Balance Activities
ONE-FOOT BALANCE
EXERCISE BALL BALANCE
BOSU BALL BALANCE
YOGA WARRIOR

2.17

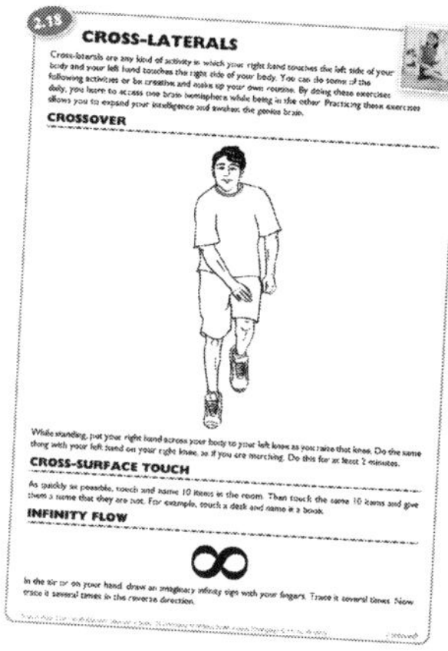
2.18 CROSS-LATERALS
CROSSOVER
CROSS-SURFACE TOUCH
INFINITY FLOW

2.18

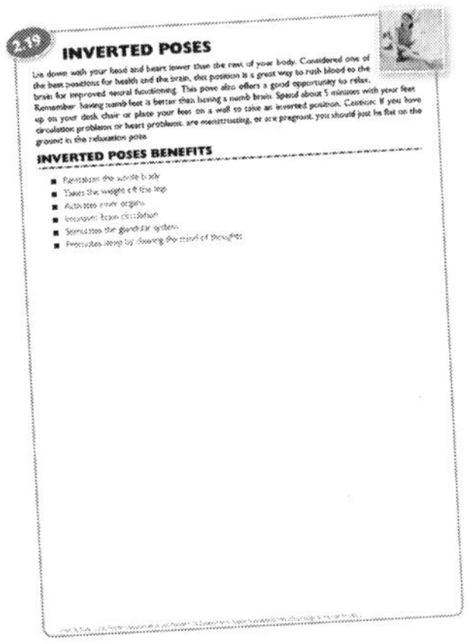
2.19 INVERTED POSES
INVERTED POSES BENEFITS

2.19

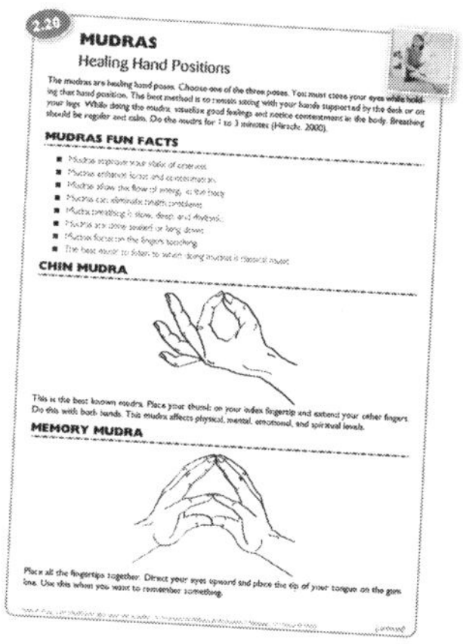
2.20 MUDRAS
Healing Hand Positions
MUDRAS FUN FACTS
CHIN MUDRA
MEMORY MUDRA

2.20

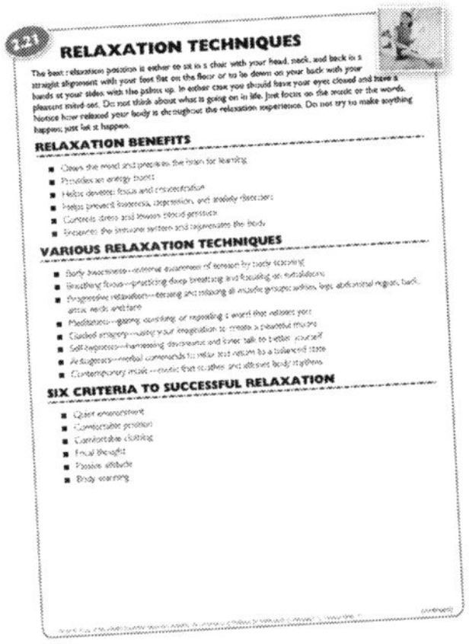
2.21 RELAXATION TECHNIQUES
RELAXATION BENEFITS
VARIOUS RELAXATION TECHNIQUES
SIX CRITERIA TO SUCCESSFUL RELAXATION

2.21

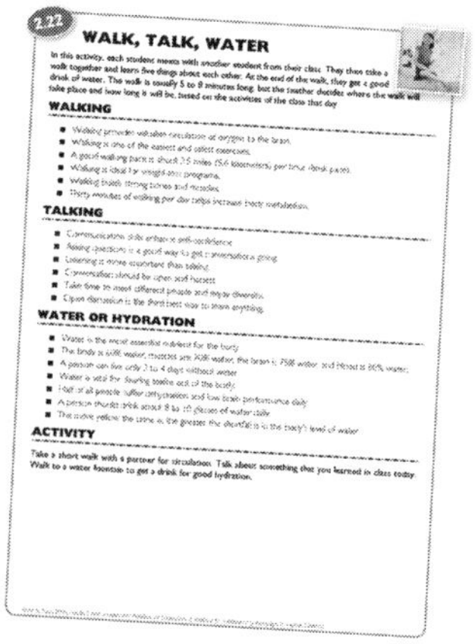
2.22 WALK, TALK, WATER
WALKING
TALKING
WATER OR HYDRATION
ACTIVITY

2.22

The Power of the Brain Test Key

OBJECTIVE

Students will be able to pass a test on the brain and learning with at least 70% accuracy.

NATIONAL STANDARD

#1 Health Promotion

INTRODUCTION

Today is test day. I hope that you are all ready and able to show that you have learned a lot about the brain and learning. The test includes true or false questions, short answer, and matching. Bring your test to the front desk when you are finished and then find something to do quietly. Raise your hand if you have any questions.

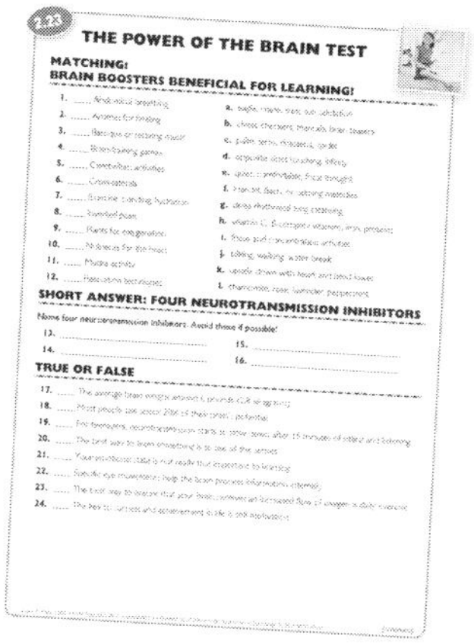
THE POWER OF THE BRAIN TEST
MATCHING: BRAIN BOOSTERS BENEFICIAL FOR LEARNING!
SHORT ANSWER: FOUR NEUROTRANSMISSION INHIBITORS
TRUE OR FALSE

2.23

HANDOUT 2.23

Matching: Brain Boosters Beneficial for Learning!

1. g
2. l
3. f
4. b
5. a
6. d
7. j
8. k
9. c
10. h
11. i
12. e

Short Answer: Four Neurotransmission Inhibitors

Questions 13–16

- drugs
- heavy metals
- alcohol
- reactive language
- animal fats
- strokes
- negativity
- stress toxins
- emotional problems, depression
- free radicals
- unchallenged
- low expectations

True or False

17. false—The average brain weighs 3 pounds (1.4 kilograms).
18. false—Most people use 5 to 10% of their brain's potential.
19. true
20. true
21. false—Your emotions have a lot to do with memory and learning.
22. true
23. true
24. true

Matching: Levels of Genius

25. a
26. c
27. d
28. b

Short Answer: Brain Facts

29. block impulses
30. 8-10 glasses
31. while sleeping
32. animal fats
33. teaching or experiencing

Matching: Brain Anatomy to General Function

34. g
35. j
36. e
37. f
38. a
39. b
40. d
41. i
42. c
43. h

Matching: Key Components to Success in Life

44. d
45. b
46. a
47. c

Short Answer: Memory Recall

Questions 48–50

- Locate part
- Say out loud
- Write word
- Write function
- Color part function
- Act out function
- Do visual tracking exercises

CLOSURE

The brain is the crucial element for learning in the human body. People who understand how the brain operates will be able to access a higher level of brain functioning.

3

Resiliency Factors

WHAT LIFE MEANS TO US IS DETERMINED, NOT SO MUCH BY WHAT LIFE BRINGS TO US AS BY THE ATTITUDE WE BRING TO LIFE; NOT SO MUCH BY WHAT HAPPENS TO US AS BY OUR REACTION TO WHAT HAPPENS.

Lewis L. Dunnington

Lesson Finder

Building Resiliency With the Power of Assets

OBJECTIVE

Students will examine the eight key factors to building resiliency in the human body and do a personal assessment.

NATIONAL STANDARDS

- #1 Health Promotion
- #7 Healthy Behaviors

INTRODUCTION

This week we are going to study resiliency. Does anyone know what *resiliency* means? Resiliency is the ability to bounce back from any situation in life! We will discuss the eight skills that help people make it through the rough times. Some people refer to these skills as assets. A person who has these assets has great power.

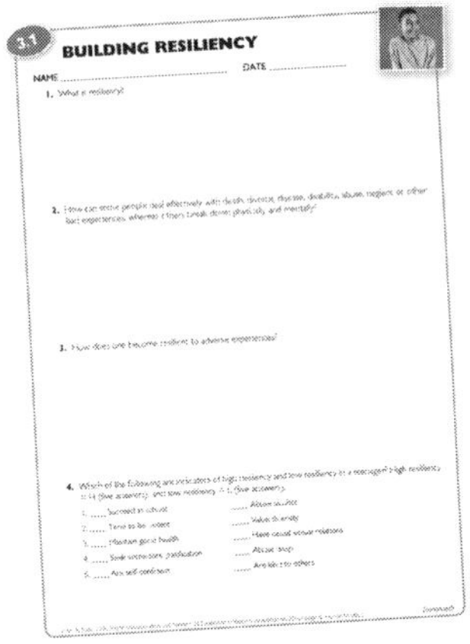
3.1 BUILDING RESILIENCY

NAME DATE

3.1

HANDOUT 3.1

1. Resiliency is the ability to bounce back and deal with any rough life situations.
2. Some people have the power! In general this means that they have some key people in their support system, believe in themselves, and have developed meaningful relationships.
3. Resiliency comes from building the eight positive assets of life. Resiliency comes from having inner strength (self-discipline) and not worrying about things that one has no control over.
4. Answers to indicators of high and low resiliency:
   1. H-L
   2. L-H
   3. H-L
   4. L-L
   5. H-H
5. The Search Institute used research to come up with a list of 40 assets that teenagers should have to become successful members of society. Visit www.search-institute.org for a list of the 40 assets. You can either direct your students to examine the list or use it yourself within the classroom for this discussion. Ask the students to consider the description of each asset and rate themselves on a scale of 1 (poor) to 5 (excellent).
6. Lead a discussion with students about how they can address certain areas that they need to work on. Do not ask for specifics. Instead, select some assets from the list that you think are suitable for class discussion. Ask students to help you brainstorm ways in which those assets are useful in daily living and ways in which they can further develop those assets.

CLOSURE

Today was a brief overview of the key components to being a resilient human being. During this week we will do activities that will help you incorporate these resiliency traits.

Positive Mind-Set and Attitude

OBJECTIVE

Students will be able to alter their mind-sets by using affirmations and eight different techniques to change their attitudes on a daily basis.

NATIONAL STANDARDS

- #1 Health Promotion
- #7 Healthy Behaviors
- #4 Communication

INTRODUCTION

Emotions are highly concentrated forms of energy consciousness that stimulate responses in the body. Emotional balance determines the sum total of all neurological and physiological processes in the body. Affirmations are ways for us to train our minds in a positive manner. The more positive things that are said about us, the better we think and feel. The more positive words that we say to our inner selves, the more effectively our minds respond to learning and healing. Practicing affirmations is one of the best ways to program the mind and body for success and happiness.

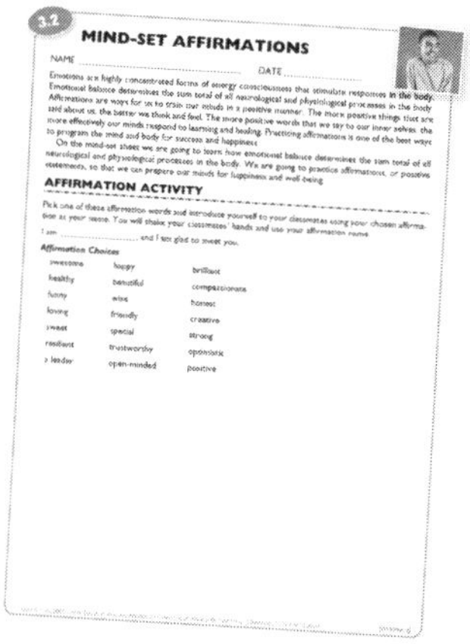

3.2

HANDOUT 3.2

You are what you think you are. Positive affirmations are important to your sense of well-being.

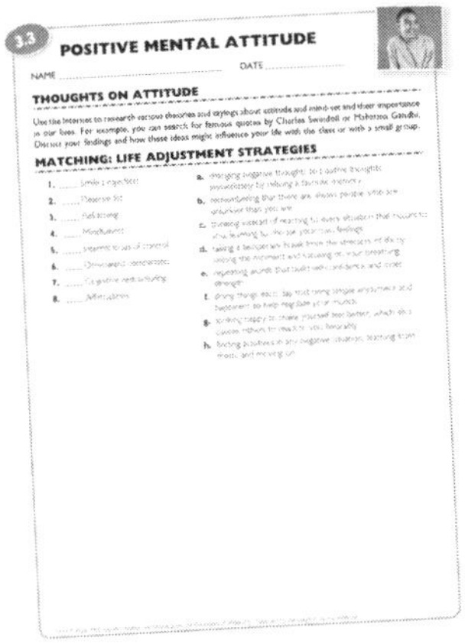

3.3

HANDOUT 3.3

Thoughts on Attitude

Have students research the importance of positive attitudes on the Internet. Remind them of safe Internet practices and monitor them if you can do this during class-time. Lead a discussion with the students about what they discovered and how they feel these ideas might influence their own lives.

Matching: Life Adjustment Strategies

1. g	**5.** c
2. f	**6.** b
3. h	**7.** a
4. d	**8.** e

CLOSURE

I hope you realize that your attitude is probably the most important aspect of life. All of us can make specific adjustments to improve our attitudes. Which techniques do you think that you would most likely use?

Goals and Dreams

OBJECTIVE

Students today will write down at least 30 dreams and goals that they want to accomplish in their lifetime.

NATIONAL STANDARDS

- #1 Health Promotion
- #7 Healthy Behaviors
- #6 Goal Setting

INTRODUCTION

Today I will tell the story of John Goddard, which appeared in Jack Canfield's book *Chicken Soup for the Soul #2*. A young man sat down at his kitchen table at age 16 and wrote a list of all the dreams that he wanted to see happen in his lifetime. He ended up writing down 128 goals that day.

The goals gave him meaning and purpose, something to look forward to. In this activity, you will list at least 30 goals and dreams that you would like to see happen in your lifetime.

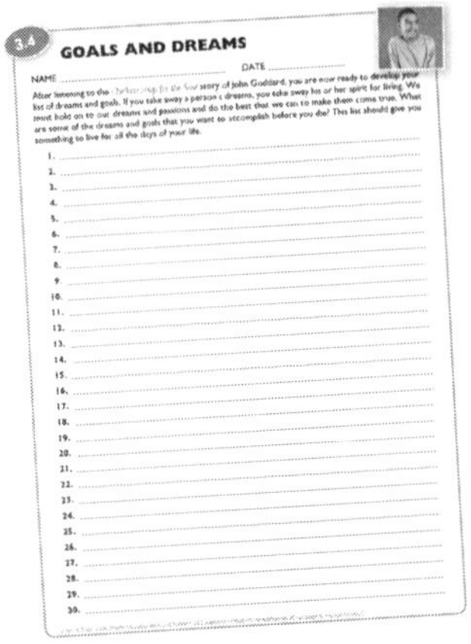
GOALS AND DREAMS

3.4

HANDOUT 3.4

You might want to put together a slideshow with images that represent some goals and dreams that your students might have. This slideshow might give your students some ideas and get them excited about their futures!

CLOSURE

I hope that you have now written down at least 30 goals and dreams. The next step is to start planning to accomplish at least one goal each year as your life passes. The fun of planning the activity and sharing the dream with others will make it more special. Do not let anyone take away your dreams. Dreams open the door to everything beautiful in the world. Remember that there are many places to go, people to meet, and things to do.

The Creative Genius

OBJECTIVE

Students will examine how to increase their creative genius by talking about creativity, doing a creativity assessment, and writing about a new invention that they think would be beneficial to society.

NATIONAL STANDARDS

- #7 Healthy Behaviors
- #5 Decision Making
- #4 Communication

INTRODUCTION

Albert Einstein said that knowledge without creativity is of little value. How well-developed are your creative talents? Do you see what life is, or do you see what it could become? Today we are going to learn about creativity and what we can do to increase our creative genius.

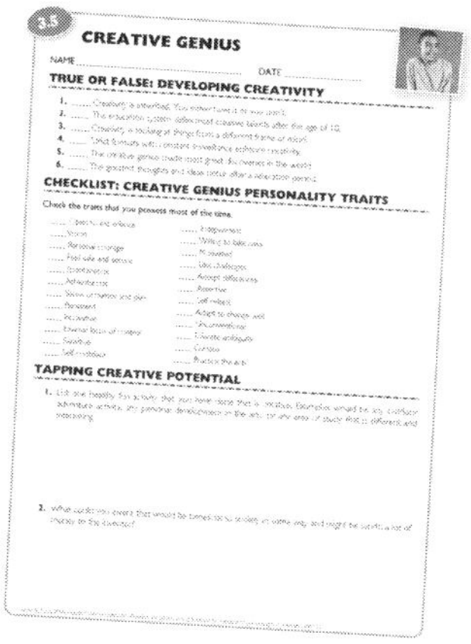
CREATIVE GENIUS

TRUE OR FALSE: DEVELOPING CREATIVITY

CHECKLIST: CREATIVE GENIUS PERSONALITY TRAITS

TAPPING CREATIVE POTENTIAL

3.5

HANDOUT 3.5

True or False: Developing Creativity

1. false—Creativity is developed in the brain by doing creative assignments and activities.
2. true
3. true
4. false—Independent thinking and a relaxing atmosphere are necessary for creativity to occur.
5. true
6. true

Checklist: Creative Genius Personality Traits

Have students raise their hands to indicate the number of personality traits that they checked.

Tapping Creative Potential

Ask students to come up with one creative fun activity and one invention for society. Their goal is to show how creative they are.

CLOSURE

Creativity is one area in life in which most people have not reached their full potential. I hope that we can help you realize and recognize your creative genius. Creativity has opened more doors to progress and led to more inventions than any other aspect of life.

The Six Pillars of Character

OBJECTIVE

Students will be able to determine which of the six pillars of character are found in their true selves by performing an assessment and participating in a value auction. The six pillars of character are described by the Josephson Institute and are the framework for CHARACTER COUNTS, the institute's prescribed approach for teaching character. For more information on the six pillars of character, visit www.charactercounts.org.

NATIONAL STANDARDS

- #1 Health Promotion
- #7 Healthy Behaviors

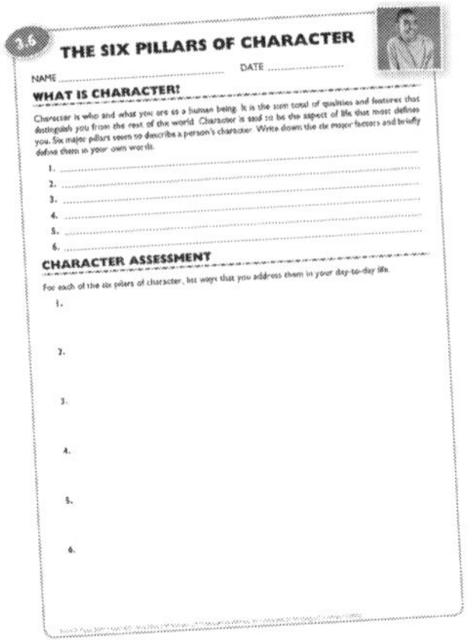

3.6 THE SIX PILLARS OF CHARACTER

NAME .... DATE ....

WHAT IS CHARACTER?

Character is who and what you are as a human being. It is the sum total of qualities and features that distinguish you from the rest of the world. Character is said to be the aspect of life that most defines you. Six major pillars seem to describe a person's character. Write down the six major factors and briefly define them in your own words.

1. ....
2. ....
3. ....
4. ....
5. ....
6. ....

CHARACTER ASSESSMENT

For each of the six pillars of character, list ways that you address them in your day-to-day life.

1.

2.

3.

4.

5.

6.

3.6

INTRODUCTION

Today we are going to examine the six pillars of character. Take the character assessment and then place the scores in the relevant categories to figure out which pillar is your strength and which pillar is your weakness.

HANDOUT 3.6

What Is Character?

The six pillars of character are trustworthy, caring, fair, respectful, responsible, and a good citizen.

Character Assessment

List the ways that you address these pillars of character in your everyday life. Then discuss the positive impact these tactics have had on yourself and others in your life.

CLOSURE

Remember that these six character values are considered the most valuable personality traits that a person can possess. All of us should do the best that we can to build these traits as strong character values.

OBJECTIVE

Students will be able to see what they really value by participating in a silent auction of the best items in life.

NATIONAL STANDARDS

- #1 Health Promotion
- #7 Healthy Behaviors
- #5 Decision Making

INTRODUCTION

We are going to conduct a silent auction today. We are auctioning off what are probably the best items in life. There is no right or wrong answer. This auction will help you understand what you really value.

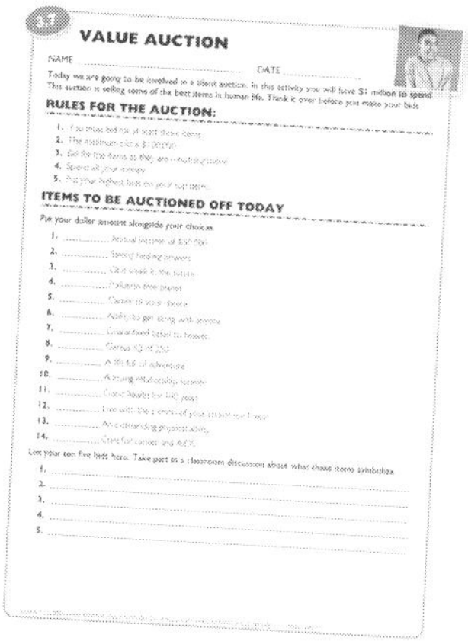
VALUE AUCTION

RULES FOR THE AUCTION:

ITEMS TO BE AUCTIONED OFF TODAY

3.7

HANDOUT 3.7

After students have filled out their bids and recorded their top 5 choices, ask how many bid on all the items, then 13, then 12, and all the way down to 3. This process will give you an idea of how many of the fourteen items were important to the class.

Review what each item generally symbolizes. To stimulate discussion, ask the students what they think each auction item might symbolize. Ideally, this exchange will encourage students to consider the different motives that people might have in selecting particular items. For example, a bid for an annual income might mean that they just want to have enough money to live comfortably (because $50,000 is not a great deal of money anymore). Alternatively, the bid might show that the bidder wants to raise money to help care for an ill parent.

Here are some possible explanations for each item:

1. Value money
2. Help others
3. Are curious or possibly want to make money
4. Are environmentally conscious
5. Seek self-satisfaction
6. Value relationships and people
7. Want life afterward to be won derful, believe in God
8. Value intelligence
9. Are interesting and creative
10. Want a great companion for life
11. Value health and life on this planet
12. Are curious and want to have a dream come true
13. Seek personal achievements
14. Care about others and want to stop their suffering

CLOSURE

By using the auction format today, we tried to see what you really value in life. There were no right or wrong answers; you made choices based only on how you feel. Sometimes we can learn a lot by finding out what our real intentions and values are. Perhaps you will change your thoughts after doing this activity and come to a better realization of what life means to you. I hope that you gained some insight into your true self today.

Resiliency Rites of Passage

OBJECTIVE

Students will practice five resiliency activities in a rites-of-passage format that will be interesting and fun.

NATIONAL STANDARDS

- #7 Healthy Behaviors
- #4 Communication

INTRODUCTION

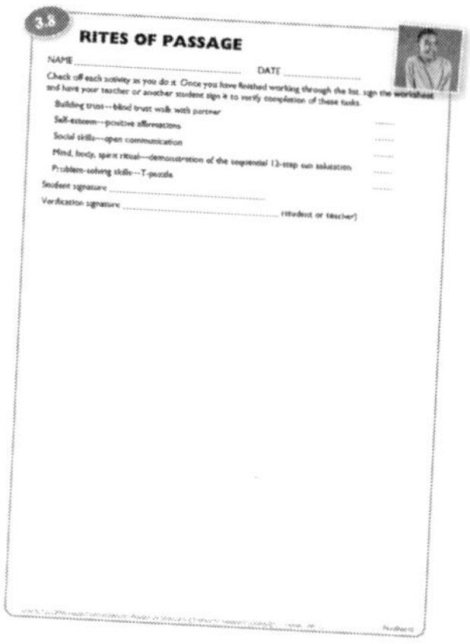
3.8
RITES OF PASSAGE
NAME .... DATE ....
Check off each activity as you do it. Once you have finished working through the list, sign the worksheet and have your teacher or another student sign it to verify completion of these tasks.
Building trust—blind trust walk with partner
Self-esteem—positive affirmations
Social skills—open communication
Mind, body, spirit ritual—demonstration of the sequential 12-step sun salutation
Problem-solving skills—T-puzzle
Student signature ....
Verification signature .... (student or teacher)

3.8

Today we are going to do five activities that lead to inner strength and resiliency. If you pass these resiliency tests, or rites of passage, you are ready to handle the complexities of emotional mature adulthood. These activities will challenge you and help you build good character. Some of the activities are rituals that are fun. Some of the activities measure your level of trust. Some check your skills and coordination. Others are based on problem solving and communication. Each is meant to enhance your well-being and build an inner strength that will help you overcome any ordeal that you have in life.

HANDOUT 3.8

Throughout life, people experience many events, both positive and negative. The ability to handle all that life offers and bounce back is called *resiliency*. These classroom activities today will test your mind, body, and spirit. These five activities are like a "rite of passage." They will show in a symbolic way if you are on track to becoming a resilient human being. The five resiliency qualities to be tested are:

1. Trust (building your support system)

   Building trust—blind trust walk with partner. Place students in pairs. One at a time, each team member puts on a blindfold. Each person is shown to trust others and also be trustworthy for his or her team member. This activity should go on without fear of injury to the participants.

2. Self-esteem (giving and receiving compliments)

   Self-esteem—positive affirmations. Each student puts his or her name on an index card. Then all the cards are passed around the classroom. Each student writes on each person's card at least one positive item about that person.

3. Social skills (practicing open communication and listening)

   Social skills—open communication. Each student finds a classmate that he or she does not know very well or at all. The pairs talk with each other for 5 minutes, and each attempt to learn five interesting facts about the other. Students write the five facts on a sheet of paper. Good communication skills build confidence in all people.

4. Mind, body, spirit ritual (12-step sun salutation sequence)

   Mind, body, spirit ritual—demonstration of the sun salutation (12-step yoga postures in sequential order). Provide a picture of the sun salutation and demonstrate it as well. (See handout 2.17 for an example.) All students will perform the 12-step yoga sequence in small groups of 3 to 5 students of their choice.

5. Problem-solving skills (completing the T-puzzle)

   Problem-solving skills—T-puzzle. Give a five-piece T-puzzle to a group of three to five students. The puzzle is meant to teach group problem solving and effective communication and listening skills. Each group must eventually put the five-piece puzzle together to form the capital letter "T," which stands for teamwork and trust.

CLOSURE

These activities are a few of the many ways of building resiliency and will start the process of preparing you for the transitions of life.

Resiliency Test Key

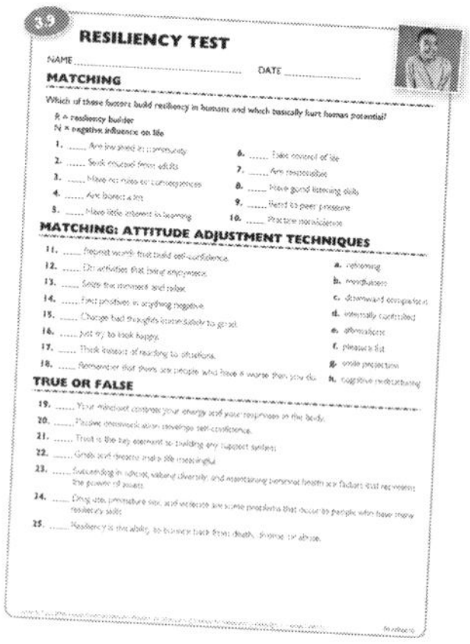

3.9

OBJECTIVE

Students will be able to pass a written test on the principles of resiliency with 70% accuracy.

NATIONAL STANDARD

#7 Healthy Behaviors

INTRODUCTION

This is a quiz on the principles of resiliency. We have covered the material well, but if you have any questions during the test, please raise your hand. Good luck!

HANDOUT 3.9

Matching

1. R	**3.** N	**5.** N	**7.** R	**9.** N
2. R	**4.** N	**6.** R	**8.** R	**10.** R

Matching: Attitude Adjustment Techniques

11. e	**13.** b	**15.** h	**17.** d
12. f	**14.** a	**16.** g	**18.** c

True or False

19. true

20. false—Active communication builds confidence.

21. true

22. true

23. true

24. false—These problems are usually for people who do not have many resiliency skills.

25. true

Short Answer

26. trustworthy

27. caring

28. fair

29. respectful

30. responsible

31. good citizen

CLOSURE

We will go over the test tomorrow to see how well you did.

4

Health and Wellness

WHY NOT SPEND TIME IN DETERMINING WHAT IS WORTHWHILE FOR US, AND THEN GO AFTER THAT?

William Ross

Lesson Finder

Health Dimensions

OBJECTIVE

Students will be able to analyze the facts concerning the five dimensions of life and ways to make healthy lifestyle changes after a class discussion.

NATIONAL STANDARD

#1 Health Promotion

INTRODUCTION

This week we are going to discuss the five dimensions of health (intellectual, physical, spiritual, emotional, and social). We will learn that we can change our health by using a three-step process that includes assessment, intervention, and reinforcement. We are also going to look at the four key factors that determine health and longevity: lifestyle, genetics, the environment, and the health care system. Let us see how much you know about health.

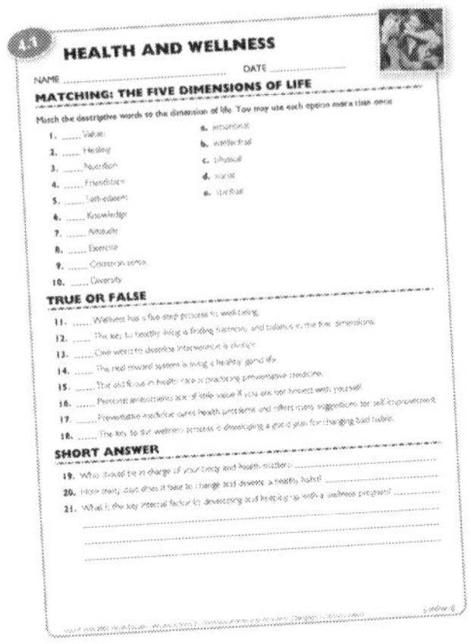

4.1

HANDOUT 4.1

Matching: The Five Dimensions of Life

Allow the students time to match the dimension of life to the descriptive word. Randomly call on students for their educated guesses. Help them if they are wrong.

1. e	**6.** b
2. c	**7.** a
3. c	**8.** c
4. d	**9.** b
5. a	**10.** d

True or False

Call on students or look for volunteers to read the true or false statements and tell the class the answer.

11. false—There is a three-step process to wellness (assessment, intervention, reinforcement).
12. true
13. false—Doing a personal assessment is the first step of the wellness process.
14. true
15. true
16. true
17. false—Preventative medicine offers clear guidelines to prevent the onset of any illness.
18. true

Short Answer

19. yourself
20. 40 days or more
21. self-motivation

Matching: Key Factors for Health and Longevity

22. b

23. c

24. a

25. d

Matching: Ultimate Goals of High-Level Wellness

26. e

27. d

28. b

29. c

30. a

HANDOUT 4.2

Matching: Teenage Major Health Risks

By using logic and the information given, students match the top health concerns to the informational data.

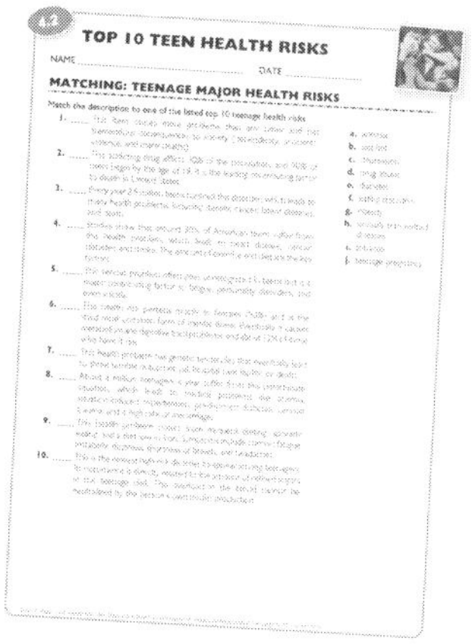
TOP 10 TEEN HEALTH RISKS

MATCHING: TEENAGE MAJOR HEALTH RISKS

4.2

1. b

2. i

3. h

4. g

5. c

6. f

7. d

8. j

9. a

10. e

CLOSURE

These facts and data on health and wellness will be the material that appears on your quiz. Do you have any questions concerning this sheet?

Total Health Assessments

OBJECTIVE

Students will be able to do accurate appraisals of their lifestyle by honestly assessing their health in 11 different areas.

NATIONAL STANDARD

#7 Healthy Behaviors

INTRODUCTION

Each of you will assess your present health status in 11 categories described by current research. Because the assessment has 110 questions, it is fairly accurate. The more elements that an assessment contains, the more accurate it is likely to be. The most comprehensive medical evaluations include 600 or more questions. This health appraisal uses several questions from other appraisals and simplifies them. Take your time and be honest.

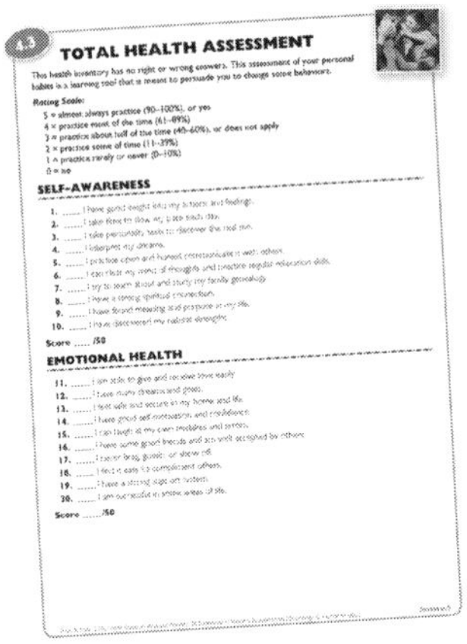

4.3

HANDOUT 4.3

At the end of each section you should tally your score in that particular section. If you have questions, ask as you work through the assessment.

At the end of the assessment, create a bar graph and graph your scores. The idea behind the graphing is to see whether any area of your health is greatly out of alignment with the others. You may want to use a program for change to work on any area that is out of alignment. Balance in the 11 dimensions is the ultimate goal.

After you finish your assessment, write your two highest scores and your two lowest scores on the board so that we can get a general appraisal of the health of the class.

CLOSURE

I hope that you found the total health assessment interesting and thought-provoking. An important part of healthy living is assessing your personal health status from time to time. This assessment is the most comprehensive one that we will do this semester.

OBJECTIVE

Students will be able to complete the intervention process by taking one area of their health and improving it over a period of 21 days.

NATIONAL STANDARD

#5 Decision Making

INTRODUCTION

In the process of changing bad habits to good habits, an intervention program is the key component. After examining your scores on the total health assessment, you will take one area of your health and improve it. Doing so will improve the quality of your life and make you happier and healthier.

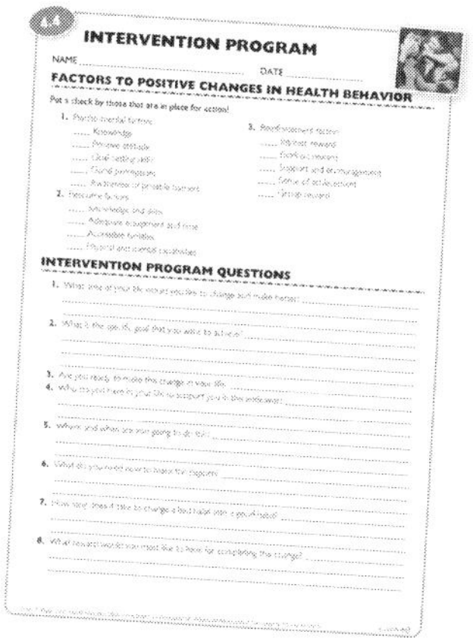
INTERVENTION PROGRAM

FACTORS TO POSITIVE CHANGES IN HEALTH BEHAVIOR

INTERVENTION PROGRAM QUESTIONS

4.4

HANDOUT 4.4

Factors to Positive Changes in Health Behavior

Ask the students to complete the checklist for the three areas necessary for behavior change: psycho-mental factors, resource factors, and reinforcement factors.

Intervention Program Questions

Have the students answer the intervention program questions. You may need to help them analyze their total health assessments. They should choose to improve a health area in which they had one of their lower scores.

Three-Week Goal

The time needed to change a bad habit into a good habit is anywhere from 40 to 180 days, depending on the person. Students will do this assignment over a period of only 21 days, but the process should give them all the skills they need to make changes in their health habits in any area of concern.

Three-Week Appraisal

Students should pick one area from the total health assessment that they need to improve and set out to make a change by altering some habits from that general category. For example, a student who selects exercise and leisure as an area of improvement might choose to do yoga or walk each day, or weight train twice a week. Students should record what they did each day to improve their chosen area of health.

CLOSURE

This intervention program gives you tools to make health changes in your life, whatever your age. The key process to any wellness program is making the changes and maintaining the good habits. I hope this makes sense to you.

Pain and Disability Act 7734

OBJECTIVE

Students will learn what it might be like to have a chronic illness or disability through an activity in which they will experience firsthand five common health disorders.

NATIONAL STANDARDS

- #1 Health Promotion
- #7 Healthy Behaviors
- #5 Decision Making

INTRODUCTION

Today I am going to make you sick. Most people take their health for granted until something happens to them or someone close to them. They then decide to change their lifestyle, but it is often too late. Consequently, they must endure pain and suffering before their time. Today you will experience firsthand several health problems. By doing so you may learn to appreciate your good health and not take it for granted.

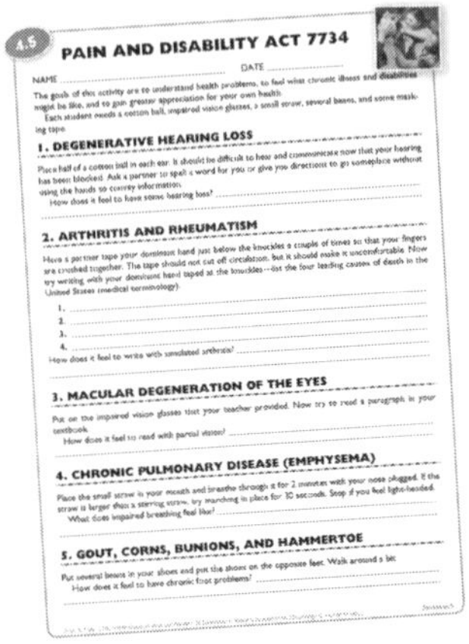
4.5

PAIN AND DISABILITY ACT 7734

NAME ________ DATE ________

The goals of this activity are to understand health problems, to feel what chronic illness and disabilities might be like, and to gain greater appreciation for your own health.

Each student needs a cotton ball, impaired vision glasses, a small straw, several beans, and some masking tape.

1. DEGENERATIVE HEARING LOSS

Place half of a cotton ball in each ear. It should be difficult to hear and communicate now that your hearing has been blocked. Ask a partner to spell a word for you or give you directions to go someplace without using the hands to convey information.

How does it feel to have some hearing loss? ________

2. ARTHRITIS AND RHEUMATISM

Have a partner tape your dominant hand just below the knuckles a couple of times so that your fingers are crushed together. The tape should not cut off circulation, but it should make it uncomfortable. Now try writing with your dominant hand taped at the knuckles—list the four leading causes of death in the United States (medical terminology).

1. ________
2. ________
3. ________
4. ________

How does it feel to write with simulated arthritis? ________

3. MACULAR DEGENERATION OF THE EYES

Put on the impaired vision glasses that your teacher provided. Now try to read a paragraph in your textbook.

How does it feel to read with partial vision? ________

4. CHRONIC PULMONARY DISEASE (EMPHYSEMA)

Place the small straw in your mouth and breathe through it for 2 minutes with your nose plugged. If the straw is larger than a stirring straw, try marching in place for 30 seconds. Stop if you feel light-headed.

What does impaired breathing feel like? ________

5. GOUT, CORNS, BUNIONS, AND HAMMERTOE

Put several beans in your shoes and put the shoes on the opposite feet. Walk around a bit.

How does it feel to have chronic foot problems? ________

HANDOUT 4.5

Talk to students about illness and disability. Ask them if they have ever been seriously ill Ask some of those who have been ill how it felt.

Hand out to each student one cotton ball, one small straw, 10 or 12 large beans, and a pair of sunglasses that impair vision. After they have completed all the tasks, have them comment on their feelings about these health problems.

1. Have the students divide their cotton balls in half and put half in each ear (hearing loss).
2. Wrap masking tape around each student's dominant hand just below the knuckles a couple of times so that the fingers are crushed together. Do not wrap so tightly that circulation is cut off, but wrap tightly enough to make it uncomfortable (arthritis).
3. Now have them do various tasks, such as writing down the four leading causes of death using medical terms. They will have difficulty hearing the terms which will be unfamiliar to them. This will be frustrating for them, which is the idea.
4. Have them put on the glasses that impair vision (macular degeneration). Ask them if they know anyone who has these problems.
5. Then have them put the small straw in their mouths and breathe through it while holding their noses so that they can feel what it is like to have emphysema. They should do this for 2 minutes. Doing this is hard, and they do not like it. You might comment, "I bet smokers never thought of this while they were smoking when they were young. You ruin some of your air sacs every time you smoke. Maybe people should appreciate their bodies more!"
6. Then have them put the beans in their shoes and put their shoes on the opposite feet to simulate gout, corns, bunions, and hammertoe. Have them walk around in the room or in the hallways to get the full effect of what foot problems are like. Doing this should be annoying.

Four Leading Causes of Death:

1. Myocardial infarction (heart disease)
2. Malignant neoplasms (cancer)
3. Cerebral vascular thrombosis (stroke)
4. Chronic obstructive pulmonary emphysema (lung disease)

CLOSURE

This lesson is meant to help you understand what it is like to have some common health problems. The lesson should also help you realize that by making positive lifestyle choices daily, you can prevent many health problems in your lifetime.

Health Vocabulary Words

OBJECTIVE

Students will learn all the major vocabulary words that will be used this semester through a teacher-led group discussion.

NATIONAL STANDARD

#1 Health Promotion

INTRODUCTION

Today we are getting the 50 new vocabulary words that we will be covering this semester. These words will be on the final exam. By going over them now, you will become familiar with them before the semester ends. By building your vocabulary and knowing the words, you will remember whole concepts of health.

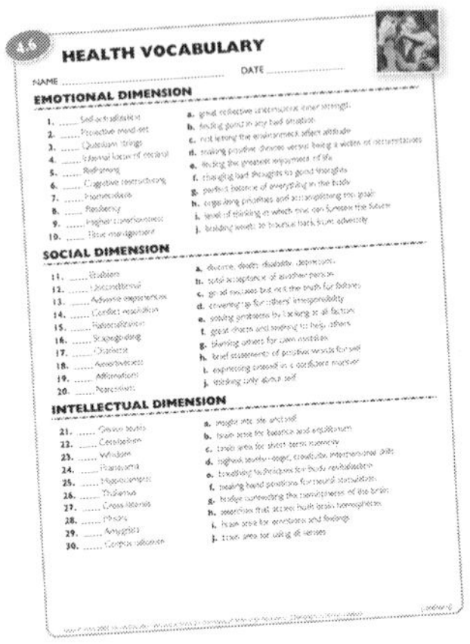

4.6

HANDOUT 4.6

Talk about each section before students match the statements and vocabulary. Ask whether anyone knows the answers and then discuss so that students can learn.

Emotional Dimension

1. e	**3.** i	**5.** b	**7.** g	**9.** a
2. d	**4.** c	**6.** f	**8.** j	**10.** h

Social Dimension

11. d	**13.** a	**15.** c	**17.** f	**19.** h
12. b	**14.** e	**16.** g	**18.** i	**20.** j

Intellectual Dimension

21. d	**23.** a	**25.** c	**27.** h	**29.** i
22. j	**24.** e	**26.** b	**28.** f	**30.** g

Physical Dimension

31. a	**35.** c	**39.** g	**43.** o	**47.** s
32. e	**36.** j	**40.** f	**44.** k	**48.** r
33. d	**37.** h	**41.** l	**45.** m	**49.** p
34. b	**38.** i	**42.** n	**46.** t	**50.** q

CLOSURE

Building your vocabulary will help you as we come across these words during the semester. Knowledge is good!

Wellness Test Key

OBJECTIVE

Students will be able to get at least 70% of the answers correct on the health and wellness test.

NATIONAL STANDARD

#1 Health Promotion

INTRODUCTION

This test covers the material that you learned during this unit. If you have any questions, please raise your hand, and I will come around to help you. Good luck.

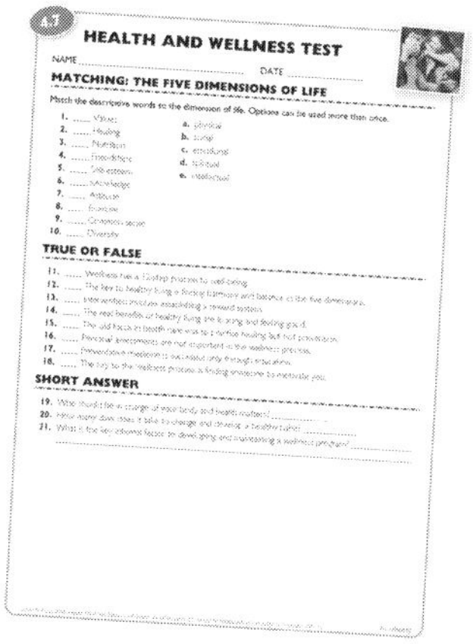
4.7
HEALTH AND WELLNESS TEST
MATCHING: THE FIVE DIMENSIONS OF LIFE
TRUE OR FALSE
SHORT ANSWER

4.7

HANDOUT 4.7

Matching: The Five Dimensions of Life

1. d	**3.** a	**5.** c	**7.** c	**9.** e
2. a	**4.** b	**6.** e	**8.** a	**10.** b

True or False

11. false—There is a three-step process to wellness (assessment, intervention, reinforcement).
12. true
13. false—Intervention is making a positive lifestyle change.
14. true
15. true
16. false—Personal assessments are important for lifestyle changes.
17. true
18. false—The key to the wellness process is self-motivation.

Short Answer

19. you
20. 40 days
21. self-motivation

Matching: Key Factors for Health and Longevity

22. a	**24.** d
23. c	**25.** b

Matching: Ultimate Goals of High-Level Wellness

26. e	**29.** c
27. d	**30.** a
28. b	

CLOSURE

Making positive lifestyle changes in your life is good. You are not doing it for someone else, but for your own well-being and happiness.

The Human Body and Medicine

> I SWEAR TO FULFILL, TO THE BEST OF MY ABILITY AND JUDGMENT, ALL OF THESE COVENANTS OF THE MEDICAL PROFESSION.
>
> **Hippocratic oath**

Lesson Finder

Amazing Facts About the Human Body

OBJECTIVE

Students will discover how amazing the human body is by discussing some interesting facts.

NATIONAL STANDARD

#1 Health Promotion

INTRODUCTION

The human body is far more miraculous than people can imagine. It is the greatest machine ever assembled. Its capabilities and potential are phenomenal. Everyone should know something about how the body works. This sheet goes over some of the amazing statistics about the human body.

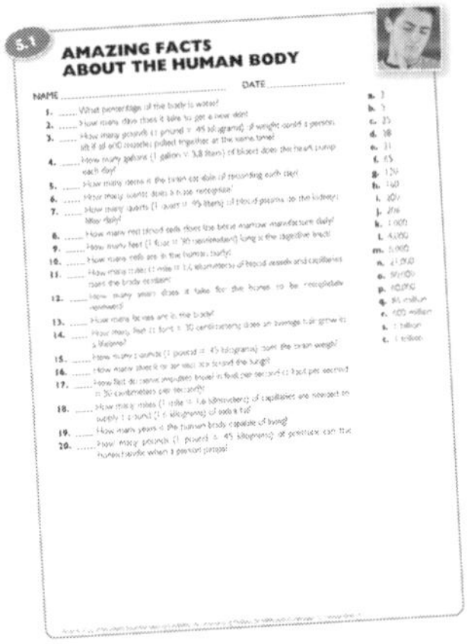

5.1

HANDOUT 5.1

Give students a few minutes to answer the questions. Then go down the list with the whole class to see how many of these interesting facts they really know. Ask students to volunteer to read the question aloud and offer an educated guess. Help them if they do not give the correct answer. Emphasize the magnificence of the human body as you go through the questions.

Matching

1. f	**6.** l	**11.** p	**16.** r
2. e	**7.** h	**12.** a	**17.** n
3. o	**8.** s	**13.** j	**18.** i
4. m	**9.** d	**14.** c	**19.** g
5. q	**10.** t	**15.** b	**20.** k

CLOSURE

I hope this activity made you realize that the human body is a magnificent machine that can last for decades if cared for properly. By the time this unit is over, you will have gained a greater appreciation for the human body and what can be done to heal it.

Medical Interns Group Project

OBJECTIVE

Students will be able to teach their classmates one system of the human body with a partner or two.

NATIONAL STANDARDS

- #5 Decision Making
- #3 Information and Services
- #4 Communication

INTRODUCTION

This exercise is a great way to learn about the human body. You will become the experts in at least one system of the body after preparing for a couple of days. Make sure that your group splits up the duties of teaching so that everyone receives a fair grade. The teaching session is worth 40 points. Your sessions will help all of us learn more about the body.

HANDOUT 5.2

Provide students with a diagram of their system (handouts 5.3 through 5.12) and set up a model of the human torso so that everyone can see it. Let the students do the teaching. Help them if necessary. Grade them while they are teaching with a separate grade for each student. After the students have finished their lessons, ask whether anyone has any questions.

HANDOUT 5.3

HANDOUT 5.4

HANDOUT 5.5

HANDOUT 5.6

HANDOUT 5.7

HANDOUT 5.8

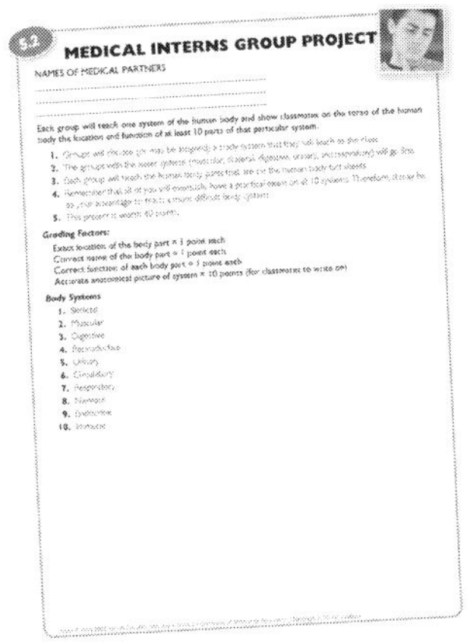

5.2

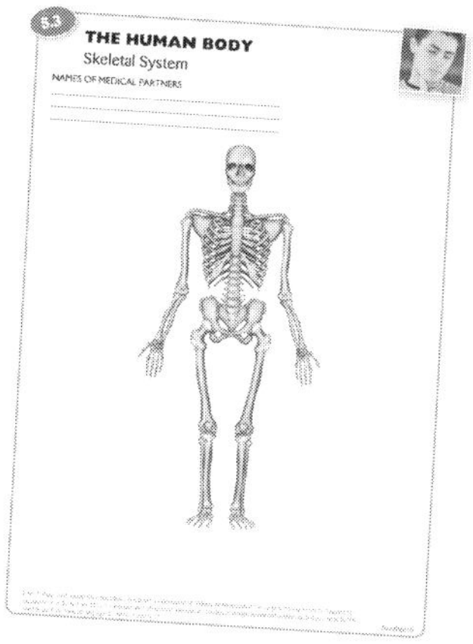

5.3

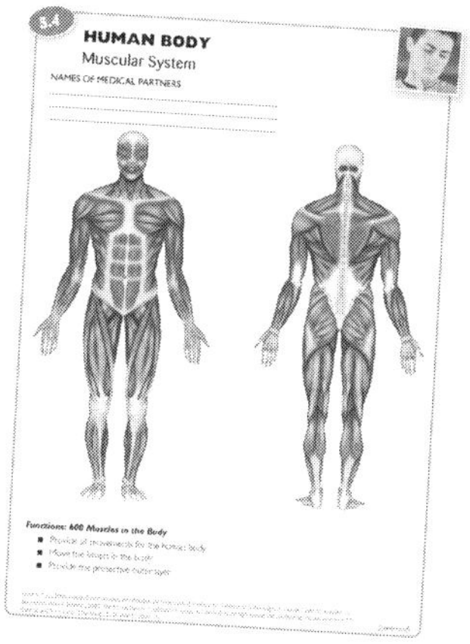

5.4

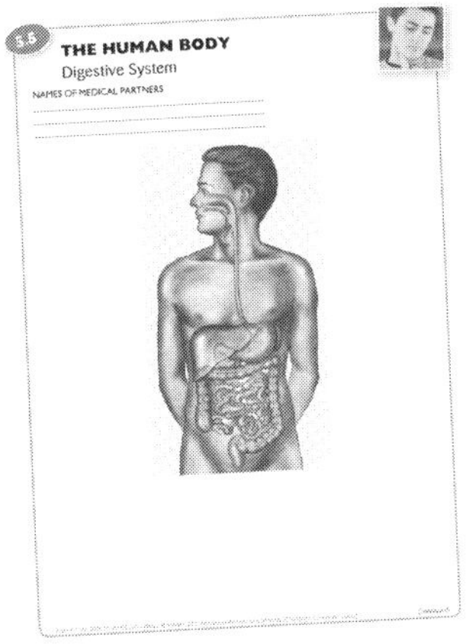

5.5

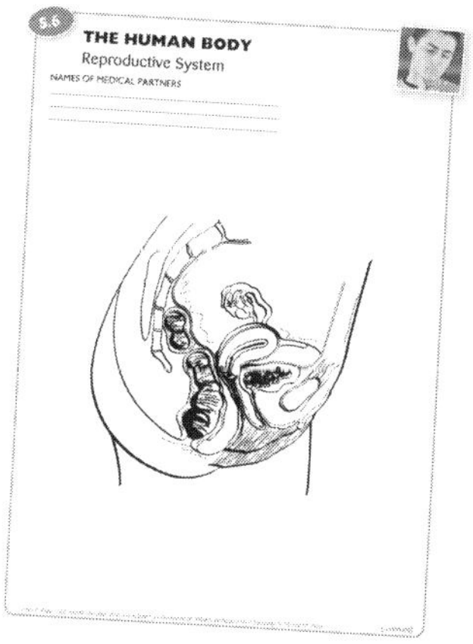

5.6

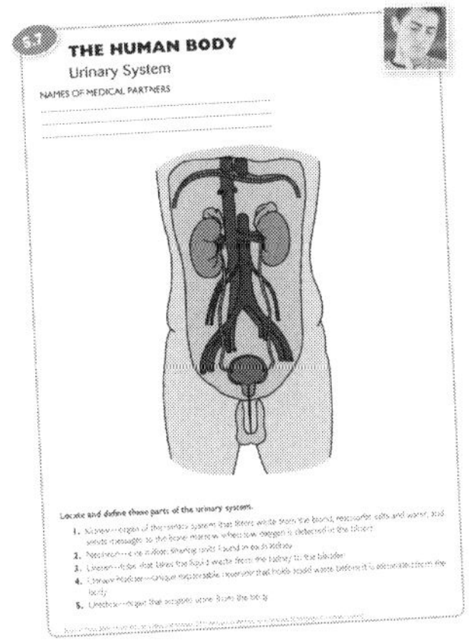

5.7

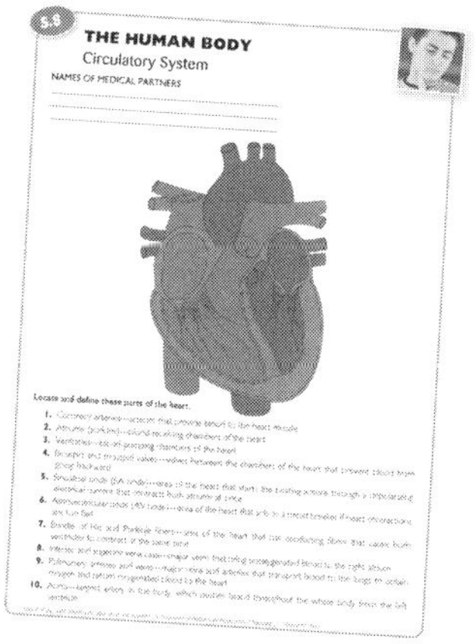

5.8

HANDOUT 5.9
HANDOUT 5.10
HANDOUT 5.11
HANDOUT 5.12

CLOSURE

Thank you, interns, for your presentations. You can take this knowledge with you as you study to become a member of the medical profession.

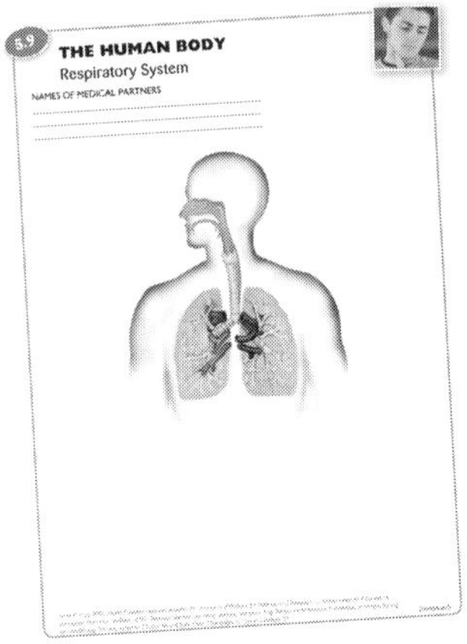

5.9

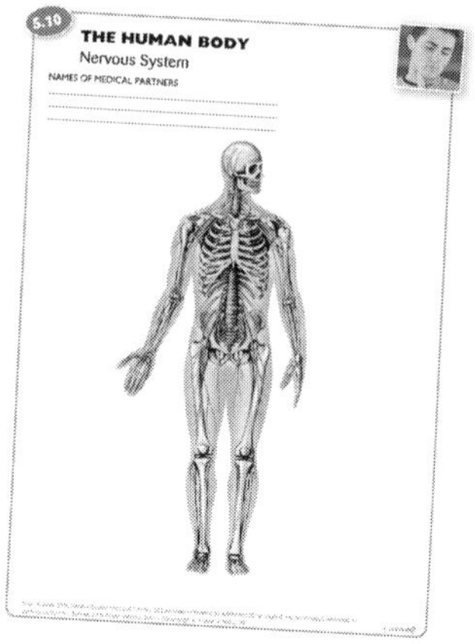

5.10

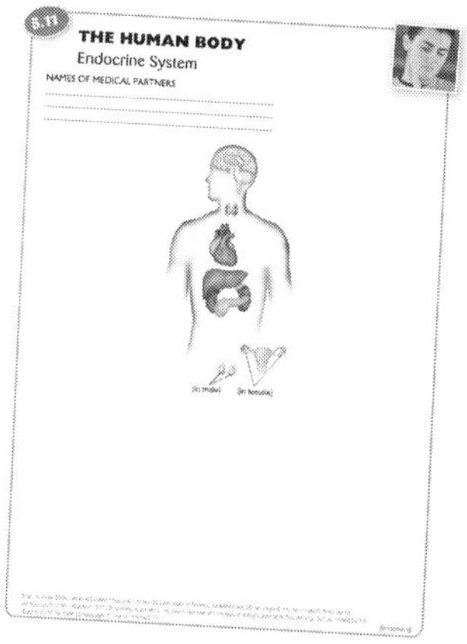

5.11

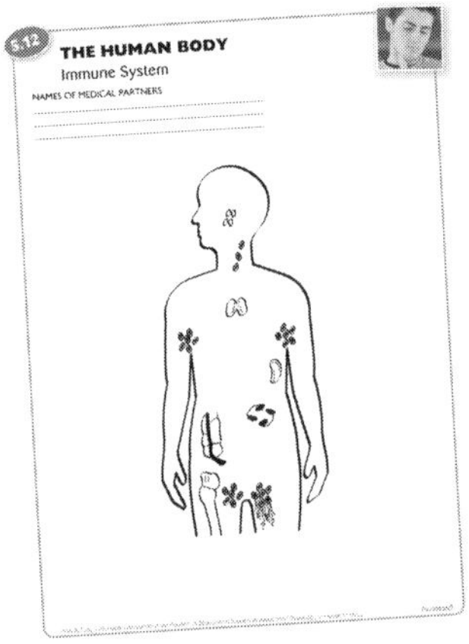

5.12

Human Body Silhouette Assignment

OBJECTIVE

Students will be able to draw and label at least 30 parts of the human body, including at least 3 parts from every system of the human body.

NATIONAL STANDARDS

- #1 Health Promotion
- #5 Decision Making
- #3 Information and Services

INTRODUCTION

This assignment will help you learn more about the human body than any other assignment. If you can draw the organs in the right place and at the right size, you will never forget that information. This task will challenge you more than you realize. You will learn where each body part is in relationship to the others. After you have studied each system well, you can report to me and identify 10 parts of a system and the function of those parts. This exercise is known as a practical exam.

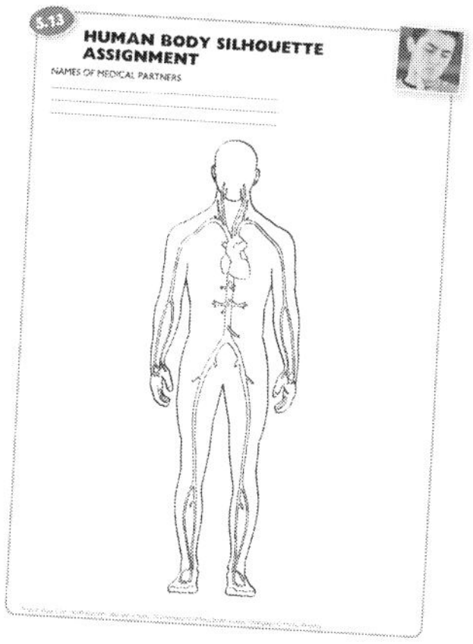

5.13

HANDOUT 5.13

This assignment will tell you exactly how much students know about the human body. You need a complete picture of the human body here, ideally with only the circulatory system shown inside. Students will draw and label everything else for the assignment—at least 30 body parts depending on your expectations. This assignment is a wonderful way for students to learn about the human body.

Make sure to give students time in class to work on this assignment. Inform them that they cannot begin the practical exam on the human body until they hand in this assignment.

CLOSURE

Great job on these human silhouettes!

Human Body Practical Exam

OBJECTIVE

Students will be able to check out on all human body systems by showing and telling the teacher or the "doctors on staff" (students in the classroom assigned by the teacher to check out other students) the location and function of all body organs on the human body teaching torso.

NATIONAL STANDARDS

- #1 Health Promotion
- #5 Decision Making
- #4 Communication

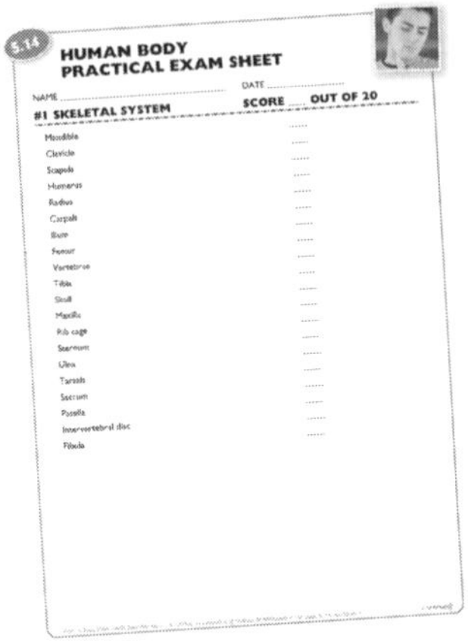
HUMAN BODY PRACTICAL EXAM SHEET
NAME DATE
#1 SKELETAL SYSTEM SCORE OUT OF 20

5.14

INTRODUCTION

Now let's see how much you have learned in the past couple of weeks. Your job is to make sure that you check off on some systems each day. You have only a week to complete this task. You can do only one system at a time, but you can check out on as many systems per day as you wish.

HANDOUT 5.14

Each day students can come up to you or one of the "doctors on staff" and ask to be checked out on a system. They should come prepared with their practical exam sheet so that you can check them off for the proper location on the torso and the function.

CLOSURE

Seeing you checking out on the human body is great. I cannot believe how well you have learned this material. This is truly a test of your knowledge on the human body. Someday some of you will be in the medical profession. We should all know what is under our skin and how those organs work. Keep up the good work!

Human Body Quiz

OBJECTIVE

Students will be able to match the facts and data to the vocabulary listed on the sheet with 70% accuracy.

NATIONAL STANDARD

- #1 Health Promotion

INTRODUCTION

This test will measure your overall knowledge about the human body and health matters. These questions focus on important points about the body and health. Read the question and write in the correct answer. Some answers are used more than once.

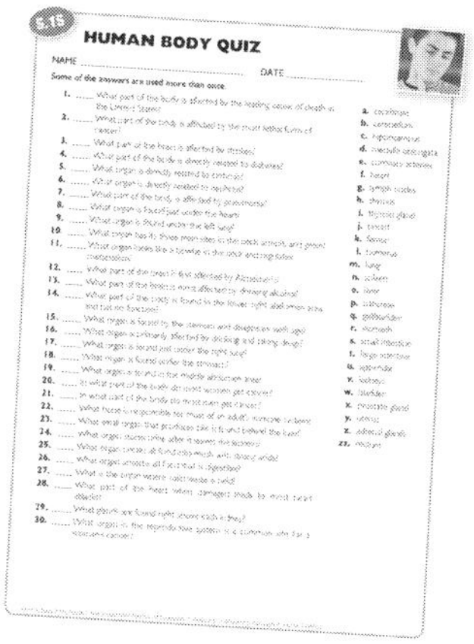

5.15

HANDOUT 5.15

Answers

1. f	**11.** i	**21.** x
2. m	**12.** c	**22.** k
3. a	**13.** b	**23.** q
4. p	**14.** u	**24.** w
5. o	**15.** h	**25.** r
6. v	**16.** o	**26.** s
7. m	**17.** o	**27.** zz
8. r	**18.** p	**28.** e
9. n	**19.** s	**29.** z
10. g	**20.** j	**30.** y

CLOSURE

The human body is a magnificent machine. I hope that this unit opened your eyes to the wonders of the human body.

Health Care System

OBJECTIVE

Students will be able to see whether they are wise health care consumers.

NATIONAL STANDARDS

- #1 Health Promotion
- #5 Decision Making

INTRODUCTION

Access to the health care system is important to your health and longevity. You should have health insurance and be a wise consumer so that you can receive proper medical care. This handout will be interesting and helpful.

HEALTH CARE SYSTEM

MATCHING: HEALTH CARE VOCABULARY

5.16

HANDOUT 5.16

Matching: Health Care Vocabulary

Let us see if you know any of the vocabulary words about the health care system. You should know some of these. Let us talk and figure them out.

1. c	**7.** l
2. k	**8.** e
3. i	**9.** g
4. a	**10.** h
5. j	**11.** b
6. f	**12.** d

Health Consumer Survey

Let us check the health consumer survey and see whether you can match the following answers to the problematic situations. After we have gone over the answers, we can discuss any questions that you might have about this consumer survey.

1. c	**6.** d
2. i	**7.** g
3. h	**8.** j
4. f	**9.** b
5. e	**10.** a

CLOSURE

How you access the health care system is vital to your health. Make sure that you have health insurance and know how to deal with health concerns at the hospital level.

Healing Through Humor and Compassion

OBJECTIVE

The students will examine the health care system by watching and discussing the movie *Patch Adams.*

NATIONAL STANDARDS

- #1 Health Promotion
- #4 Communication

INTRODUCTION

This movie tells a wonderful story about a man named Patch Adams. The movie shows how he became interested in the field of medicine and what prompted his idea to provide health care for the people who do not have insurance or access to affordable health care. The story is about healing with love and compassion. We will talk each day about the segment that we watched and will answer the questions on the Patch Adams worksheet. Try to answer them as we go along.

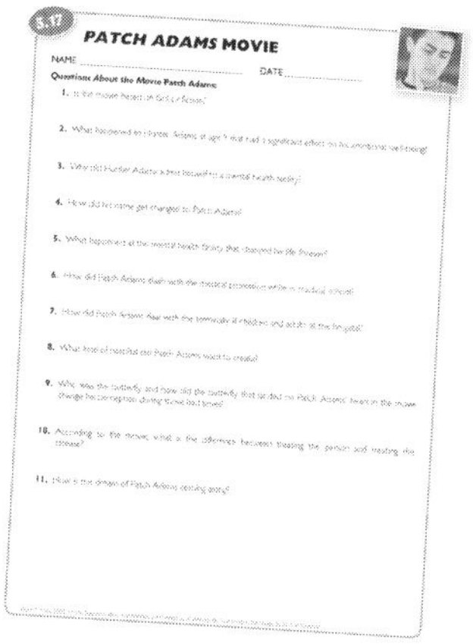

5.17

HANDOUT 5.17

1. It is based on fact.
2. His father died, and he realized that his father didn't hate him.
3. He was going to commit suicide.
4. He fixed up and helped people.
5. He saw through the problem to the source, helped another person with a problem.
6. He used humor and compassion as well as healing, treated the whole person.
7. Patch made them laugh and helped them attain their last wishes. He was there for them in their last days.
8. A free hospital where patients learned from each other and humor and compassion were used as therapy.
9. The butterfly symbolized Carin. Carin was free (sexually abused as child), and was saying to not give up, that passions are good.
10. When you treat the whole person it is win–win; treating a disease is win–lose!
11. Patch is still raising money for his facility in West Virginia called Gesundheit.

CLOSURE

Patch Adams is still trying to build a hospital in rural West Virginia for people who have no health care. His movie and talks around the country are providing funds for this dream. His hospital, called Gesundheit, is based on sound health care and includes a lot of humor and compassion.

Medical Terminology and Health Examination

HISTORY OF MEDICINE

Twenty-Four Hundred Years of Progress

MATCHING: GREAT MEDICAL MARVELS

MATCHING: RECENT MEDICAL MARVELS

5.18

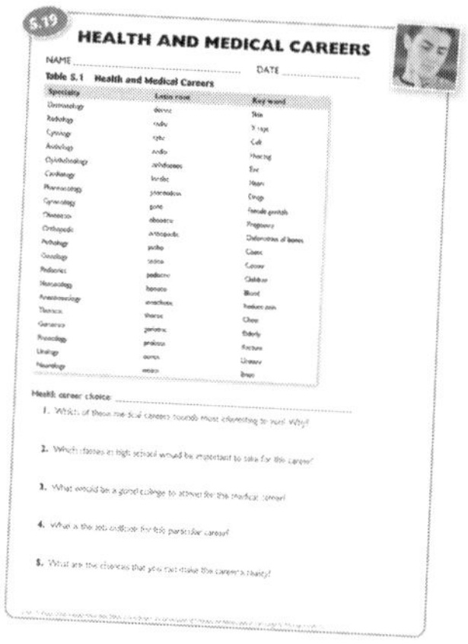
HEALTH AND MEDICAL CAREERS

Table 5.1 Health and Medical Careers

5.19

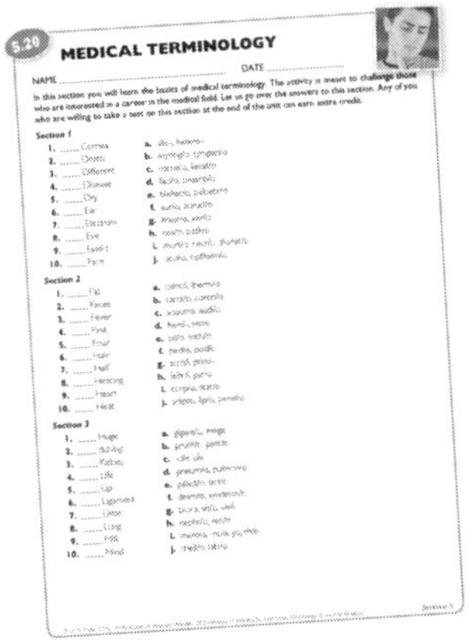
MEDICAL TERMINOLOGY

5.20

OBJECTIVE

Students will learn medical careers, terminology, and the basics of a health examination through personal research and open discussions.

NATIONAL STANDARDS

- #1 Health Promotion
- #7 Healthy Behaviors
- #5 Decision Making
- #3 Information and Services
- #4 Communication

INTRODUCTION

Medicine is a rewarding profession in our culture. Medical practitioners are those who want to heal and help those with pain, disease, and infirmity. This part of the unit will be a learning experience for those who are thinking about the medical field as a career.

HANDOUT 5.18

Examine some of the famous men and women in medical history by discussing the sheet about the history of medicine.

Matching: Great Medical Marvels

1. i	**3.** g	**5.** b	**7.** j	**9.** d
2. h	**4.** f	**6.** c	**8.** e	**10.** a

Matching: Recent Medical Marvels

1. a	**3.** c	**5.** e	**7.** g	**9.** i
2. b	**4.** d	**6.** f	**8.** h	**10.** j

HANDOUT 5.19

Learn the 20 health career specialty areas and do some research about the area that is most interesting to you.

HANDOUT 5.20

Examine the 70 most common medical terms and their Latin roots for a better understanding of medical terminology.

Section 1

1. c	**3.** a	**5.** g	**7.** b	**9.** e
2. i	**4.** h	**6.** f	**8.** j	**10.** d

Section 2

1. j	**3.** h	**5.** f	**7.** d	**9.** b
2. i	**4.** g	**6.** e	**8.** c	**10.** a

Section 3

1. a	**3.** h	**5.** j	**7.** c	**9.** e
2. b	**4.** g	**6.** f	**8.** d	**10.** i

Section 4

1. d	**3.** f	**5.** i	**7.** e	**9.** j
2. c	**4.** b	**6.** g	**8.** a	**10.** h

Section 5

1. d	**3.** c	**5.** e	**7.** g	**9.** b
2. i	**4.** a	**6.** j	**8.** h	**10.** f

Section 6

1. c	**3.** i	**5.** f	**7.** b	**9.** j
2. e	**4.** h	**6.** d	**8.** a	**10.** g

Section 7

1. c	**3.** f	**5.** h	**7.** g
2. d	**4.** b	**6.** a	**8.** e

CLOSURE

This section on health careers and medical terminology was meant to give you an in-depth study of the healing arts. I hope that the study was fun, challenging, and interesting. The medical profession is one of the most revered professions in our society.

6

Longevity and Death

THERE IS NO CURE FOR BIRTH AND DEATH SAVE TO ENJOY THE INTERVAL.

George Santayana

Lesson Finder

Leading Causes of Death

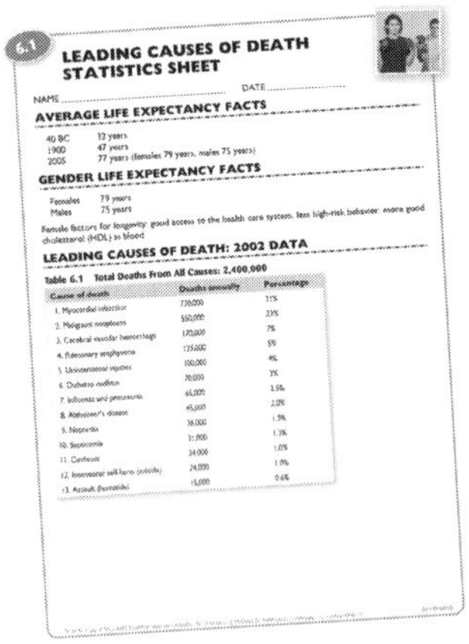
LEADING CAUSES OF DEATH STATISTICS SHEET

NAME .... DATE ....

AVERAGE LIFE EXPECTANCY FACTS

40 BC 22 years
1900 47 years
2005 77 years (females 79 years, males 75 years)

GENDER LIFE EXPECTANCY FACTS

Females 79 years
Males 75 years

Female factors for longevity: good access to the health care system, less high-risk behavior, more good cholesterol (HDL) in blood

LEADING CAUSES OF DEATH: 2002 DATA

Table 6.1 Total Deaths From All Causes: 2,400,000

Cause of death	Deaths annually	Percentage
1. Myocardial infarction	720,000	[illegible]
2. Malignant neoplasms	550,000	23%
3. Cerebral vascular hemorrhage	170,000	7%
4. Pulmonary emphysema	125,000	5%
5. Unintentional injuries	100,000	4%
6. Diabetes mellitus	70,000	3%
7. Influenza and pneumonia	65,000	2.5%
8. Alzheimer's disease	45,000	2.0%
9. Nephritis	36,000	1.5%
10. Septicemia	31,000	1.3%
11. Cirrhosis	24,000	1.0%
12. Intentional self-harm (suicide)	24,000	1.0%
13. Assault (homicide)	15,000	0.6%

6.1

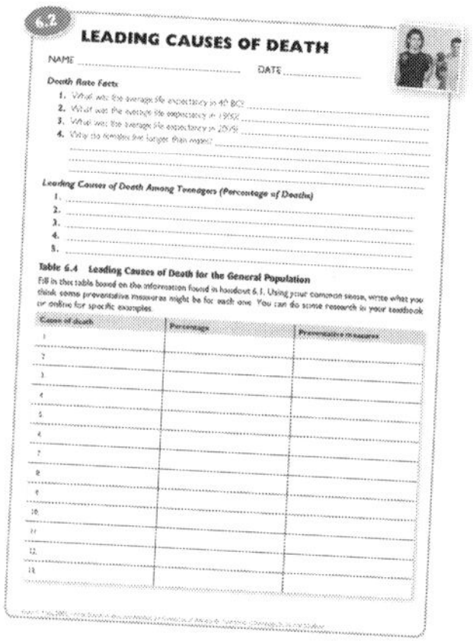
LEADING CAUSES OF DEATH

NAME .... DATE ....

Death Rate Facts

1.
2.
3.
4.

Leading Causes of Death Among Teenagers (Percentage of Deaths)

1.
2.
3.
4.
5.

Table 6.4 Leading Causes of Death for the General Population

Fill in this table based on the information found in handout 6.1. Using your common sense, write what you think some preventative measures might be for each one. You can do some research in your textbook or online for specific examples.

Cause of death	Percentage	Preventative measures
1		
2		
3		
4		
5		
6		
7		
8		
9		
10		
11		
12		
13		

6.2

OBJECTIVE

By examining the data sheet, students will be able to identify the leading causes of death in the United States and name some preventive measures.

NATIONAL STANDARDS

- #1 Health Promotion
- #7 Healthy Behaviors
- #5 Decision Making

INTRODUCTION

The human body is capable of living more than 120 years. Today we are going to examine the leading causes of death in the United States and discover what we can do to slow the process of aging and add years to our lives.

HANDOUT 6.1

HANDOUT 6.2

1. Have the students use the statistic sheet (handout 6.1) to figure out death rate facts, causes of death among teenagers, and causes of death among adults. They can then use it to complete handout 6.2.
2. Discuss the sheet after students have completed it.
3. Show them pictures or slides of the leading causes of death in the United States.

CLOSURE

Preventative measures could make a huge difference in the life span of Americans. This week we will examine the leading causes of death and identify what people can do to avoid dying early from these complications.

Fountain of Youth

OBJECTIVE

Students will be able to determine the 10 key factors to living a long life and delaying the onset of degenerative disease by processing data on longevity and death.

NATIONAL STANDARDS

- #1 Health Promotion
- #7 Healthy Behaviors
- #3 Information and Services
- #4 Communication

INTRODUCTION

People have talked forever about the fountain of youth that Ponce de Leon searched for in America. He was looking for the water that would keep people young for a long time. He never found the well, but you can find a fountain of youth by observing a particular lifestyle. You can be younger than your years. We are going to study the key factors that determine health and longevity. Then, to find the fountain of youth, you will pick out the 10 factors that are more important than any others.

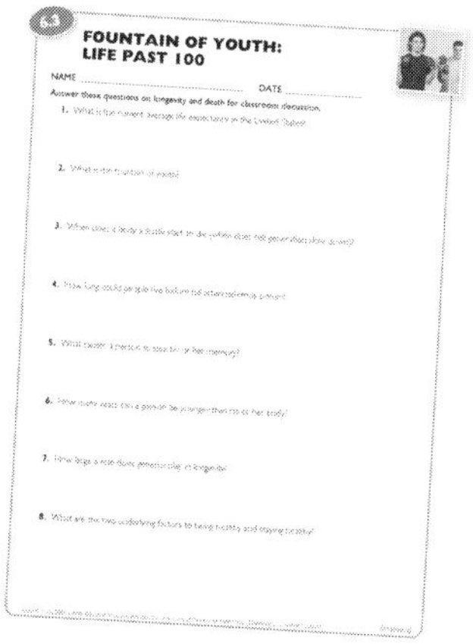
FOUNTAIN OF YOUTH: LIFE PAST 100

6.3

HANDOUT 6.3

Discuss the 10 questions related to aging and death.

1. 77
2. lifestyle of healthy habits
3. age 30
4. 120 to 130 years
5. failure to use the brain each day
6. 25 to 30 years
7. 25%
8. self-esteem and medical knowledge
9. stress
10. genetics and lifestyle

The following five factors contribute the most to lowering life expectancy:

tobacco smoking

diet and obesity

lack of exercise

alcohol abuse

infectious agents

HANDOUT 6.4

Examine the fountain of youth assessment and discuss with the class how these habits help longevity and how not doing these things can hurt it.

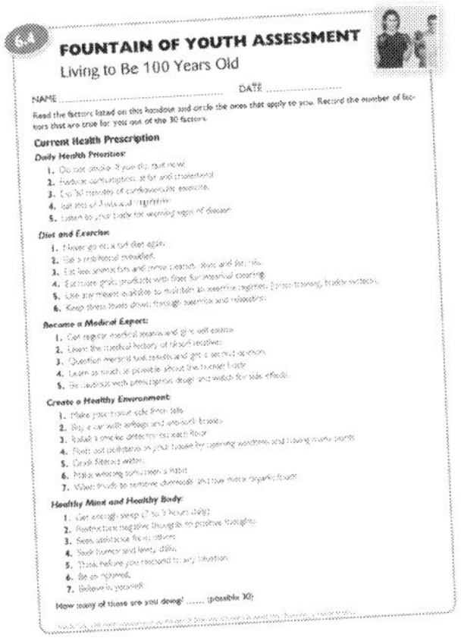
FOUNTAIN OF YOUTH ASSESSMENT

Living to Be 100 Years Old

6.4

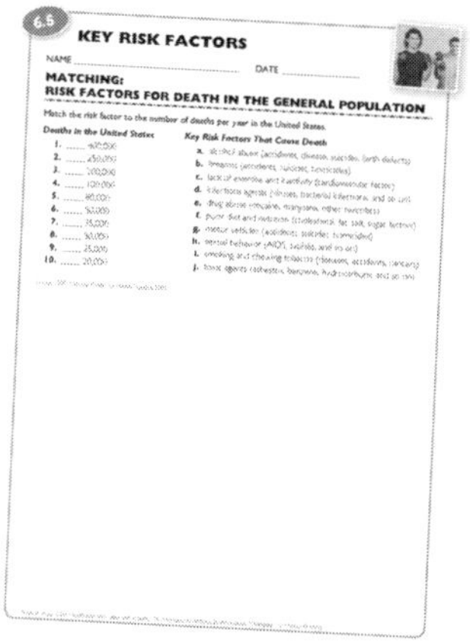

6.5

HANDOUT 6.5

Determine the 10 key factors and the number of deaths that they cause yearly. Then examine the data sheet answers and come up with some conclusions.

1. i
2. f
3. c
4. a
5. d
6. j
7. b
8. g
9. e
10. h

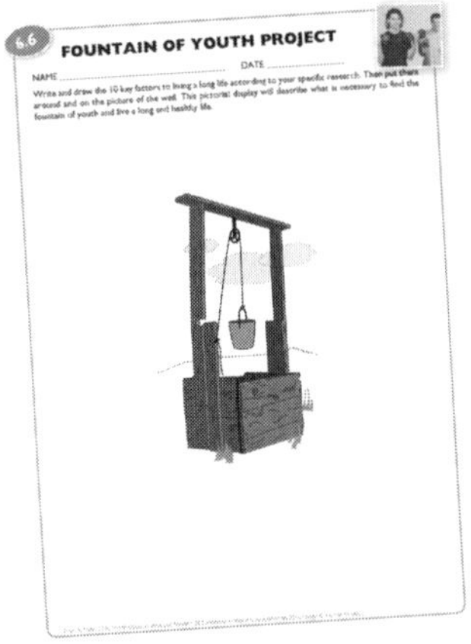

6.6

HANDOUT 6.6

Using what you have learned from handouts 6.4 and 6.5, identify the 10 key factors to health and well-being and list them on the fountain of youth sheet.

CLOSURE

After looking at all the data and facts, you should come up with at least 10 key factors to finding the fountain of youth. These factors can make you look young and feel great even into your older years. Is it worth the time and effort to develop habits conducive to living longer? That is a question you will have to ponder. Remember that having good habits will also improve your quality of life. You make the choice!

Longevity and Death Test Key

OBJECTIVE

Students will be able to complete the test on longevity and death with 70% accuracy.

NATIONAL STANDARD

#1 Health Promotion

INTRODUCTION

This test covers the material that we discussed and studied in this unit. If you have any questions, please raise your hand so that I can help you.

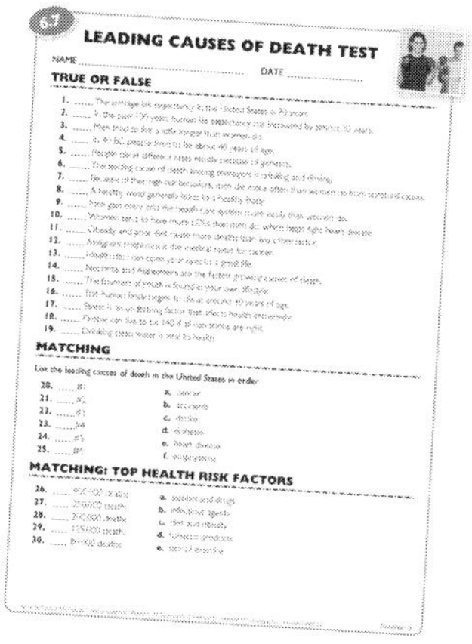
6.7 LEADING CAUSES OF DEATH TEST
TRUE OR FALSE
MATCHING
MATCHING: TOP HEALTH RISK FACTORS

6.7

HANDOUT 6.7

True or False

1. false—The average life expectancy in the United States is 77 years.
2. true
3. false—Women tend to live 4 years longer than men do.
4. false—In 40 BC life expectancy was 32 years.
5. false—Death rates are related more to lifestyle than they are to any other factor.
6. true
7. true
8. true
9. false—Women gain entry into the health care system more easily than men do.
10. false—Women have more HDLs to fight against heart disease.
11. false—Smoking causes more illnesses and death than any other factor.
12. true
13. true
14. true
15. true
16. false—The decline of cell reproduction in the body occurs around age 30.
17. true
18. false—The longest-living people in the world are around 120 years old.
19. true

Matching

20. e
21. a
22. c
23. f
24. b
25. d

Matching: Top Health Risk Factors

26. d

27. c

28. e

29. a

30. b

Matching: Causes of Death Among Teenagers

31. e

32. b

33. a

34. c

35. d

CLOSURE

I hope that you all did well on the test. The habits that you choose and the way that you think are key ingredients to living a long and happy life.

7

Nutrition and Body Image

EAT BREAKFAST LIKE A KING, EAT LUNCH LIKE A PRINCE, AND EAT SUPPER LIKE A PAUPER.

Adelle Davis

Lesson Finder

Nutrition Awareness

OBJECTIVE

Students will be able to analyze the facts concerning foods and risk elements in the diet through a discussion and personal evaluation.

NATIONAL STANDARDS

- #1 Health Promotion
- #7 Healthy Behaviors
- #4 Communication

INTRODUCTION

A poor diet is the most easily preventable factor concerning your health. The old saying "You are what you eat" is true. What are you then? Most people do not think about what they put into their bodies on a regular basis.

How would your car run if you did not put the right fuel in the tank? Many people take better care of their cars than they do their bodies. All of us need to recognize how important diet is to our life and health.

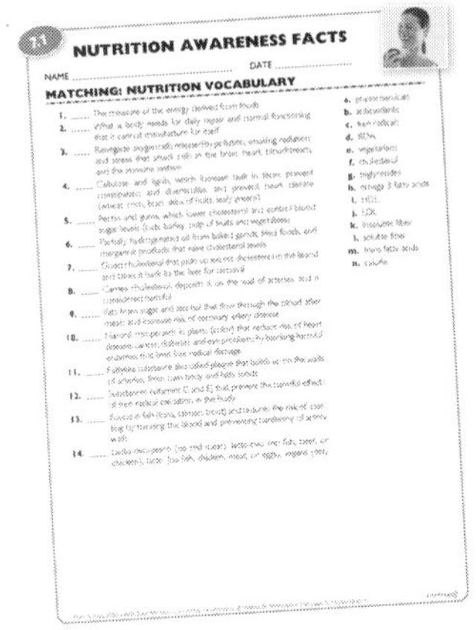
7.1 NUTRITION AWARENESS FACTS
MATCHING: NUTRITION VOCABULARY

7.1

HANDOUT 7.1

Matching: Nutrition Vocabulary

1. n	**5.** l	**9.** g	**13.** h
2. d	**6.** m	**10.** a	**14.** e
3. c	**7.** i	**11.** f	
4. k	**8.** j	**12.** b	

Matching: Essential Nutrients

1. b	**5.** a
2. e	**6.** g
3. d	**7.** c
4. f	

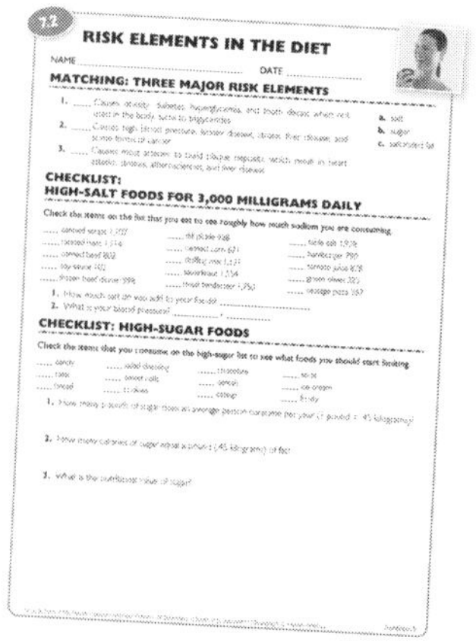
7.2 RISK ELEMENTS IN THE DIET
MATCHING: THREE MAJOR RISK ELEMENTS
CHECKLIST: HIGH-SALT FOODS FOR 3,000 MILLIGRAMS DAILY
CHECKLIST: HIGH-SUGAR FOODS

7.2

HANDOUT 7.2

Matching: Three Major Risk Elements

1. b
2. a
3. c

Checklist: High-Sugar Foods

1. over 100
2. 1 pound (.45 kilograms) of fat = 3,500 calories of sugar
3. zero

Checklist: High Saturated Fats (Cholesterol) for 60 to 70 Fat Grams per Day

1. less than 60 grams per day
2. fish, peanuts, olive oil, soybeans
3. less than 200
4. greater than 40
5. less than 100

CLOSURE

You need to know more about foods and think about what you are putting into your human machine every day. You are what you eat!

Body Image and a Healthy Diet

OBJECTIVE

Students will be able to list the 10 best ways to keep weight at a healthy and desirable level.

NATIONAL STANDARDS

- #1 Health Promotion
- #7 Healthy Behaviors

INTRODUCTION

Looking good and feeling good are important aspects of healthy living. You will need a lot of self-discipline and willpower to modify your diet for the prevention of degenerative diseases. You can do several things every day to keep your weight within desirable limits. Let us see what we can learn today.

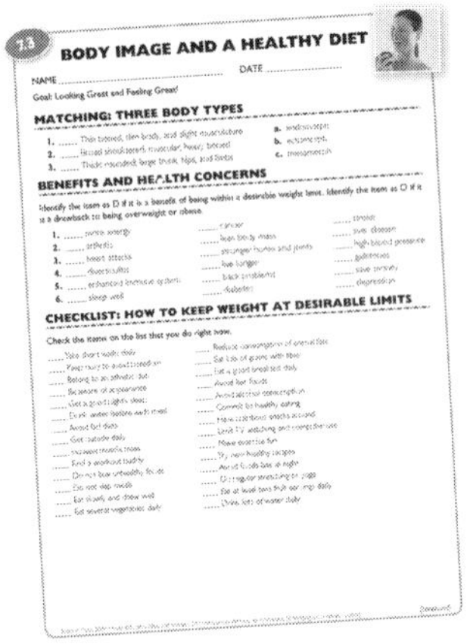
BODY IMAGE AND A HEALTHY DIET

MATCHING: THREE BODY TYPES

BENEFITS AND HEALTH CONCERNS

CHECKLIST: HOW TO KEEP WEIGHT AT DESIRABLE LIMITS

7.3

HANDOUT 7.3

Matching: Three Body Types

1. b
2. c
3. a—The endomorph will always be big because of the large bone frame and never really slender, so genetics has something to do with body size.

Benefits and Health Concerns

1. D-O-O
2. O-D-O
3. O-D-O
4. O-D-O
5. D-O-D
6. D-O-O

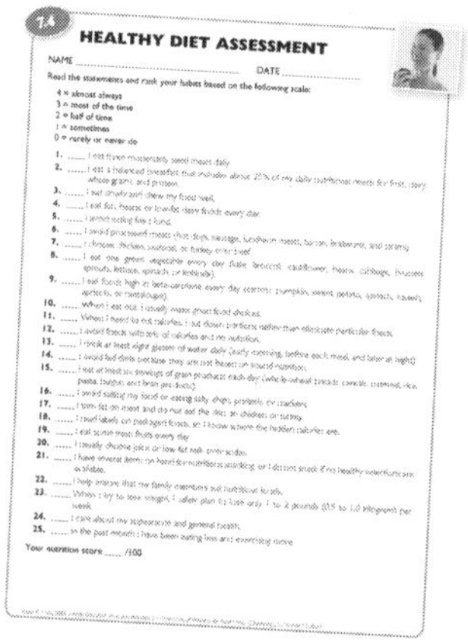
HEALTHY DIET ASSESSMENT

7.4

HANDOUT 7.4

Complete the healthy diet assessment and check out your nutrition score. The score indicates a general dietary appraisal for your food consumption at this time in your life. The more of these habits you have, the better your chances of having a healthy body.

CLOSURE

You should start to make healthy eating choices at a young age, even if your family does not practice healthy eating. You may even be able to persuade your parents to make some changes for their health. Eating good foods takes a conscious effort on the part of the whole family.

Break the Fast

OBJECTIVE

Students will be able to find the best sources of quick and easy foods for breakfast, the most important meal of the day.

NATIONAL STANDARDS

- #1 Health Promotion
- #7 Healthy Behaviors
- #5 Decision Making
- #3 Information and Services
- #4 Communication

HANDOUT 7.5

Breakfast Questions

1. increases body metabolism, mental alertness, and performance
2. 25%
3. 2 weeks
4. eating late the night before
5. 5 minutes
6. cereal
7. 30%
8. 50%

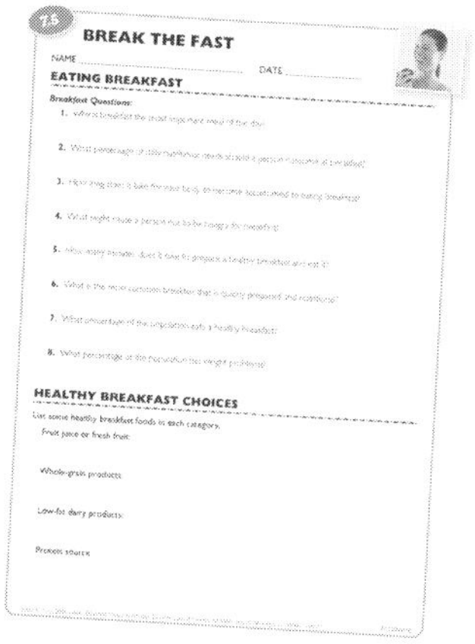

7.5

CLOSURE

If you are going to improve your eating habits, you need to start with the most important meal first. I hope that all of you will start eating a nutritional breakfast so that you feel energized, look good, and can perform well mentally in school. Eating a nutritious breakfast is a great way to change every day of your life.

Healing Foods

OBJECTIVE

Students will be able to recognize which foods in the American diet are the most beneficial for health and well-being.

NATIONAL STANDARDS

- #1 Health Promotion
- #5 Decision Making
- #8 Advocacy

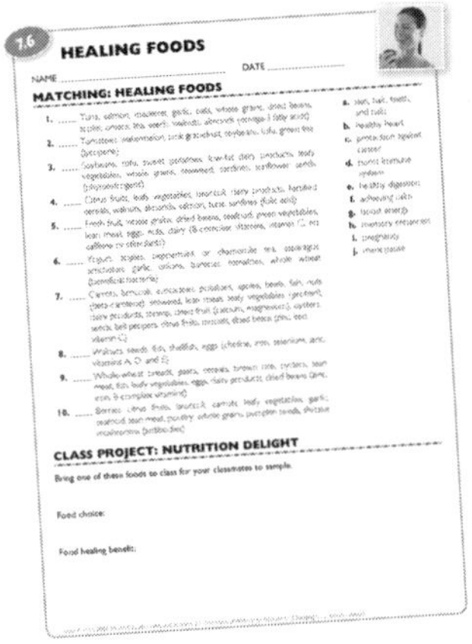
HEALING FOODS

MATCHING: HEALING FOODS

CLASS PROJECT: NUTRITION DELIGHT

7.6

HANDOUT 7.6

Matching: Healing Foods

1. f	**6.** e
2. c	**7.** a
3. j	**8.** h
4. i	**9.** g
5. b	**10.** d

Class Project: Nutrition Delight

Each of you must bring one healing food to class on the designated day so that we can sample a variety of healthy foods. Some of you may wish to put your resources together and make something with a mix of foods. You will be eating one of the most nutritional meals of your life in this class. You will find that these foods taste good and are great for you. Maybe you will find some new foods that you can add to your regular diet. Talk with me if there is some reason why you will not be able to bring food for our nutrition delight day.

CLOSURE

You must sign up on this sheet today for the nutrition delight meal this later this week. We are doing this so that everyone does not bring the same foods. We could also use some plates, forks, bowls, or napkins for the meal. Those of you who bring those items will earn extra credit.

Nutrition Awareness Test Key

OBJECTIVE

Students will pass a written evaluation on nutrition after a unit on nutrients, risk elements in the diet, and healthy foods.

NATIONAL STANDARDS

- #1 Health Promotion
- #7 Healthy Behaviors

INTRODUCTION

This is the test on Nutrition Awareness. If there are any questions, please raise your hand. Once you are finished, please hand the test to the instructor.

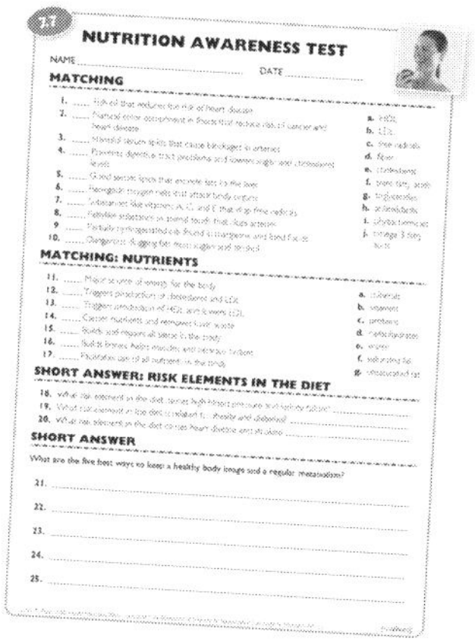
NUTRITION AWARENESS TEST
NAME DATE
MATCHING
MATCHING: NUTRIENTS
SHORT ANSWER: RISK ELEMENTS IN THE DIET
SHORT ANSWER
What are the five best ways to keep a healthy body image and a regular metabolism?

7.7

HANDOUT 7.7

Matching

1. j
2. i
3. b
4. d
5. a
6. c
7. h
8. e
9. f
10. g

Matching: Nutrients

11. d
12. f
13. g
14. e
15. c
16. a
17. b

Short Answer: Risk Elements in the Diet

18. salt
19. sugar
20. cholesterol

Short Answer

Questions 21–25.

- Eat breakfast.
- Exercise regularly.
- Drink lots of water daily.
- Eat healthy snacks.
- Do outside activities.
- Avoid fad diets.
- Avoid eating late.
- Buy healthy foods.
- Avoid fast foods.
- Eat three meals a day.

Short Answer

Questions 26–35.

- sweet potato
- skim milk
- spinach
- broccoli
- cantaloupe
- tomato
- nuts
- salmon or other fish
- beans
- cereals
- dried fruit
- garlic
- nonfat yogurt
- organic foods
- berries

CLOSURE

The information covered in this unit will prepare you for a healthy lifestyle and help you to make knowledgeable decisions regarding your food choices and habits.

8

Total Fitness

> THOSE WHO DO NOT FIND TIME FOR EXERCISE NOW WILL HAVE TO FIND TIME FOR ILLNESS.
>
> **The Earl of Derby, 1873**

Lesson Finder

Exercise and Fitness Facts

OBJECTIVE

Students will become acquainted with lots of information on fitness by playing a game called Panel of Experts.

NATIONAL STANDARDS

- #1 Health Promotion
- #5 Decision Making
- #4 Communication

INTRODUCTION

Exercise is a basic necessity for human life, like food, air, water, and shelter. Let us see how much you know about exercise and total fitness. Today we are going to play a game called Panel of Experts. In this game we will find out about all aspects of fitness.

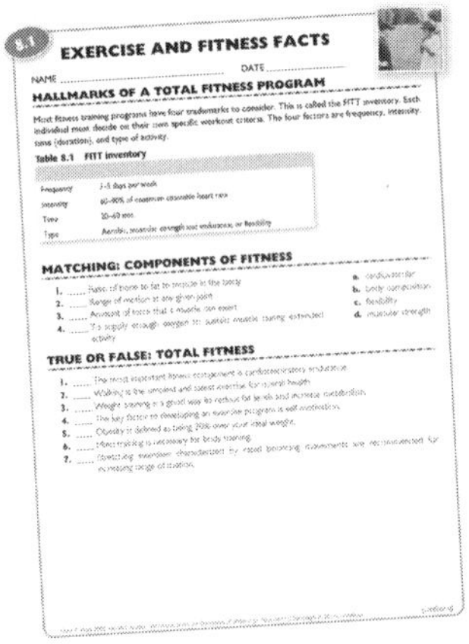
EXERCISE AND FITNESS FACTS

HALLMARKS OF A TOTAL FITNESS PROGRAM

MATCHING: COMPONENTS OF FITNESS

TRUE OR FALSE: TOTAL FITNESS

8.1

HANDOUT 8.1

Ask for five volunteers to come to the front of class today to start as exercise experts. Each expert starts with 5 extra credit points. The experts keep their points unless someone from the class can ask them a question from the two sheets on exercise that they cannot answer. Then the student who asked the question gets the point. Students should ask questions that can be answered with one word or a phrase. No trick questions are allowed.

If an expert loses all his or her points, a new expert from the class takes his or her place on the panel.

Monitor the game and be sure that questions have only one answer. Also make sure that everyone asks at least one question. Call on students if necessary. The questions to the panel are to go in order. The questions continue until the class is out of questions or time is up. This activity is a different way to go over material with lots of fun and involvement.

Matching: Components of Fitness

1. b
2. c
3. d
4. a

True or False: Total Fitness

1. true
2. true
3. true
4. true
5. true
6. true
7. false—Avoid bouncing because of muscle pulls and injury.

Matching: Fitness Vocabulary

1. o	**5.** m	**9.** n	**13.** b
2. i	**6.** e	**10.** a	**14.** k
3. h	**7.** p	**11.** l	**15.** j
4. d	**8.** g	**12.** c	**16.** f

Matching: Great Benefits of Exercise

1. g	**5.** a	**9.** e	**13.** i
2. l	**6.** h	**10.** d	
3. c	**7.** m	**11.** k	
4. f	**8.** j	**12.** b	

Matching: Fitness IQ Test

1. a	**5.** j	**9.** l	**13.** s	**17.** h
2. i	**6.** k	**10.** m	**14.** n	**18.** t
3. p	**7.** e	**11.** q	**15.** o	**19.** c
4. g	**8.** d	**12.** r	**16.** f	**20.** b

CLOSURE

Being physically fit includes many facets. Exercise is vital to your health and well-being. I hope that you learned a lot about fitness today.

Mind Over Matter: Fitness Training Program

OBJECTIVE

Students will be able to list the five key components to getting the mind involved in a fitness training program after a discussion and a general fitness appraisal.

NATIONAL STANDARDS

- #1 Health Promotion
- #7 Healthy Behaviors
- #4 Communication

INTRODUCTION

The mind controls the body, so to develop habits and succeed in any endeavor, you need to develop a particular mind-set. Today you are going to learn how to train your mind—so that it can train your body.

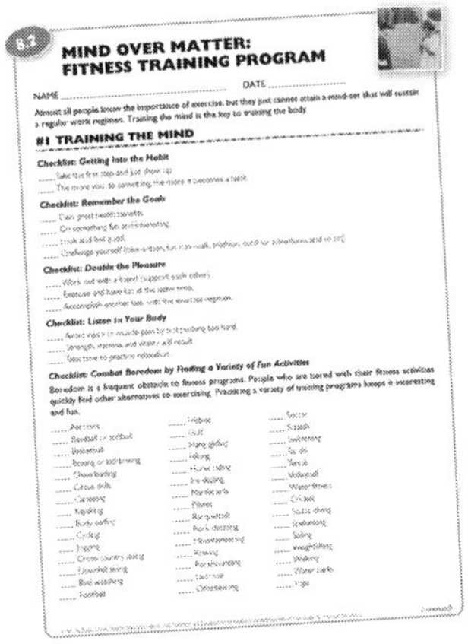
MIND OVER MATTER: FITNESS TRAINING PROGRAM

#1 TRAINING THE MIND

8.2

HANDOUT 8.2

Discuss the five factors that can help students develop a successful training program that will involve the mind. Go through the points one at a time. Have students list the factors and activities that they believe would help them make an exercise program a permanent part of their lifestyle. These five factors are integral to training the brain for success.

CLOSURE

Developing and maintaining an exercise training program is difficult. First, get your mind ready and then work on all five components for optimal success. These five factors will help you make exercise a fun and rewarding part of your daily life.

Total Body Workout

OBJECTIVE

Students will be able to experience the three most common exercise programs by going to the gym or a weight-training room for a workout.

NATIONAL STANDARD

#7 Healthy Behaviors

INTRODUCTION

We are going to the gym to practice the three major components of physical fitness. This activity will help you to understand and feel the benefits of regular exercise on your body.

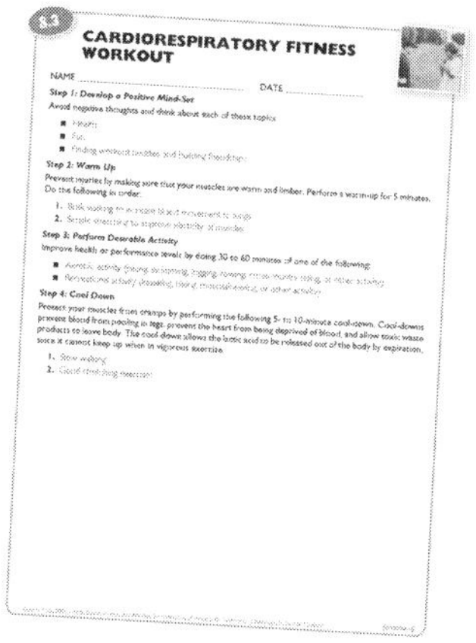

8.3

HANDOUT 8.3

Matching: Top Five Cardiorespiratory Exercises

1. a
2. e
3. b
4. c
5. d

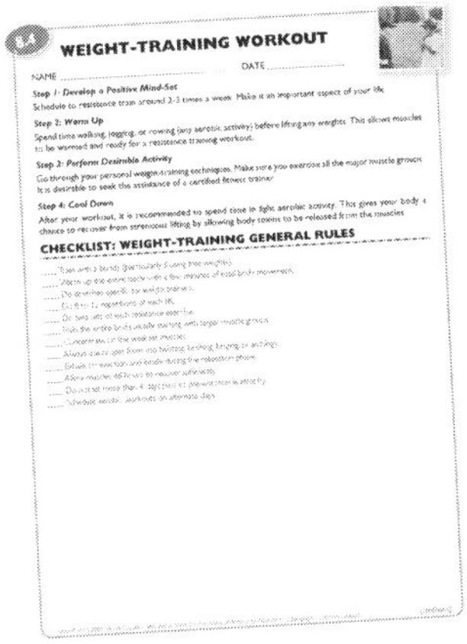

8.4

HANDOUT 8.4

HANDOUT 8.5

Matching: Types of Stretching

1. a
2. b
3. c
4. d

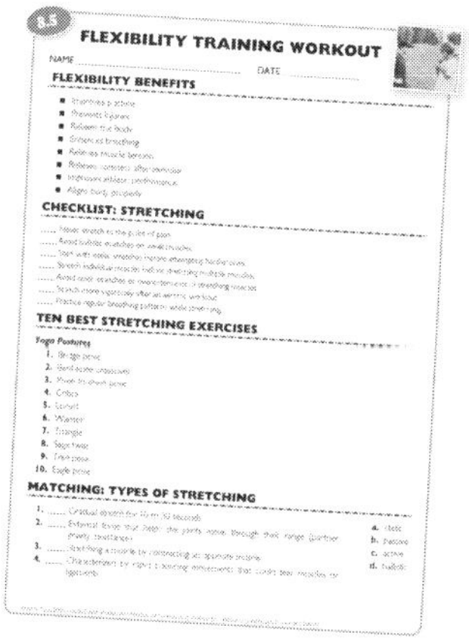

8.5

In each case, go over the worksheet the day before you take the students to the designated site for personal experience.

CLOSURE

I hope that you learned more about this component of physical fitness and that you are more confident about incorporating this activity into your daily lifestyle.

Exercise and Fitness Test Key

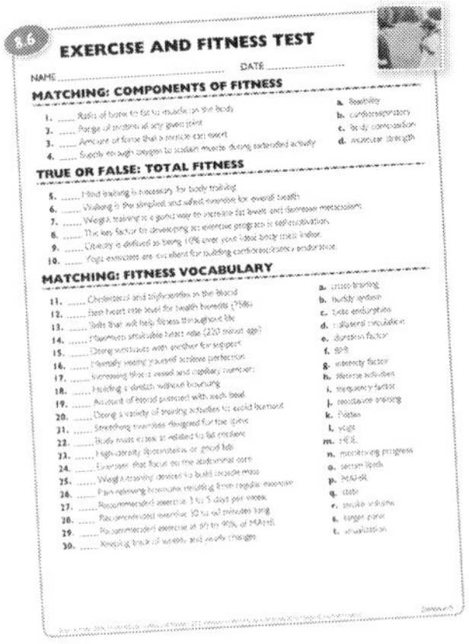

8.6

OBJECTIVE

Students will pass a written evaluation of facts and data on a total fitness program.

NATIONAL STANDARDS

- #1 Health Promotion
- #7 Healthy Behaviors

INTRODUCTION

This is the written test on a total fitness training program.

HANDOUT 8.6

Matching: Components of Fitness

1. c　**3.** d
2. a　**4.** b

True or False: Total Fitness

5. true
6. true
7. false—Weight training decreases fat levels and increase metabolism.
8. true
9. false—Obesity is defined as being 20% or more over your ideal weight.
10. false—Yoga builds strength and flexibility.

Matching: Fitness Vocabulary

11. o	**16.** t	**21.** l	**26.** c
12. s	**17.** d	**22.** f	**27.** i
13. h	**18.** q	**23.** m	**28.** e
14. p	**19.** r	**24.** k	**29.** g
15. b	**20.** a	**25.** j	**30.** n

Short Answer

Questions: 31-35

- greater longevity
- stronger heart
- cancer prevention
- prevents osteoporosis
- enhanced immunity
- higher level of endorphins
- weight reduction
- emotional strength
- strong spine
- delays aging
- less insomnia
- sense of well-being
- social connections

CLOSURE

The test will be returned as soon as possible to check your score.

9

Sleep, Dreams, and Relaxation

IF YOU CAN'T GET TO SLEEP AT NIGHT, CHECK YOUR PILLOW. IF YOU CAN'T GET TO SLEEP FOR TWO NIGHTS, CHECK YOUR MATTRESS. IF YOU CAN'T GET TO SLEEP FOR THREE NIGHTS, CHECK YOUR CONSCIENCE.

Anonymous

Lesson Finder

Sleep Time

OBJECTIVE

Students will be able to list the key factors to getting a good night's sleep and the problems from sleep deprivation through a classroom discussion.

NATIONAL STANDARDS

- #1 Health Promotion
- #7 Healthy Behaviors
- #5 Decision Making
- #4 Communication

INTRODUCTION

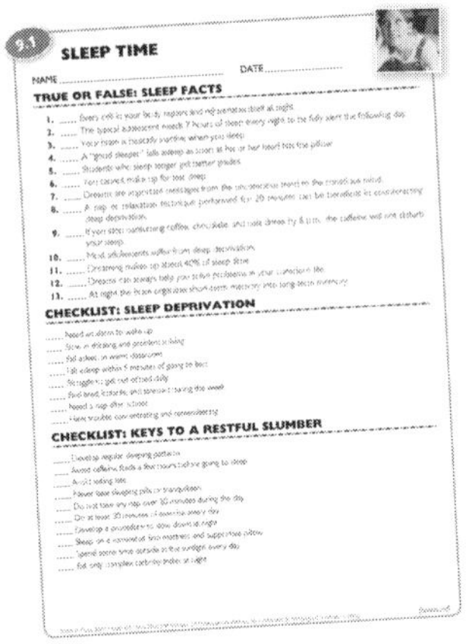
SLEEP TIME
TRUE OR FALSE: SLEEP FACTS
CHECKLIST: SLEEP DEPRIVATION
CHECKLIST: KEYS TO A RESTFUL SLUMBER

9.1

Sleep is essential to survival, and you spend one-third of your life sleeping. We need to find out what the important functions of sleep are and what people can do to ensure a good night's sleep. According to statistics, about 50 million Americans regularly have trouble sleeping.

How many of you know someone who has trouble sleeping at night? How many of you have trouble sleeping from time to time yourself? Let us look at what happens at night while you sleep.

HANDOUT 9.1

True or False: Sleep Facts

Have students take turns reading the questions. Make sure that they get the right answer after an explanation or discussion.

1. true
2. false—On average, 9 hours of sleep are needed.
3. false—The unconscious brain is very active.
4. false—This is a sign of being overtired.
5. true
6. true
7. true
8. false—A nap or relaxation technique lasting under 20 minutes can be beneficial.
9. true
10. true
11. false—Dreaming makes up about 20% of sleep time.
12. false—Dreams do not always help with problems.
13. true

Checklist: Sleep Deprivation

Have students check the sleep deprivation factors that are true for them. The more of these symptoms they have, the more likely it is that they are not getting enough sleep each night and are thus experiencing a lower quality of life each day. Have students share how many are true for them. The more symptoms they check, the more of a problem they have.

Checklist: Keys to a Restful Slumber

In this checklist have students check which patterns they use each night. These are the key ingredients to getting a good's night's sleep. Have them share how many are true for them. The more they have, the better off they are.

Assignment

Tomorrow we are going to talk more about dreams. You must write down at least one dream that you can remember.

CLOSURE

Most people do not realize how important getting a good night's sleep is to their health, their school work, and their relationships. Talking about the facts on sleeping may help you gain some insights about what you or others can do to lessen problems with sleeping at night. Sleep tight tonight!

Sleep and Dreaming

OBJECTIVE

Students will be able to discuss the interesting conditions related to sleeping and dreaming.

NATIONAL STANDARDS

- #1 Health Promotion
- #4 Communication

INTRODUCTION

Today is going to be an interesting day. You will find the answers to the most common problems related to sleeping and what dreams really mean. Understand this first about dreaming—most dreams have to do with your anxieties and fears. They are about what is going on in your life now, about problems that you are not solving. Dreams usually exaggerate what you feel deep inside. They are messages from the unconscious to the conscious to help you deal with life. They are trying to help you!

SLEEP AND DREAMING
NAME DATE
MATCHING: VOCABULARY
MATCHING: SLEEP ELEMENTS AND SOME DREAM MEANINGS

9.2

HANDOUT 9.2

Matching: Vocabulary

1. b	**6.** m	**11.** e	**16.** i
2. c	**7.** n	**12.** a	**17.** h
3. s	**8.** q	**13.** d	**18.** g
4. l	**9.** r	**14.** j	**19.** p
5. k	**10.** o	**15.** f	

Matching: Sleep Elements and Some Dream Meanings

1. e	**6.** j
2. d	**7.** f
3. h	**8.** i
4. c	**9.** g
5. b	**10.** a

Key Factors to Dream Recall and Interpretation

1. I	**6.** R
2. R	**7.** I
3. R	**8.** I
4. R	**9.** I
5. I	**10.** R

CLOSURE

The interpretation of dreams is complicated. In most cases you need to look into your present life and try to figure out how your dreams connect to it. There are many ways to interpret dreams. The viewpoints that we discussed today are only examples of ways to interpret dreams. You may find it interesting to do some research of your own to discover other interpretations.

Dream Analysis

OBJECTIVE

Students will be able to remember and figure out what their dreams mean through a discussion of the facts concerning dreams.

NATIONAL STANDARDS

- #1 Health Promotion
- #5 Decision Making
- #4 Communication

INTRODUCTION

Dreams are important messages that you should try to understand. Dreams arise from the unconscious state and reveal more about our life and character than any other self-awareness technique.

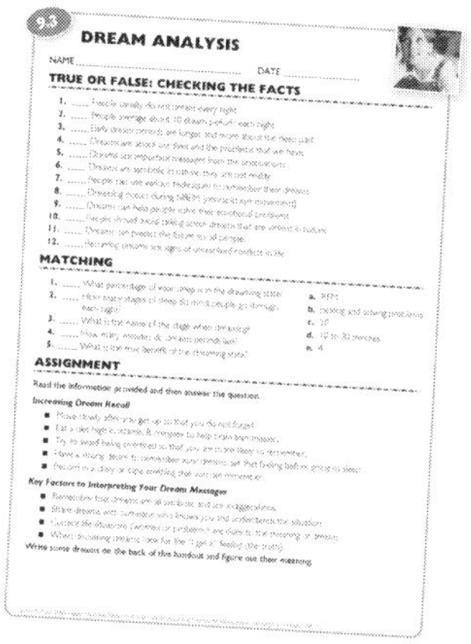
DREAM ANALYSIS
TRUE OR FALSE: CHECKING THE FACTS
MATCHING
ASSIGNMENT

9.3

HANDOUT 9.3

True or False: Checking the Facts

1. false—People usually dream each night.
2. false—People average about five dream periods each night.
3. false—Early dream periods are usually shorter and about the recent past.
4. true
5. true
6. true
7. true
8. false—Dreaming occurs during REM.
9. true
10. false—People should talk about dreams that are violent in nature.
11. false—Dreams cannot predict the future for most people.
12. true

Matching

1. c	**3.** a	**5.** b
2. e	**4.** d	

Assignment

Dreams are important messages from the unconscious mind to the conscious mind. Dreams are exaggerations of mostly unresolved conflicts and worries in life. Do what you can to get the students to solve the meaning of their dreams. They should look at what is going on in their lives.

CLOSURE

Dreams are important messages that you should try to understand. Interpreting your dreams may help you solve some of your personal problems.

Relaxation Techniques

OBJECTIVE

Students will be able to practice a relaxation technique after a short teacher-led discussion on the criteria for successful relaxation.

NATIONAL STANDARDS

- #1 Health Promotion
- #5 Decision Making

INTRODUCTION

Relaxation techniques are one of the best ways to clear the mind and perform better at any task. It is one of the best ways to register stress long before the conscious mind does. Some of the greatest minds in history used these skills. Albert Einstein, Ben Franklin, and Thomas Edison, to name a few, had cots set up so that they could take so-called power naps. What a great way to rejuvenate the mind and the body.

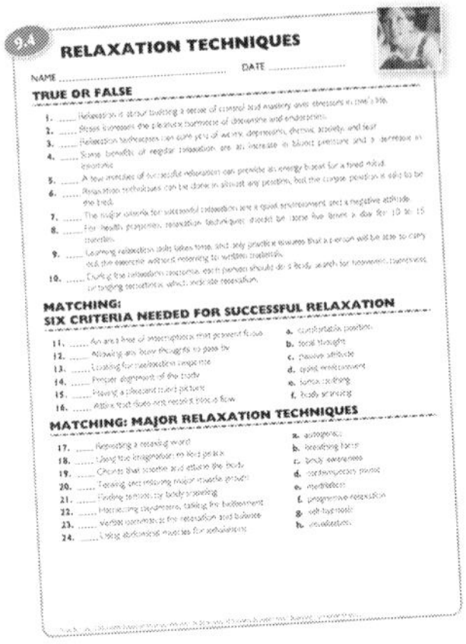
RELAXATION TECHNIQUES

TRUE OR FALSE

MATCHING: SIX CRITERIA NEEDED FOR SUCCESSFUL RELAXATION

MATCHING: MAJOR RELAXATION TECHNIQUES

9.4

HANDOUT 9.4

True or False

1. true
2. false—It decreases pleasure hormones in the body.
3. true
4. false—Regular relaxation can often decrease blood pressure.
5. true
6. true
7. false—A passive attitude is needed for successful relaxation.
8. false—Twice a day is better.
9. true
10. true

Matching: Six Criteria Needed for Successful Relaxation

11. d	**14.** a
12. c	**15.** b
13. f	**16.** e

Matching: Major Relaxation Techniques

17. e	**20.** f	**23.** a
18. h	**21.** c	**24.** b
19. d	**22.** g	

HANDOUT 9.5

Relaxation Techniques

Have students practice one of these relaxation techniques. Ask how many have done a relaxation technique before. All students will need to cooperate for this to be successful. Students can get into the corpse position (show them), or you can have them sit as comfortably as possible in their chairs with their bodies supported. Go over the six criteria again for successful relaxation.

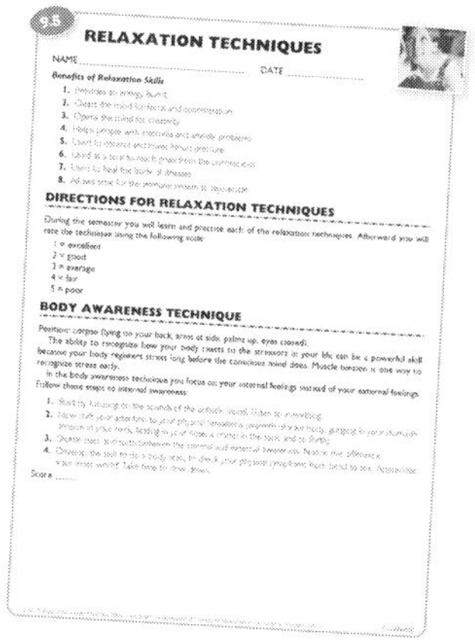
RELAXATION TECHNIQUES

DIRECTIONS FOR RELAXATION TECHNIQUES

BODY AWARENESS TECHNIQUE

9.5

CLOSURE

I appreciate your being considerate of others. Even if you could not relax, you did not interrupt the session for your classmates. How many of you achieved a successful relaxation? How many had trouble keeping thoughts out of your mind? Mastering these skills takes practice. Perhaps we can try another technique on a different day.

Sleep and Dream Test Key

OBJECTIVE

Students will be able to pass a written test on the facts and data on sleep, dreams, and relaxation techniques.

NATIONAL STANDARDS

- #1 Health Promotion
- #7 Healthy Behaviors

INTRODUCTION

This is the test on sleep, dreams, and relaxation.

SLEEP AND DREAMS TEST

TRUE OR FALSE: SLEEP FACTS

9.6

HANDOUT 9.6

True or False: Sleep Facts

1. true
2. false—The average adolescent requires 8 or 9 hours.
3. false—Strangers usually represent a quality you don't like.
4. true
5. true
6. true
7. true
8. true
9. true
10. true
11. false—Dreaming makes up about 20% of sleep.
12. false—Dreams can sometimes help solve life issues.
13. true
14. true
15. true
16. false—Exercise and sunshine assist in sleeping.
17. true
18. true
19. false—Animal fats are generally bad for the body.
20. true

Matching: Vocabulary

21. g	**26.** r	**31.** e	**36.** i
22. q	**27.** b	**32.** h	**37.** k
23. d	**28.** s	**33.** p	**38.** n
24. l	**29.** t	**34.** j	**39.** m
25. a	**30.** o	**35.** f	**40.** c

CLOSURE

We will go over the test the next time we meet.

10

Heart Disease

THERE ARE 60,000 MILES OF BLOOD VESSELS, CAPILLARIES, ARTERIES AND VEINS IN THE BODY. . . . WHAT ARE YOU DOING TO KEEP THIS BLOOD FLOWING TO THE VITAL ORGANS?

Anonymous

Lesson Finder

Heart Disease and Stroke Facts

OBJECTIVE

Students will be able list the six types of heart disease and the key risk factors contributing to the leading cause of death in the United States through a discussion.

NATIONAL STANDARDS

- #1 Health Promotion
- #4 Communication

INTRODUCTION

Because heart disease and stroke kill approximately 40 out of 100 people, we should spend some time learning about the major contributing factors to cardiovascular disease in the United States.

10.1
HEART DISEASE AND STROKE FACTS
NAME DATE
TRUE OR FALSE
MATCHING: CARDIOVASCULAR DISEASE VOCABULARY
MATCHING: TYPES OF HEART DISEASE

10.1

HANDOUT 10.1

True or False

1. true
2. false—Even adolescents are starting to show signs of coronary artery disease.
3. true
4. true
5. false—Most blood circulation problems are due to arteriosclerosis.
6. true
7. true
8. false—Over 200 milligrams per deciliter of blood is considered high.
9. false—Stress does contribute to heart problems, but can't really be measured.
10. true

Matching: Cardiovascular Disease Vocabulary

1. a
2. f
3. h
4. e
5. i
6. b
7. g
8. k
9. d
10. j
11. c

Matching: Types of Heart Disease

1. e
2. b
3. f
4. a
5. c
6. d

Six most common conditions leading to heart failure and death

1. Thrombus—blood clot in a coronary artery
2. Aortic aneurysm—a bulge in an artery
3. Ventricular fibrillation—an irregular beating pattern originating in the SA node
4. Heart murmur—a leaky valve going to the ventricles (bicuspid/triaspid valve)
5. Defective septum—usually a hole in the heart wall separating the left side from the right
6. Congestive heart failure—enlarged, weak heart resulting from age and various conditions

CLOSURE

Today you learned about what happens when someone has a heart attack or stroke. Our goal this week is to see what we can do to prevent these situations from happening so early in life.

High Blood Pressure

RISK FACTORS FOR HEART DISEASE

CHECKLIST: CONTROLLABLE RISK FACTORS

CHECKLIST: UNCONTROLLABLE RISK FACTORS

CHECKLIST: NEW RISK FACTORS

10.2

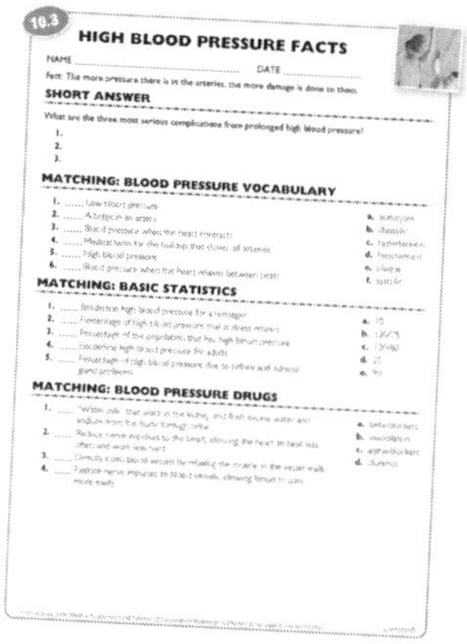
HIGH BLOOD PRESSURE FACTS

SHORT ANSWER

MATCHING: BLOOD PRESSURE VOCABULARY

MATCHING: BASIC STATISTICS

MATCHING: BLOOD PRESSURE DRUGS

10.3

OBJECTIVE

Students will be able to determine the causes, problems, and treatment of high blood pressure through an open discussion.

NATIONAL STANDARDS

- #1 Health Promotion
- #5 Decision Making
- #4 Communication

INTRODUCTION

Has anyone ever heard of the silent killer? High blood pressure is the silent killer because it has no symptoms and damages the arteries beyond repair. Many young people already have high blood pressure. We need to find out what this is all about.

HANDOUT 10.2

HANDOUT 10.3

Short Answer

1. stroke
2. heart disease
3. kidney disease

Matching: Blood Pressure Vocabulary

1. d
2. a
3. f
4. e
5. c
6. b

Matching: Basic Statistics

1. b
2. e
3. d
4. c
5. a

Matching: Blood Pressure Drugs

1. d
2. c
3. b
4. a

Blood Pressure Management

1. Manage stress.
2. Do not smoke.
3. Eat a diet low in saturated fat and cholesterol.
4. Keep weight within desirable limits.
5. Restrict salt in the diet.
6. Get regular exercise.

Give students time to take their blood pressure: ________ /_________

Teach students how to take their blood pressure. Have a speaker come in to take blood pressure.

CLOSURE

Regular monitoring of blood pressure is important for heart health. Your life is too important to be cut short by this silent killer. Practice the blood pressure control measures.

Cholesterol Facts

OBJECTIVE

Students will be able to understand the effect of high cholesterol on health and learn which foods to eat and which to avoid through a classroom discussion.

NATIONAL STANDARDS

- #1 Health Promotion
- #5 Decision Making
- #4 Communication

INTRODUCTION

An element in the American diet causes major plaque buildup in the arteries. The culprit is cholesterol. We are going to examine cholesterol today.

CHOLESTEROL FACTS

MATCHING: CHOLESTEROL VOCABULARY

MATCHING: BLOOD PROFILE FOR GOOD HEALTH

MATCHING: DRUG TREATMENT FOR CHOLESTEROL

MATCHING: MEASURES TO MANAGE HIGH CHOLESTEROL

TRUE OR FALSE

10.4

HANDOUT 10.4

Matching: Cholesterol Vocabulary

1. d
2. c
3. a
4. b
5. e

Matching: Blood Profile for Good Health

6. b
7. c
8. a
9. d

Matching: Drug Treatment for Cholesterol

10. a
11. b
12. c
13. d

Matching: Measures to Manage High Cholesterol

14. e
15. c
16. a
17. d
18. b

True or False

19. false—All people can lower their cholesterol levels.
20. true

Checklist: Food Choices

1.	H	L	L	H
2.	H	L	L	H
3.	L	L	L	H
4.	L	H	L	H
5.	H	H	L	L
6.	H	H	L	L
7.	L	H	L	L

CLOSURE

Watching the amount of cholesterol that you eat daily is important. Cholesterol builds up on artery walls and causes blockages. Keep your arteries clean and flexible by exercising and eating a low-cholesterol diet.

Tobacco and Atherosclerosis

OBJECTIVE

Students will be able to draw an artery and the seven-step progression to artery disease in the human body after a classroom discussion.

NATIONAL STANDARDS

- #1 Health Promotion
- #5 Decision Making

INTRODUCTION

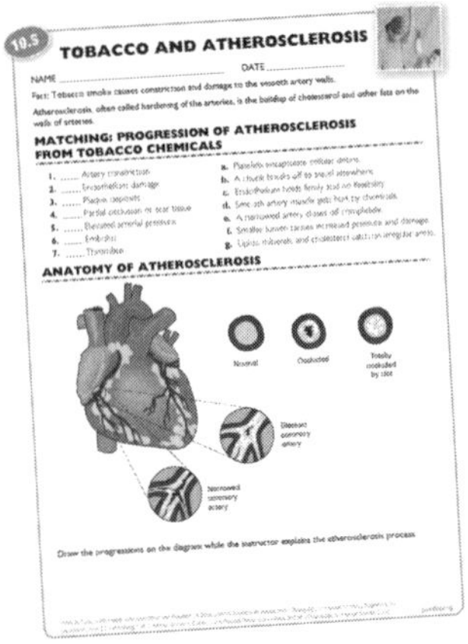

10.5

The tobacco habit is the leading preventable cause of death and heart disease in the United States. Take some time to examine this extremely unhealthy habit. Let us examine how artery disease progresses in the vascular system.

HANDOUT 10.5

Matching: Progression of Atherosclerosis From Tobacco Chemicals

1. c
2. d
3. g
4. a
5. f
6. b
7. e

Anatomy of Atherosclerosis

Draw a diagram about artery disease progression for the students to follow.

True or False

1. true
2. false—It is the most important risk factor of all.
3. false—Smoking cuts around 10 years off your longevity.
4. false—Nicotine is most responsible.
5. true
6. true
7. true

Discussion Questions

These thought-provoking questions should help you realize that smoking is a bad habit that affects both the smoker and many other people. It is difficult to understand why we allow an industry to keep making a product that is the number one killer in the United States. Kick the habit . . . for your own sake!

CLOSURE

Does anyone have any questions about how tobacco chemicals cause heart disease and strokes?

Heart Disease Test Key

OBJECTIVE

Students will be able to pass a written test on heart disease at the end of the unit.

NATIONAL STANDARDS

- #1 Health Promotion
- #7 Healthy Behaviors

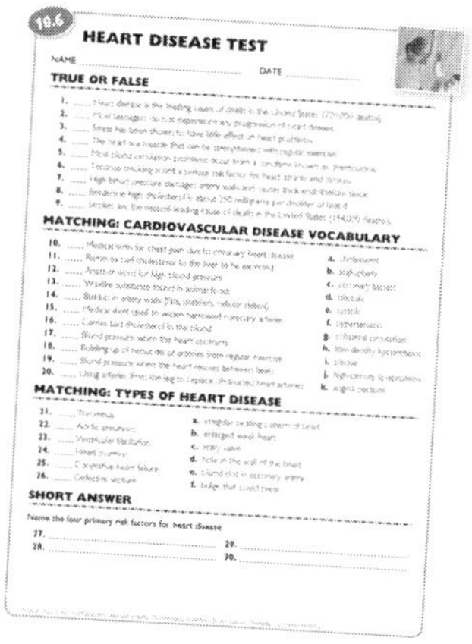
10.6

HEART DISEASE TEST

TRUE OR FALSE

MATCHING: CARDIOVASCULAR DISEASE VOCABULARY

MATCHING: TYPES OF HEART DISEASE

SHORT ANSWER

INTRODUCTION

This is the test on heart disease.

HANDOUT 10.6

True or False

1. true
2. false—Even adolescents are now experiencing early arteriosclerosis.
3. false—Stress affects the entire body.
4. true
5. false—Atherosclerosis causes most blood circulation problems.
6. false—Tobacco is the number one risk factor.
7. true
8. false—Borderline high cholesterol is about 200 milligrams per deciliter of blood.
9. true

Matching: Cardiovascular Disease Vocabulary

10. k	**13.** a	**16.** h	**19.** d
11. j	**14.** i	**17.** e	**20.** c
12. f	**15.** b	**18.** g	

Matching: Types of Heart Disease

21. e	**24.** c
22. f	**25.** b
23. a	**26.** d

Short Answer

27. tobacco
28. cholesterol
29. high blood pressure
30. lack of exercise

CLOSURE

We will go over the test next class period.

11

Cancer Prevention

TAKE A MENTAL
WALK THROUGH THE
CANCER WARDS,
THE INSANE ASYLUMS,
THE HOMELESS
GHETTOES,
THE CHILDREN'S
HOSPITALS . . .
AND THEN RE-ASK
YOURSELF WHAT IS
BOTHERING YOU.

G.W.F.

Lesson Finder

Cancer Facts

OBJECTIVE

Students will gain insight into the deadly disease of cancer by discussing vocabulary, stages, treatment, and prevention measures.

NATIONAL STANDARD

#1 Health Promotion

INTRODUCTION

Cancer does not discriminate. It can affect anyone at any age. We should learn as much as we can about this deadly disease. Probably no other disease brings as much fear as cancer.

11.1
CANCER FACTS
Malignant Neoplasms
TRUE OR FALSE
MATCHING: CANCER VOCABULARY
MATCHING: CLASSIFICATIONS OF CANCER
MATCHING: CANCER STAGES

11.1

HANDOUT 11.1

True or False

1. false—Incidence is increasing and survival rates are increasing.

2. true

3. true

4. false—The survival rate is around 40%.

5. true

6. true

7. true

8. true

9. true

Matching: Cancer Vocabulary

1. d	**5.** e
2. c	**6.** h
3. f	**7.** b
4. g	**8.** a

Matching: Classifications of Cancer

1. a

2. b

3. c

4. d

Matching: Cancer Stages

1. b

2. c

3. a

Matching: Cancer Treatment

1. a
2. b
3. c
4. d
5. e
6. f
7. g

Annual Death Rates of Cancer

Male	Female
1. a	**1.** a
2. b	**2.** b
3. e	**3.** d
4. c	**4.** c
5. f	**5.** g

Checklist: Cancer Prevention Techniques

How many out of 10 are true for you?

Cancer Warning Signs

C Change in bowel or bladder habits
A A sore that does not heal
U Usually bleeding or discharge
T Thickening or lump in the breast or elsewhere
I Indigestion or difficulty in swallowing
O Obvious change in wart or mole
N Nagging cough or hoarseness

Antioxidant Foods

Options that students might select as good antioxidant foods.

- strawberries
- tomatoes
- peppers
- broccoli
- blueberries
- cabbage
- carrots
- brussels sprouts
- collard greens
- peaches
- cauliflower
- cantaloupe
- sweet potatoes
- spinach
- squash
- potatoes
- asparagus
- papaya
- oranges
- bananas
- watermelon
- apples
- grapes
- onions

HANDOUT 11.2

Cancer Risk Assessment

Take this assessment to estimate your risk of developing cancer.

11.2 CANCER RISK ASSESSMENT
NAME DATE

11.2

CLOSURE

This is an overview of the cancer facts and figures for the United States.

Tobacco and Cancer

OBJECTIVE

Students will be able to analyze the major chemicals in tobacco and the diseases that they can cause in the human body through an open discussion.

NATIONAL STANDARDS

- #1 Health Promotion
- #4 Communication

TOBACCO AND CANCER

MATCHING: PRINCIPAL POISONS IN TOBACCO SMOKE

MATCHING: DISEASES AND TOBACCO SMOKE

11.3

INTRODUCTION

Tobacco is the primary cause of cancer in the United States. Tobacco products have over 401 toxic chemicals and 43 carcinogens. Tobacco causes more diseases and complications than any other lifestyle factor.

HANDOUT 11.3

Matching: Principal Poisons in Tobacco Smoke

1. d	**6.** b	**11.** a
2. o	**7.** i	**12.** c
3. n	**8.** j	**13.** h
4. m	**9.** e	**14.** g
5. k	**10.** f	**15.** l

Matching: Diseases and Tobacco Smoke

1. c	**6.** j
2. f	**7.** g
3. h	**8.** b
4. d	**9.** a
5. e	**10.** i

CLOSURE

Tobacco smoke has several hundred poisons that harm us every time we smoke. Forty-three chemicals are known to cause cancer. The survival rate of those who get cancer is 40%. Why would you take the chance of getting cancer or some other disease from this addictive habit? Best tip: Don't start! Last tip: Kick the habit before it kicks you!

OBJECTIVE

Students will examine their eating habits and eventually bring one anticancer food to share with the class.

NATIONAL STANDARDS

- #7 Healthy Behaviors
- #5 Decision Making
- #8 Advocacy

INTRODUCTION

Today we will examine the importance of the diet and cancer prevention. The foods that you eat contribute to the possibility that cancer will develop in your body. What kind of foods are you eating every day? It may be about time to make some subtle changes to lower your cancer risk. Foods high in antioxidants taste good as well.

HANDOUT 11.4

Eat Smart Survey

Take the Eat Smart Survey to see how you are doing with cancer prevention.

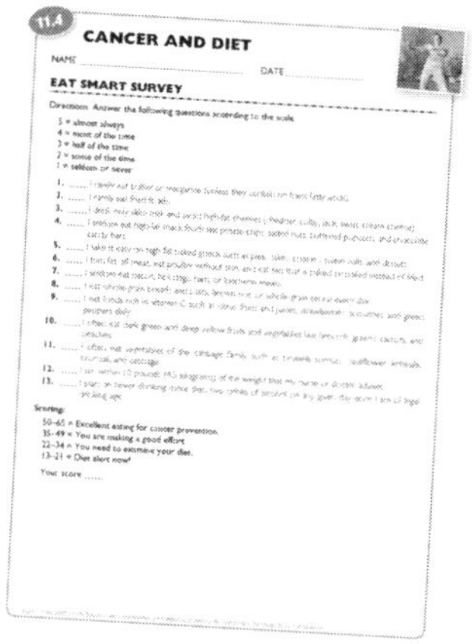
11.4
CANCER AND DIET
EAT SMART SURVEY

11.4

HANDOUT 11.5

Cancer and Foods Antioxidant Day

On the antioxidant sheet, note all the benefits of foods in preventing cancer. You must sign up to bring a sampling of food for the next class period.

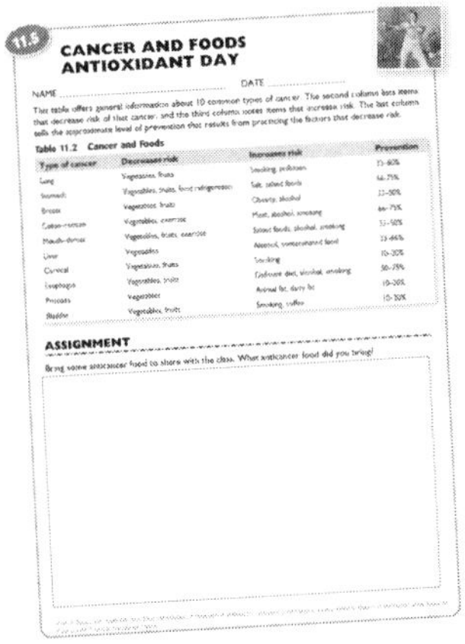
11.5
CANCER AND FOODS ANTIOXIDANT DAY
ASSIGNMENT

11.5

CLOSURE

The food that you put in your body is more important than you realize. Cancer, the most feared disease of all, can be prevented, altered, and changed by the foods that you eat. Take time to assess your diet for the good foods and bring a sample to class to share. This assignment is worth 20 points.

Cancer Education and Intervention

OBJECTIVE

Students will be able to teach another person about cancer and either take the Tobacco Pledge themselves or persuade someone else to take the Tobacco Pledge.

NATIONAL STANDARDS

- #5 Decision Making
- #8 Advocacy

INTRODUCTION

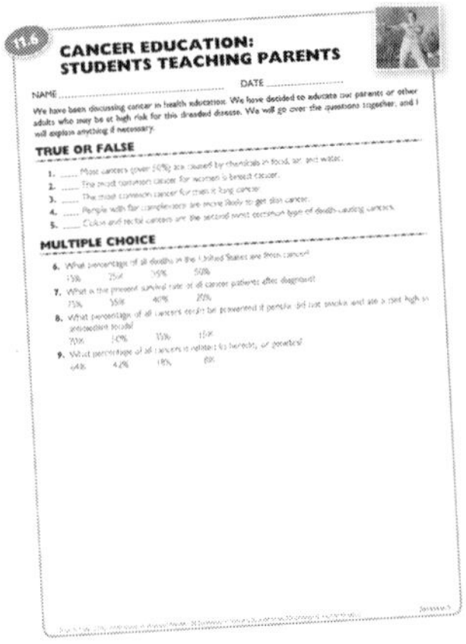
CANCER EDUCATION: STUDENTS TEACHING PARENTS

TRUE OR FALSE

MULTIPLE CHOICE

11.6

You have one assignment to do this week: educate one of your parents or some other adult about cancer. This assignment could make a difference to a family member or someone else you care about. Take the time to educate the person and have him or her sign the bottom of the sheet. The answers are on the bottom of the sheet, but you will probably know most of them without looking or without letting your "student" look. See how much your parent or other adult really knows about cancer.

HANDOUT 11.6

Students Teaching Parents

Look over the cancer education sheet and prepare to educate an adult. Answers appear on the sheet so that you can review them with the adult you educate.

HANDOUT 11.7

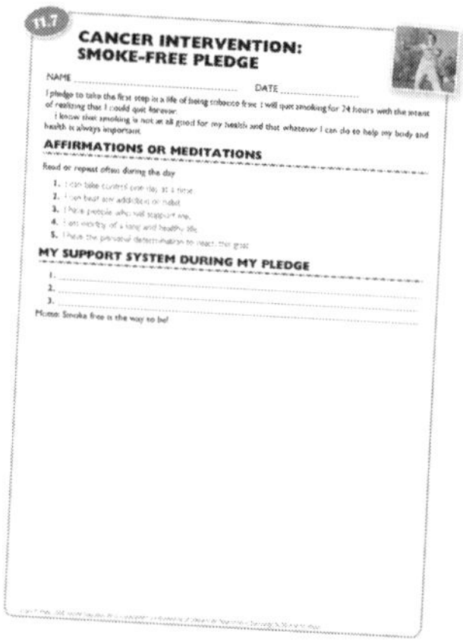
CANCER INTERVENTION: SMOKE-FREE PLEDGE

AFFIRMATIONS OR MEDITATIONS

MY SUPPORT SYSTEM DURING MY PLEDGE

11.7

Smoking is a bad habit. Smokers are not bad people; they are just addicted to the nicotine in the tobacco product. Try to help someone stop smoking for 24 hours or more. Keep track of how well the person does. You could also quit yourself if you are a smoker or tobacco chewer. Talk to the teacher before you do this.

Smoke-Free Pledge

Ask the tobacco user to refrain for 24 hours or more. Be the person's support system if he or she needs you. Most people want to quit. This activity could prove to be the start of their success story.

CLOSURE

Remember that anything you can do to educate others about cancer might save a life. Smoking is the biggest cause of poor health, so this activity would be a great way to help someone you care about.

Cancer Test Key

OBJECTIVE

Students will pass a written test on cancer after studying this unit.

NATIONAL STANDARDS

- #1 Health Promotion
- #7 Healthy Behaviors

INTRODUCTION

Take your time and complete all the questions on the test.

HANDOUT 11.8

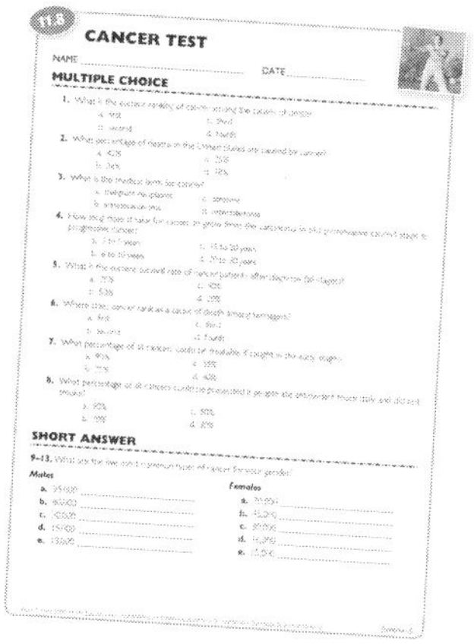
CANCER TEST

MULTIPLE CHOICE

SHORT ANSWER

11.8

Multiple Choice

1. b
2. c
3. a
4. c
5. c
6. d
7. a
8. b

Short Answer

Questions 9–13

Males	Females
a. lung	**a.** lung
b. prostate	**b.** breast
c. colon	**c.** colon
d. pancreatic	**d.** pancreatic
e. lymphoma	**e.** ovarian

Matching

14. a
15. f
16. d
17. g
18. b
19. c
20. e

Matching

21. d
22. c
23. b
24. a

Short Answer

Questions 25–31

- **a.** sweet potatoes
- **b.** broccoli
- **c.** cantaloupe
- **d.** spinach
- **e.** tomatoes
- **f.** strawberries
- **g.** carrots

Matching

32. a

33. b

34. d

35. c

Short Answer: Cancer Vocabulary

36. cancer

37. carcinogens

38. biopsy

39. malignant

40. oncologist

CLOSURE

We will go over the test as soon as possible so you can see your results.

12

Environmental Health

TAKE CARE OF
MOTHER EARTH.
FOR IT IS UP TO US
TO CONSERVE.
PLEASE DO NOT
BE FOOLED.
OR GENERATIONS
MAY BE DOOMED.

Puza

Lesson Finder

Environmental Health Facts

OBJECTIVE

Students will be able to realize that taking care of nature is a priority for the survival of the planet through reading and discussing the current situation.

NATIONAL STANDARDS

- #1 Health Promotion
- #7 Healthy Behaviors
- #4 Communication

INTRODUCTION

Sometimes we get caught up in the small world—in ourselves and our lives. We should never forget that we are only one small part of the big picture. If we do not take care of our planet it will not be here for future generations. That is a sad perspective. Mother Earth needs our help now!

Environmental Truths

The planet is still suffering from the effects of the Industrial Revolution and the environmental disasters of the past.

- Rivers in some industrial towns actually caught on fire because of pollution.
- Some lakes in America were completely dead; no species of fish could live in them.
- Air pollution disasters occurred in several cities during temperature inversions.
- Twenty thousand toxic waste sites buried in landfills leaked into the groundwater.
- The list of extinct species grew at its fastest rate ever.
- CFCs were ruining the ozone layer that protects humans from the sun.
- World population continued to soar, threatening the limits of the planet.

Despite this history, people can take many steps toward environmental solutions.

- Practice zero population growth by limiting the number of people in families.
- Do their share to help save the environment by recycling, bicycling instead of driving or riding in a car, not littering, and planting trees.
- Elect governments that monitor industrial sites and establish stricter pollution standards.
- Build public awareness about how vital the environment is to the future of the planet.
- Use alternative sources of energy to replace or reduce emissions from fossil fuels.

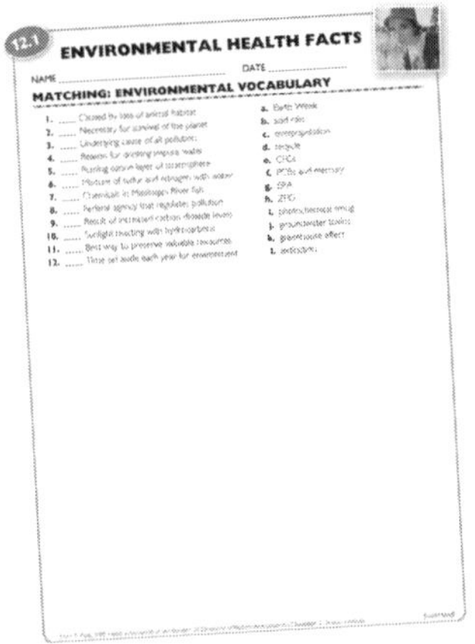

12.1

HANDOUT 12.1

Matching: Environmental Vocabulary

1. l	**7.** f
2. c	**8.** b
3. h	**9.** j
4. e	**10.** i
5. k	**11.** d
6. g	**12.** a

Matching: Earth Facts

1. g
2. d
3. p, q, or r
4. u
5. l
6. k
7. j
8. b
9. e
10. i
11. n
12. p, q, or r
13. t
14. c
15. m
16. p, q, or r
17. s
18. o
19. f
20. a
21. h

HANDOUT 12.2

Environmental Health Assessment

What is your score?

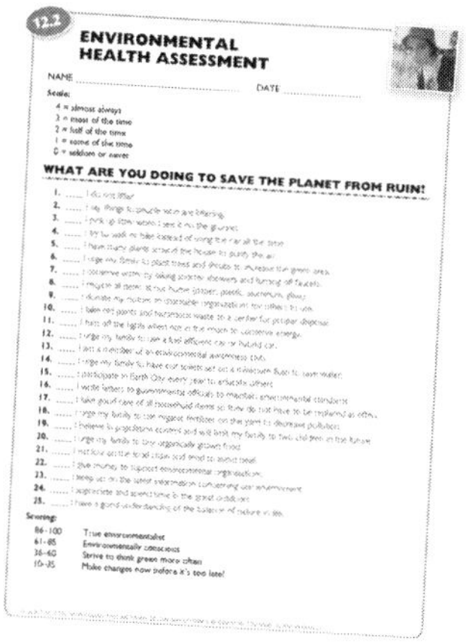
ENVIRONMENTAL HEALTH ASSESSMENT

WHAT ARE YOU DOING TO SAVE THE PLANET FROM RUIN!

12.2

CLOSURE

Today you have learned about the importance of taking care of our planet on a daily basis. This is the most important priority for the survival of the world. What can we all do to make it happen?

Environmental Pollutants

OBJECTIVE

Students will discuss the major pollutants that affect the health of Americans every day and find ways to avoid being subject to serious exposure.

NATIONAL STANDARDS

- #1 Health Promotion
- #5 Decision Making

INTRODUCTION

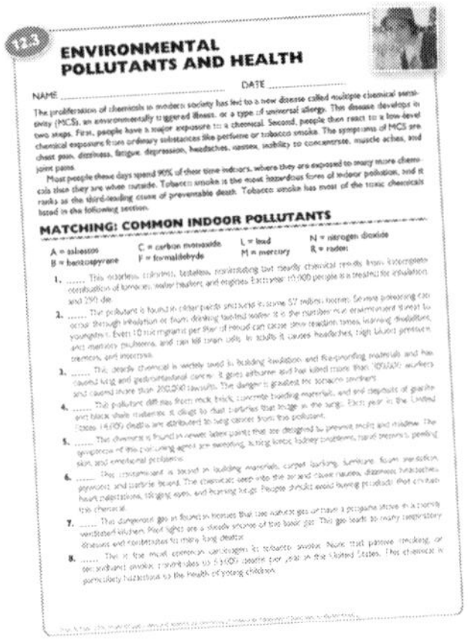
ENVIRONMENTAL POLLUTANTS AND HEALTH
NAME DATE
MATCHING: COMMON INDOOR POLLUTANTS

12.3

The proliferation of chemicals in modern society has had a major effect on the health and well-being of all Americans. Most of these chemicals are found inside, which is important because many people spend 90% of their time indoors. Let us find out more about the major environmental pollutants.

HANDOUT 12.3

Environmental Pollutants and Health

Read a little about multiple chemical sensitivity. A discussion may follow. Note that tobacco smoke is by far our biggest hazard.

Matching: Common Indoor Pollutants

1. C	**5.** M
2. L	**6.** F
3. A	**7.** N
4. R	**8.** B

CLOSURE

All of us should be aware of the serious pollutants that affect Americans these days. These eight chemicals contribute to many disabling diseases and thousands of deaths yearly in the United States. Tell your parents about these substances because they may be in your homes right now.

Earth Awareness Project

OBJECTIVE

Students will be able to show their creative talents by completing a project on an environmental health issue.

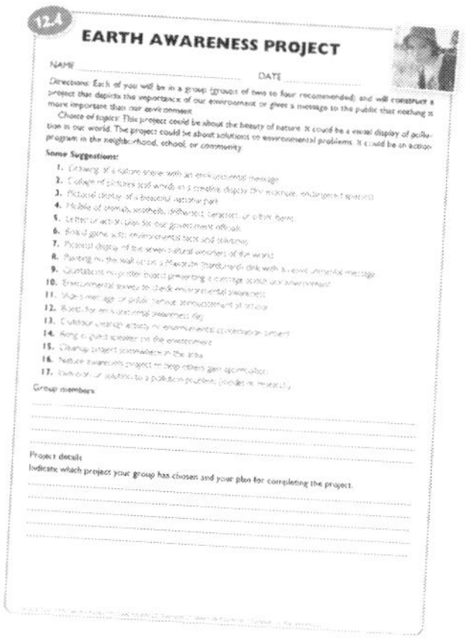
EARTH AWARENESS PROJECT

12.4

NATIONAL STANDARDS

- #5 Decision Making
- #3 Information and Services
- #4 Communication
- #8 Advocacy

INTRODUCTION

We will be working on a major project throughout this week. You need to decide what you would like to do to enlighten the world about the importance of taking care of our planet. We need to be active participants in keeping this planet safe for generations to come. We must look into the future and make some adjustments now.

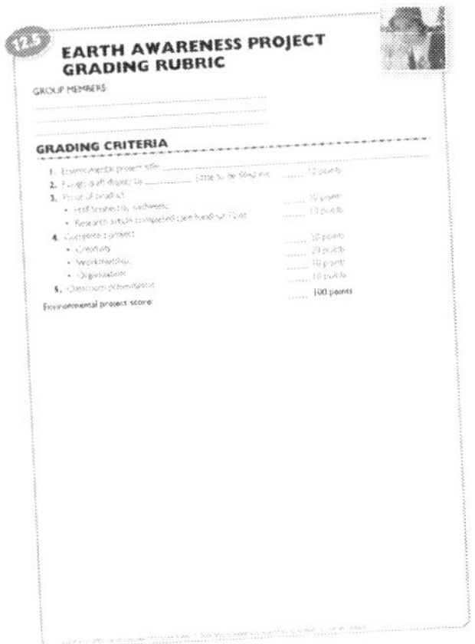
EARTH AWARENESS PROJECT
GRADING RUBRIC

12.5

HANDOUT 12.4

Earth Awareness Project

Find a partner or two and pick an earth awareness project. This activity should be fun and interesting. Many options are available, so no two projects should be alike. You must let me know soon who is in your group and which project you are planning to do. This project is worth 100 points, and you have all week to complete it. Good luck! Let me know if I can help you in any way.

HANDOUT 12.5

Earth Awareness Project Grading Rubric

Explain the format and grading rubric.

HANDOUT 12.6

Earth Awareness Project Research Article

Remind students to read and report on at least one research article. Let them know that you will check on their progress halfway to the due date.

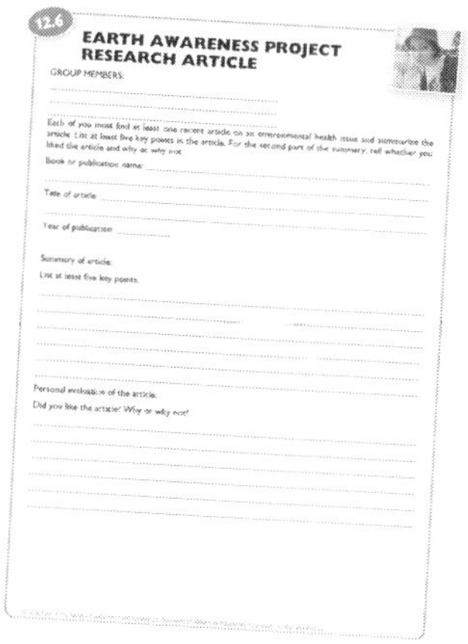
EARTH AWARENESS PROJECT
RESEARCH ARTICLE

12.6

CLOSURE

This activity will help you learn about the major environmental conditions facing the world and give you the opportunity to teach others about the problems and solutions to the predicaments facing our planet.

The Naturalist

OBJECTIVE

Students will gain an appreciation for and awareness of nature by discussing survival skills and the common wildlife found in the United States.

NATIONAL STANDARDS

- #1 Health Promotion
- #4 Communication

INTRODUCTION

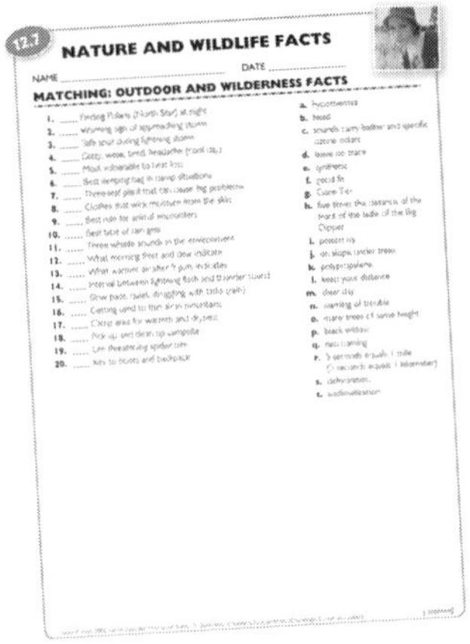

12.7

Today we will learn about nature and becoming comfortable when outside. These facts will help you enjoy nature and all that it has to offer. I think that you will find the information interesting and valuable for future adventures. If you learn to appreciate nature, you will take better care of the environment.

HANDOUT 12.7

Nature and Wildlife Facts

Let us talk about survival skills in the outdoors and wildlife. See how many wilderness facts you can match in section one and how many common animals in nature you can match in section two. Then we will talk.

Matching: Outdoor and Wilderness Facts

1. h	**6.** e	**11.** n	**16.** t
2. c	**7.** i	**12.** m	**17.** j
3. o	**8.** k	**13.** q	**18.** d
4. s	**9.** l	**14.** r	**19.** p
5. b	**10.** g	**15.** a	**20.** f

Matching: Animals in the Wild

1. x	**6.** e	**11.** p	**16.** f	**21.** h
2. s	**7.** u	**12.** i	**17.** t	**22.** k
3. w	**8.** l	**13.** d	**18.** m	**23.** o
4. j	**9.** y	**14.** r	**19.** q	**24.** b
5. g	**10.** a	**15.** c	**20.** n	**25.** v

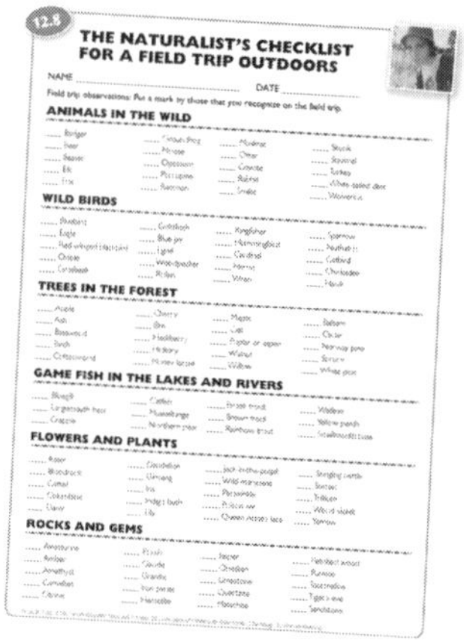

12.8

HANDOUT 12.8

The Naturalist's Checklist for a Field Trip Outdoors

A field trip into nature is also possible. This sheet is a checklist that students can use to identify some of the elements in nature. They should take time to see, hear, and watch for nature at its best. Because the flora and fauna in each region of the country are different, you will need to adapt the list to your area.

CLOSURE

You should spend some time outside every day to enhance both your health and your appreciation for nature and wildlife. Nature is soothing to the soul. We need to take care of our planet so that future generations will be able to enjoy what we have now.

Environmental Health Test Key

OBJECTIVE

Students will be able to pass a written test after studying the environment during this unit.

NATIONAL STANDARDS

- #1 Health Promotion
- #7 Healthy Behaviors

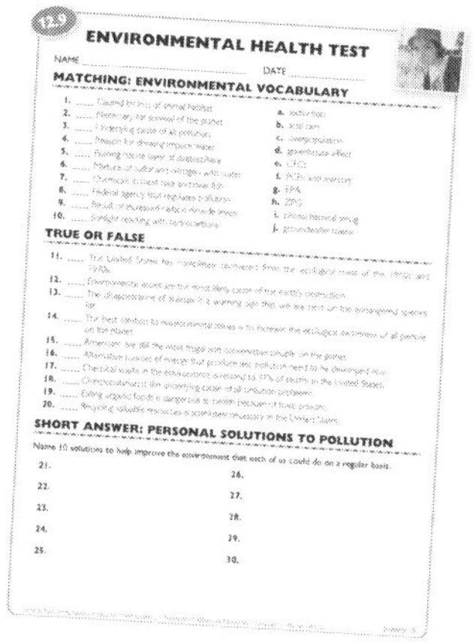
ENVIRONMENTAL HEALTH TEST

MATCHING: ENVIRONMENTAL VOCABULARY

TRUE OR FALSE

SHORT ANSWER: PERSONAL SOLUTIONS TO POLLUTION

12.9

INTRODUCTION

Please complete this test and hand it in when you are finished.

HANDOUT 12.9

Matching: Environmental Vocabulary

1. a	**6.** b
2. h	**7.** f
3. c	**8.** g
4. j	**9.** d
5. e	**10.** i

True or False

11. false—Not exactly, but we have made great strides over the years.
12. true
13. true
14. true
15. false—We are more wasteful than any nation on the planet.
16. true
17. false—Around 68% of deaths have chemical waste in the environment as a contributing factor.
18. true
19. false—Organic foods do not have pesticides or herbicides used on them.
20. true

Short Answer: Personal Solutions to Pollution

Questions 21–30. Many answers will be acceptable for this question. See environmental health assessment for potential answers.

Matching: Earth Problems

31. i	**36.** c
32. g	**37.** e
33. h	**38.** j
34. f	**39.** a
35. d	**40.** b

CLOSURE

We will go over the test in the next class period.

13

Spiritual Health

BY HAVING A REVERENCE FOR LIFE, WE ENTER INTO A SPIRITUAL RELATION WITH THE WORLD. BY PRACTICING REVERENCE FOR LIFE WE BECOME GOOD, DEEP, AND ALIVE.

Albert Schweitzer

Lesson Finder

Spiritual Health

OBJECTIVE

Students will be able to define spirituality and what that means to them through an interactive discussion.

NATIONAL STANDARDS

- #1 Health Promotion
- #7 Healthy Behaviors
- #5 Decision Making
- #4 Communication

INTRODUCTION

This chapter is about the inner core, or spirit, of a person. Even the literature of antiquity speaks to the mind, body, and of the spirit of humans. The spirit is the essence of one's character. Let us examine the area of spiritual health.

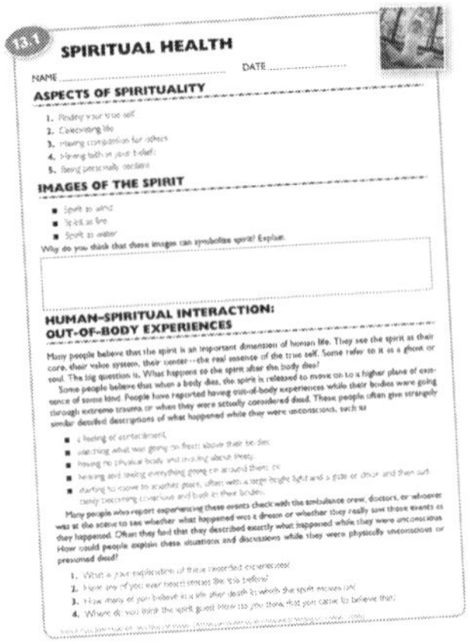
SPIRITUAL HEALTH
NAME DATE
ASPECTS OF SPIRITUALITY
IMAGES OF THE SPIRIT
HUMAN–SPIRITUAL INTERACTION: OUT-OF-BODY EXPERIENCES

13.1

HANDOUT 13.1

Spiritual Health

Together with the students, read the spiritual health handout. Go over the five aspects of spirituality, the examples of images of the spirit, and human–spiritual interaction. Moderate a discussion in which students can give their ideas or feelings on each of the five questions.

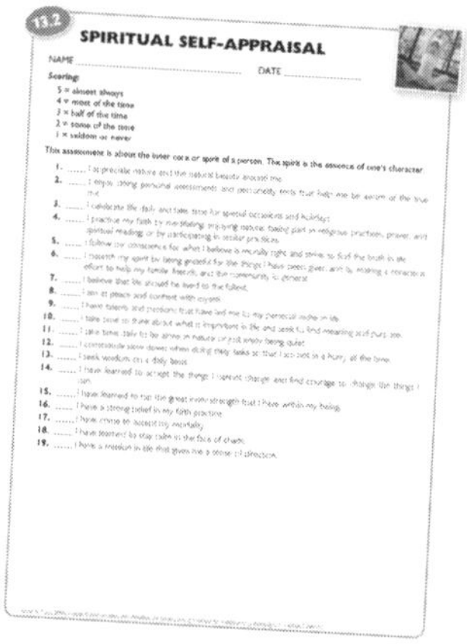
SPIRITUAL SELF-APPRAISAL
NAME DATE

13.2

HANDOUT 13.2

Spiritual Self-Appraisal

Have the students complete the spiritual self-appraisal to get them thinking about their level of spirituality. You can discuss as a class or simply allow the students to ponder these questions on their own.

CLOSURE

Maintaining a balance in life is important. Your spiritual health, whatever your beliefs, may be one of the most important areas.

OBJECTIVE

Students will be able to freely discuss their ideas and beliefs about spirituality with their classmates in a roundtable discussion.

NATIONAL STANDARDS

- #5 Decision Making
- #4 Communication

INTRODUCTION

Today we will talk about our ideas and beliefs concerning spirituality. Your ideas and beliefs may not be like anyone else's. There are no right or wrong answers. Your answers are just your feelings at this time in your life based on your experiences. Share your feelings on the questions that you feel comfortable with and be a good listener when others are talking.

If students are not comfortable taking part in a discussion about this topic, make it easy for them to go to another section of the room or to the library to study. Do not force students to share or listen if they are uncomfortable doing so.

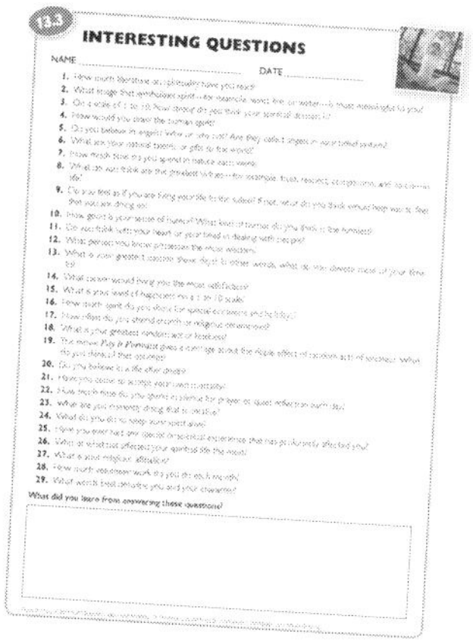

13.3

HANDOUT 13.3

Interesting Questions

Have the class form a circle. Start the discussion by picking any question off the handout titled "Interesting Questions" and answering it. Then go around the circle and ask students to share their answers if they feel comfortable doing so. To have a different person start each time, ask the next person in line to choose a question to discuss. Go through the questions until the class is over or the questions run out.

CLOSURE

I hope that you all learned some interesting facts about spiritual health today and that the activity was fun and interesting. Thank you for being respectful of each other's answers.

Living Your Dreams

OBJECTIVE

Students will explore the seven disciplines for living their dreams and finding spiritual happiness and fulfillment.

NATIONAL STANDARDS

- #7 Healthy Behaviors
- #5 Decision Making

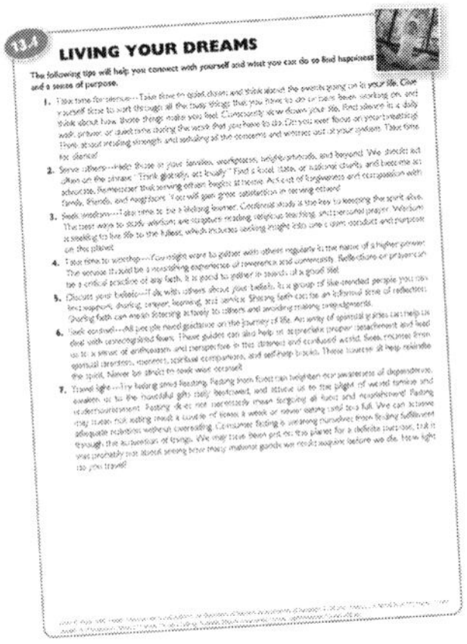
LIVING YOUR DREAMS

The following tips will help you connect with yourself and what you can do to find happiness and a sense of purpose.

13.4

INTRODUCTION

An important aspect of spiritual health is taking time for personal reflection. Today we will explore seven ways to keep our spirits happy.

HANDOUT 13.4

Living Your Dreams

Read the sheet titled "Living Your Dreams."

CLOSURE

The spiritual aspect of life is important. These seven disciplines can help guide you to keeping your spirit alive.

14

Self-Awareness

> THERE IS BUT ONE STRAIGHT COURSE IN LIFE, AND THAT IS TO SEEK THE TRUTH AND PURSUE IT STEADILY.
>
> **George Washington**

Lesson Finder

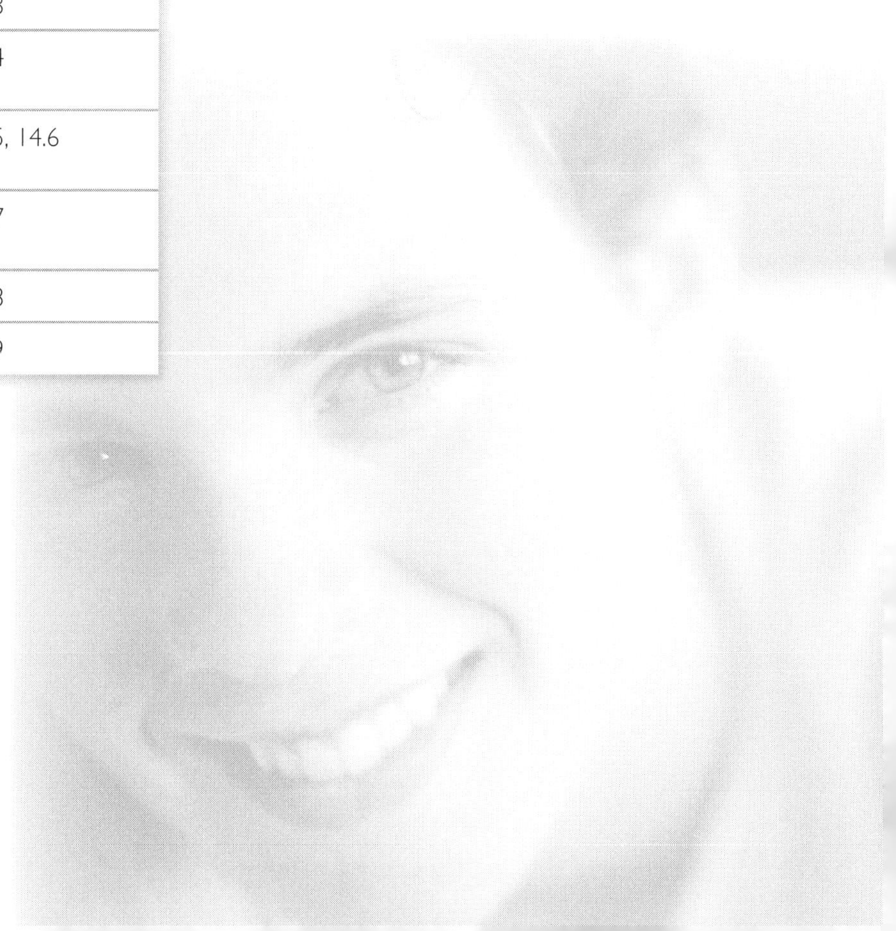

Self-Awareness Facts

14.1

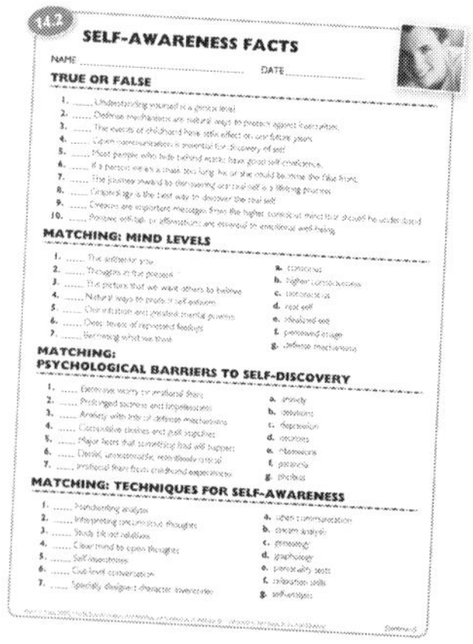

SELF-AWARENESS FACTS

NAME DATE

TRUE OR FALSE

MATCHING: MIND LEVELS

MATCHING: PSYCHOLOGICAL BARRIERS TO SELF-DISCOVERY

MATCHING: TECHNIQUES FOR SELF-AWARENESS

14.2

OBJECTIVE

Students will be able to learn the key factors that determine intrapersonal intelligence through a classroom discussion.

NATIONAL STANDARDS

- #1 Health Promotion
- #4 Communication

INTRODUCTION

One level of genius is called intrapersonal intelligence—having knowledge and insight into oneself. Solving the riddle of self takes self-confidence and self-respect. We will do many fun and interesting activities in this unit that will give you insight into your own being.

HANDOUT 14.1

Show or draw the bull's-eye figure, shown in handout 14.1. This figure symbolizes how the real self emerges as the fake image we portray to others is no longer necessary.

HANDOUT 14.2

True or False

1. true
2. true
3. false—Childhood events are a major influence.
4. true
5. false—People with low self-esteem often hide themselves behind masks.
6. true
7. true
8. false—Dream analysis is the best way to discover the real self.
9. false—Dreams are important messages from the unconscious that should be understood.
10. true

Matching: Mind Levels

1. d
2. a
3. f
4. g
5. b
6. c
7. f

Matching: Psychological Barriers to Self-Discovery

1. a
2. c
3. d
4. e
5. f
6. b
7. g

Matching: Techniques for Self-Awareness

1. d
2. b
3. c
4. f
5. g
6. b
7. e

Questions to Ask Yourself

1. fear of rejection
2. lots of answers
3. communication, personality tests, dream analysis

CLOSURE

This week challenges us to see the masks and fronts that almost all of us wear. The goal is not to discover the fake fronts of others but to see our own masks. Seek the truth and pursue it steadily.

Personality Test

OBJECTIVE

Students will be able to understand a little more about their true self by taking a personality test and discussing the meaning of their answers.

NATIONAL STANDARD

#1 Health Promotion

INTRODUCTION

This is a personality test that will help you to discover the "trueself." There are no right or wrong answers. Just be honest and mark the answers the way you really feel. Then we will discuss the different questions.

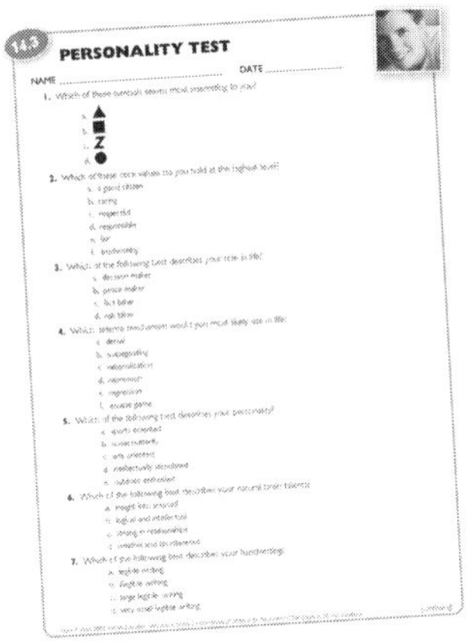

14.3

HANDOUT 14.3

Meaning of the Answers

1. Share the interpretations for the answers with students so that they can see what their answers mean.
   - a. high achiever, spiritual
   - b. leader, creative
   - c. solid, dependable
   - d. well balanced, harmonious
2. All are great core values.
3. General role
4. Use of defense mechanisms
5. General personality types
6. Share the interpretations for the answers with students so that they can see what their answers mean.
   - a. intrapersonal
   - b. logical
   - c. interpersonal
   - d. creative
7. Graphology (handwriting analysis)—legible writing is good.
8. Colors tell feelings and moods.
9. Emotional needs—together these fulfilled emotional needs create a sense of well-being.
10. Typical lifestyle
11. Five dimensions
12. Environmental areas suited to them
13. Like the qualities of the animal

14. Share the interpretations for the answers with students so that they can see what their answers mean.

a. materialistic

b. humanitarian

c. career focus

d. compassionate

e. creative

f. adventurous

15. What is your natural niche?

16. Share the interpretations for each answer with students so they can see what their answers mean.

a. energy

b. environmental

c. spiritual

d. nourishing

17. Multiple intelligences test

18. Meaning of astrological signs:

- Aries (March 21–April 20)—friendly, impulsive, and energetic; avoid the tendency to bully others.
- Taurus (April 21–May 21)—Stubborn, hardworking, warm-hearted, and loyal; avoid becoming self-indulgent.
- Gemini (May 22–June 21)—adaptable, communicative, witty, and a clever intellectual; avoid the tendency to become nervous and tense.
- Cancer (June 22–July 22)—nurturing, family-oriented, imaginative, and emotional; avoid a tendency to become overly possessive because of personal insecurities.
- Leo (July 23–August 22)—creative, optimistic, warm-hearted, and confident; avoid giving in to arrogance by becoming selfish, patronizing, or bossy.
- Virgo (August 23–September 22)—analytical, practical, reliable, and a perfectionist; avoid becoming overcritical or too worrisome.
- Libra (September 23–October 23)—balanced, easygoing, peaceable, romantic, and gullible; avoid becoming indecisive by overanalyzing all of the angles.
- Scorpio (October 24–November 22)—intuitive, intense, and passionate; avoid jealousy and a tendency to become obsessive.
- Sagittarius (November 23–December 22)—optimistic, honest, and enthusiastic; avoid being tactless or outspoken.
- Capricorn (December 23–January 20)—success-driven, disciplined, hardworking, patient, and humorous; avoid appearing overly reserved or rigid.
- Aquarius (January 21–February 19)—friendly, honest, original, independent, and an intellectual; avoid appearing detached and unemotional or being contrary.
- Pisces (February 20–March 20)—imaginative, compassionate, and sensitive; avoid being easily led and a tendency to turn a blind eye to the defects in those you love.

CLOSURE

This was meant to be an interesting activity and a good way to reveal some of your true feelings, ideas, beliefs, and talents.

True Colors Personality Test

OBJECTIVE

Students will be able to identify their dominant color by taking a personality test that measures natural brain talent.

NATIONAL STANDARD

#7 Healthy Behaviors

INTRODUCTION

There are four main brain dominances. This personality test will help you discover which area seems to be your natural talent. There are no right or wrong answers. Personality tests are a good way to determine who you really are.

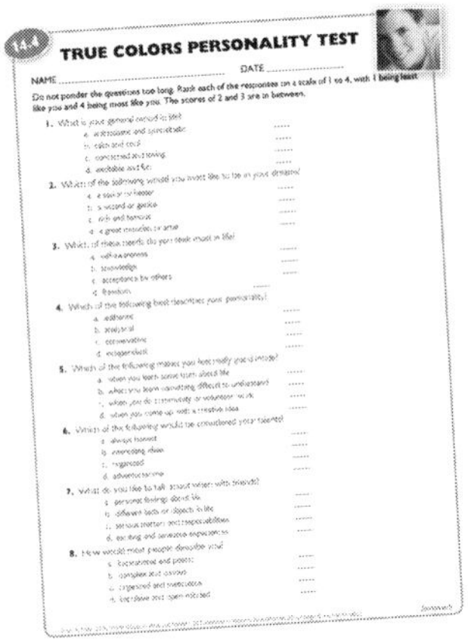
TRUE COLORS PERSONALITY TEST

14.4

HANDOUT 14.4

True Colors Personality Test

Read the directions and do the first question together. There are no right or wrong answers. Then have students complete the rest of the test on their own.

This test is supposed to show which area of the brain is accessed the most by natural ability. A student's high score is his or her dominant color; the low score is the student's least accessed color.

At the end of the test, after students have added up their points to see what their natural brain dominance is, have them come to the board and mark both their primary color, or high score, and their lowest color, or their area least accessed. Everyone can then see how the class as a whole scored on the personality test.

The brain has four quadrants. The colors represent different types of brain intelligence, known as the four levels of genius.

a. Blue = intrapersonal IQ, or self-awareness

b. Yellow = logical IQ, or brain reasoning

c. Red = interpersonal IQ, or social skills

d. Orange = creative IQ, or innovative talents

Discuss any questions that students have about this personality test and what it means.

CLOSURE

This short personality test identifies the area of the brain that seems to be your dominant talent. If the test is valid, the results are like this:

a. Blue has good insight into self.

b. Yellow has good common sense and logic.

c. Red has great people skills.

d. Orange is creative and independent.

Graphology (Handwriting Analysis)

OBJECTIVE

Students will give a sample of their handwriting and decipher some information about their real self.

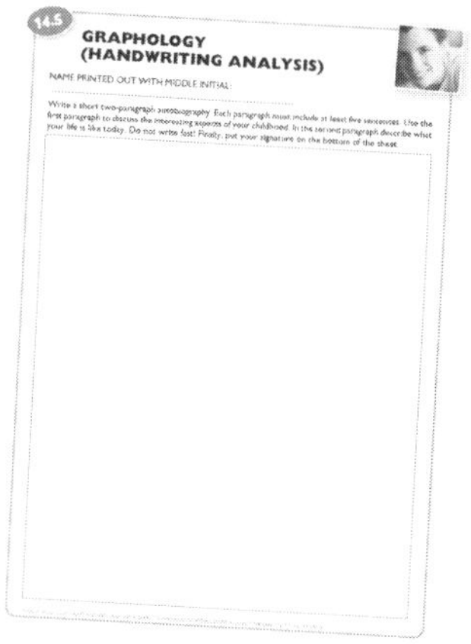

14.5

NATIONAL STANDARDS

- #5 Decision Making
- #6 Goal Setting

INTRODUCTION

Handwriting has been used for years as an investigative tool and for psychoanalysis. A lot can be determined by an analysis of your handwriting. Each person has a very specific writing style. This activity is to help you reveal a little more about the "real you."

HANDOUT 14.5

HANDOUT 14.6

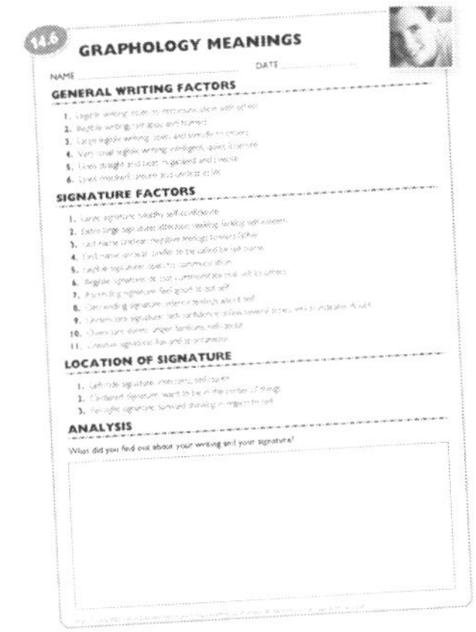

14.6

CLOSURE

There are many ways to increase self-awareness. Maybe this handwriting analysis provided you with insight into your real self.

Open and Honest Communication

OBJECTIVE

Students will be able to share their personal feelings with a group of classmates on a variety of questions about life.

NATIONAL STANDARDS

- #5 Decision Making
- #4 Communication

INTRODUCTION

One of the best ways to understand yourself is to answer a variety of difficult questions about life. These questions generally do not come up in normal conversation. Each answer reveals a bit about you. Remember that there are no right or wrong answers.

We are asking you to be open and honest and not to hide yourself from the rest of the class. Why are people afraid to tell others what they are really like inside? (Answer: fear of rejection.)

I want you to be able to talk with honesty and self-confidence, to be unafraid. This has been an interesting and successful activity over the years.

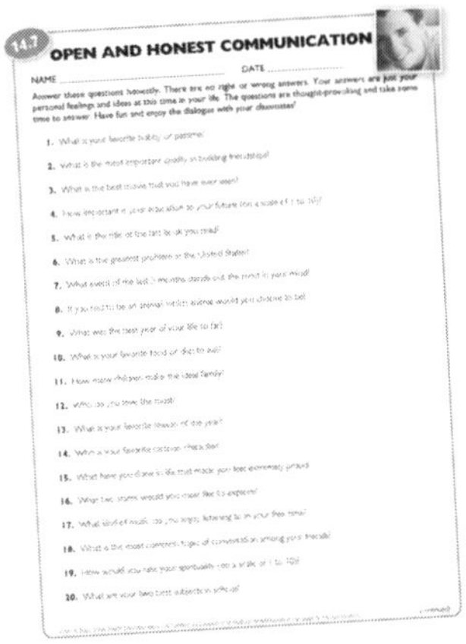
OPEN AND HONEST COMMUNICATION

14.7

HANDOUT 14.7

Open and Honest Communication

Each student must answer all 70 questions before the activity starts. Tell the students that there are no right or wrong answers; they just give their opinions. Have them form groups of 10 or so. A whole-class circle can also work. Have one person start by picking any question that he or she thinks is interesting. The student tells his or her response, and the others all follow with their responses (have a different person start each question). Go through as many questions as time permits. You may need 2 days to complete the activity.

At the end of the class discussion have the students do the synthesis set, which checks their listening level.

CLOSURE

This activity helps you communicate openly and honestly. You learned a lot about your classmates and a lot about yourself. You should never be afraid to reveal your personality. Self-awareness is an important part of emotional well-being.

Coat of Arms Assignment

OBJECTIVE

Students will complete a coat of arms assignment after some research and personal analysis.

NATIONAL STANDARDS

- #7 Healthy Behaviors
- #5 Decision Making
- #4 Communication

INTRODUCTION

This interesting assignment allow you to describe your character at this time in life. The project has six parts:

1. Put your surname (last name) on top in bold letters.
2. Color the coat of arms with your favorite color.
3. Put at least one animal that you like on the side of the shield.
4. Put at least three symbols that describe your character inside the shield.
5. Put your motto for life at the bottom.
6. Write an explanation about the meaning of each part of your shield on the back of this handout.

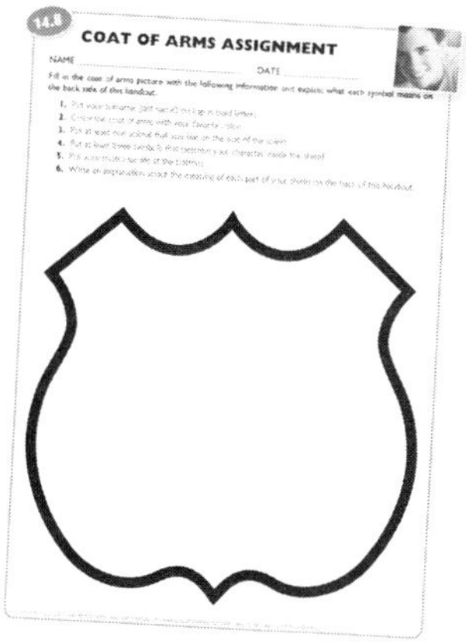

14.8

HANDOUT 14.8

Coat of Arms Assignment

Fill in the information as shown on the coat of arms assignment sheet. Share your coat of arms with the class or at least a few of your classmates. This assignment is meant to be a meaningful and proud reflection of your character.

CLOSURE

Thanks for sharing your coat of arms with the class.

Self-Awareness Test Key

OBJECTIVE

Students will pass a written test on the key factors related to self-awareness.

NATIONAL STANDARDS

- #1 Health Promotion
- #7 Healthy Behaviors

INTRODUCTION

Please complete this test and turn it in as soon as you are finished.

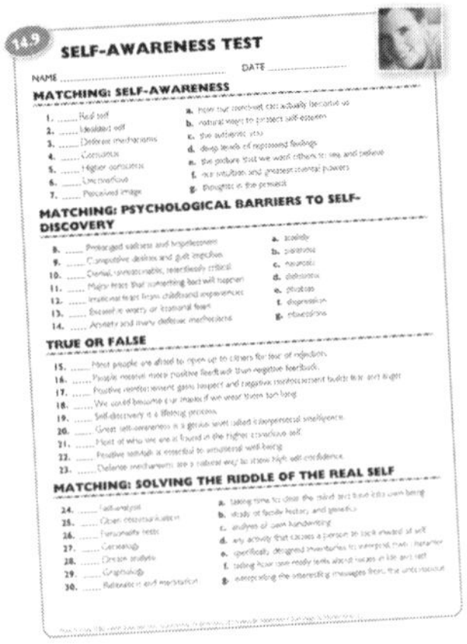
14.9 SELF-AWARENESS TEST

MATCHING: SELF-AWARENESS

MATCHING: PSYCHOLOGICAL BARRIERS TO SELF-DISCOVERY

TRUE OR FALSE

MATCHING: SOLVING THE RIDDLE OF THE REAL SELF

14.9

HANDOUT 14.9

Matching: Self-Awareness

1. c
2. e
3. b
4. g
5. f
6. d
7. a

Matching: Psychological Barriers to Self-Discovery

8. f
9. g
10. d
11. b
12. e
13. a
14. c

True or False

15. true
16. false—People get more negative feedback than positive messages in life.
17. true
18. true
19. true
20. false—Great self-awareness is a genius level called intrapersonal intelligence.
21. false—Most of who we are is found in the unconscious self.
22. true
23. false—Defense mechanisms are a natural way to show low self-confidence.

Matching: Solving the Riddle of the Real Self

24. d

25. f

26. e

27. b

28. g

29. c

30. a

CLOSURE

We will go over the test the next time we meet.

15

The Gift of Wisdom

GREAT IS WISDOM;
INFINITE IS THE
VALUE OF WISDOM.
IT CANNOT BE
EXAGGERATED;
IT IS THE HIGHEST
ACHIEVEMENT
OF MAN.

Thomas Carlyle

Lesson Finder

Seeking Wisdom

OBJECTIVE

Students will be able to write down at least seven qualities for developing wisdom.

NATIONAL STANDARDS

- #1 Health Promotion
- #7 Healthy Behaviors
- #4 Communication

INTRODUCTION

Wisdom is considered one of the great virtues in life. This week we will examine the many facets of wisdom. I think the topic will be of great interest to you. Always seek counsel from the wise when making serious choices in life.

SEEKING WISDOM

MATCHING: WISDOM VOCABULARY

FILL IN THE BLANK

CHECKLIST: FINDING MEANING AND PURPOSE IN LIFE

How many of these do you do?

15.1

HANDOUT 15.1

Matching: Wisdom Vocabulary

1. f
2. c
3. j
4. e
5. i
6. a
7. g
8. b
9. d
10. h

Fill in the Blank

1. listen
2. gain
3. slowly
4. right
5. admit
6. truth
7. teach

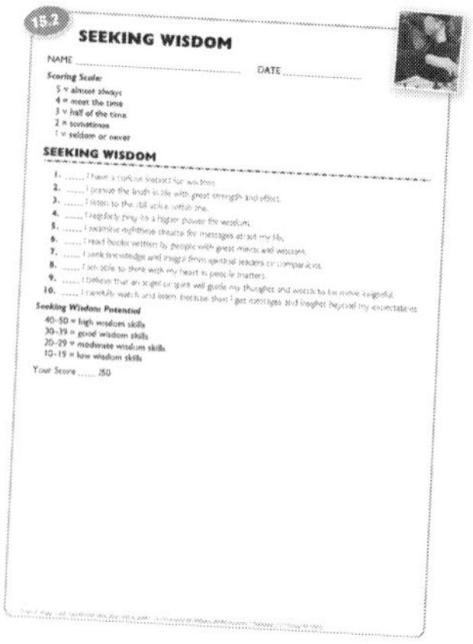
SEEKING WISDOM

SEEKING WISDOM

15.2

Checklist: Finding Meaning and Purpose in Life

How many of these do you practice?

HANDOUT 15.2

CLOSURE

Wisdom is the greatest achievement in life, and those who seek wisdom will find it. Wouldn't it be terrific to be able to make good choices about life decisions and live life to your fullest potential?

Finding Wisdom

OBJECTIVE

Students will examine the highest level of intelligence—wisdom—by discussing the facts and finding answers to difficult questions in life.

NATIONAL STANDARDS

- #1 Health Promotion
- #5 Decision Making
- #4 Communication

INTRODUCTION

There are many levels of intelligence in life. The highest level that a person is able to reach is called wisdom. Wouldn't it be wonderful to be able to come up with all the right solutions to the many problems that people must face? Today we will examine the stages of intelligence and the facts concerning wisdom. We will also try to answer some of the tough questions as a wise person might answer them.

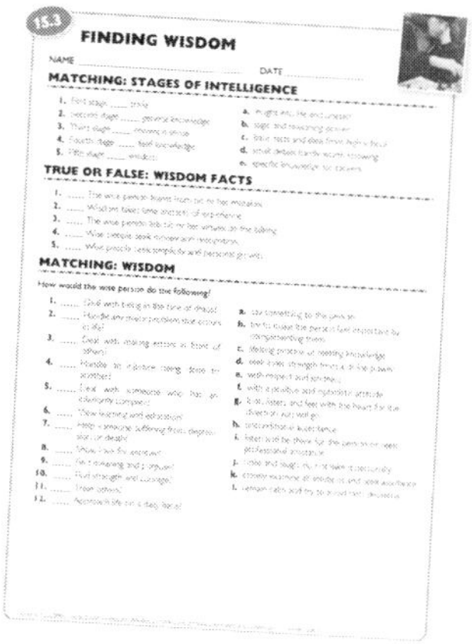
FINDING WISDOM
MATCHING: STAGES OF INTELLIGENCE
TRUE OR FALSE: WISDOM FACTS
MATCHING: WISDOM

15.3

HANDOUT 15.3

Matching: Stages of Intelligence

The five stages of intelligence can be ordered from the lowest level to the highest level. Let us try to match definitions to the five stages of intelligence. Do any of you know which definitions match the various levels of intelligence?

1. d
2. c
3. b
4. e
5. a

True or False: Wisdom Facts

Go over a few facts concerning the highest level of intelligence—wisdom. Talk a little about each and give the correct answer.

1. true
2. true
3. true
4. false—The wise are humble.
5. true

Matching: Wisdom

This section helps us think as a wise person would about the following situations.

1. l	**7.** i
2. k	**8.** h
3. j	**9.** g
4. a	**10.** d
5. b	**11.** e
6. c	**12.** f

15.4

HANDOUT 15.4

Matching: Questions About Wisdom

With a partner, see whether you can now figure out the section on finding wisdom with the 13 different questions.

1. e	**8.** d
2. f	**9.** i
3. g	**10.** j
4. h	**11.** k
5. a	**12.** l
6. b	**13.** m, n, o, p
7. c	

CLOSURE

One of the greatest honors is to have gained insight into all aspects of life. This ability comes with time and patience. Finding wisdom is a lifelong process. Only those who really want to know the truth will gain wisdom.

Divine Wisdom Project

OBJECTIVE

Students will be able to design and create their own poems, songs, quotes, or pictures that present profound wisdom to the observer.

NATIONAL STANDARDS

- #5 Decision Making
- #8 Advocacy

INTRODUCTION

Now that we have analyzed wisdom, your assignment is to come up with an inspirational project that invokes wisdom to the observer. You can do this project with a partner.

Today we will answer any questions that you might have about wisdom. Then you will have time to design your wisdom project, which you will present to the class.

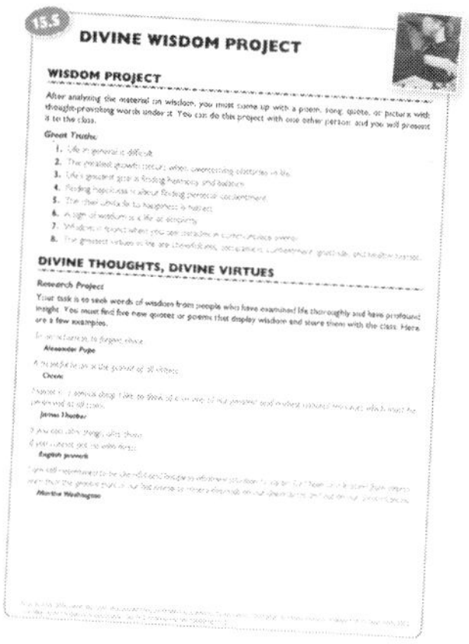
DIVINE WISDOM PROJECT

WISDOM PROJECT

DIVINE THOUGHTS, DIVINE VIRTUES

15.5

HANDOUT 15.5

Great Truths

We have eight great truths to examine today to see whether you really understand the concepts of wisdom.

Divine Thoughts, Divine Virtues Research Project

Now you have time to determine what project you are going to do. Tell me about it before you leave class today.

CLOSURE

The finished products about wisdom will be interesting to see. You will be presenting them to the class instead of taking a test.

Quantum Transformation

OBJECTIVE

Students will be able to practice a new concept of tapping an unlimited power source found within them by using a mental programming technique for success and happiness.

NATIONAL STANDARDS

- #1 Health Promotion
- #5 Decision Making

INTRODUCTION

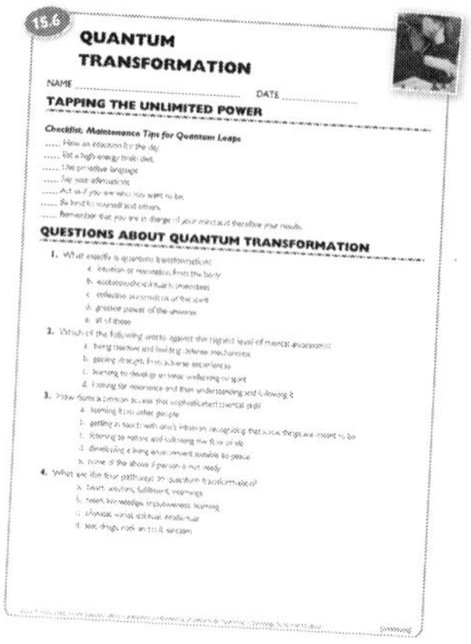

15.6

This is a relatively new concept of programming ourselves for success and happiness. We all have an unlimited power source known as the quantum strings. This lesson is about learning how to tap this source of energy for great power and resiliency. The ability to tap this inner wellspring will help us understand the deepest form of inner awareness.

HANDOUT 15.6

Checklist: Maintenance Tips for Quantum Leaps

Ask for a show of hands to learn how many students are practicing each of these tips on a daily basis.

Questions About Quantum Transformation

1. e
2. a
3. e
4. a
5. Good choices:
    a. Enhance your spiritual dimension.
    b. Find meaning and purpose in life.
    c. Practice imagery and meditation.
    e. Listen to music that brings inner contentment.
    f. Seek to listen to your special silent voice.
    i. Seek to be noble and find absolute truths.

15.7

HANDOUT 15.7

Quantum Transformation Mental Programming Technique

We are going to practice a mental programming technique called visualization. Have any of you ever done any visualization techniques? Let us follow the warm-up criteria and then try this mental programming skill.

After students have completed the mental programming technique, comment on the activity sheet and talk about what they learned from this activity.

CLOSURE

This material on quantum transformation is interesting, although it can be difficult to understand. Just remember that your mind programs your body and that there are ways to program yourself for happiness, healing, success, and a good life. Most people end up being programmed by the many negative aspects that they hear and feel in their lives. Let us learn to change the program.

16

Emotional Health

> THE MIND IS LIKE A RIVER; UPON ITS WATER THOUGHTS FLOAT THROUGH IN A CONSTANT PROCESSION EVERY CONSCIOUS MOMENT. YOU CAN STAND ON A BRIDGE OVER IT AND CAN STOP AND TURN BACK ANY THOUGHT THAT COMES ALONG. THE ART OF CONTENTMENT IS TO LET NO THOUGHT PASS THAT IS GOING TO DISTURB YOU.
>
> **Dr. Frank Crane**

Lesson Finder

Emotional Health Facts

OBJECTIVE

Students will be able to analyze the facts and data related to emotional health through a classroom discussion.

NATIONAL STANDARDS

- #1 Health Promotion
- #4 Communication

INTRODUCTION

Emotional health is probably the most important topic in the study of health and well-being. Emotions determine more of our behavior than any other single factor. Keeping your emotional health strong is vital for learning and happiness.

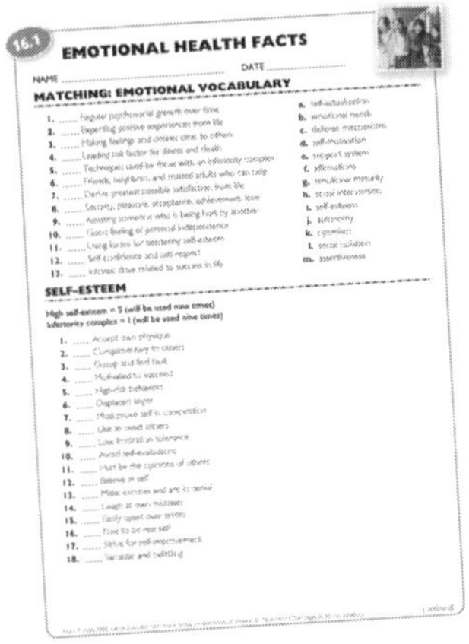
EMOTIONAL HEALTH FACTS

MATCHING: EMOTIONAL VOCABULARY

SELF-ESTEEM

16.1

HANDOUT 16.1

Matching: Emotional Vocabulary

1. g	**8.** b
2. k	**9.** h
3. m	**10.** j
4. l	**11.** f
5. c	**12.** i
6. e	**13.** d
7. a	

Self-Esteem

1. S	**7.** I	**13.** I
2. S	**8.** S	**14.** S
3. I	**9.** I	**15.** I
4. S	**10.** I	**16.** S
5. I	**11.** I	**17.** S
6. I	**12.** S	**18.** I

Matching: Dealing With Adverse Transitions

1. d
2. b
3. a
4. e
5. c

Matching: Common Defense Mechanisms

1. d
2. f
3. g
4. a
5. b
6. c
7. e

HANDOUT 16.2

Emotional Health and Life

Read aloud and tell students who the people were.

Case 1: Albert Einstein

Case 2: Eleanor Roosevelt

Case 3: Thomas Edison

Case 4: Winston Churchill

1. accepted by significant others
2. believed in self
3. inner wellspring of strength
4. wanted to prove others wrong

The moral of the story is that no matter how bad your life is, you can turn it around, but to do so you must believe in yourself and know that you have the inner strength to prove others wrong. Determination and hard work can overcome all obstacles.

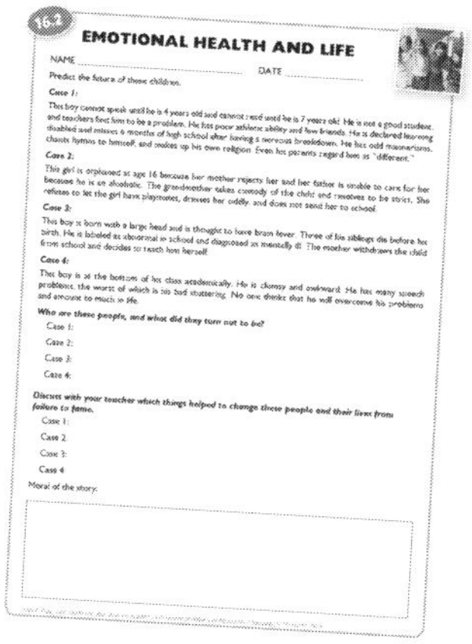
16.2 EMOTIONAL HEALTH AND LIFE

NAME .... DATE ....

Predict the future of these children.

Case 1:

This boy cannot speak until he is 4 years old and cannot read until he is 7 years old. He is not a good student and teachers find him to be a problem. He has poor athletic ability and few friends. He is declared learning disabled and misses 6 months of high school after having a nervous breakdown. He has odd mannerisms, chants hymns to himself, and makes up his own religion. Even his parents regard him as "different."

Case 2:

This girl is orphaned at age 16 because her mother rejects her and her father is unable to care for her because he is an alcoholic. The grandmother takes custody of the child and resolves to be strict. She refuses to let the girl have playmates, dresses her oddly, and does not send her to school.

Case 3:

This boy is born with a large head and is thought to have brain fever. Three of his siblings die before his birth. He is labeled as abnormal in school and diagnosed as mentally ill. The mother withdraws the child from school and decides to teach him herself.

Case 4:

This boy is at the bottom of his class academically. He is clumsy and awkward. He has many speech problems, the worst of which is his bad stuttering. No one thinks that he will overcome his problems and amount to much in life.

Who are these people, and what did they turn out to be?

Case 1:

Case 2:

Case 3:

Case 4:

Discuss with your teacher which things helped to change these people and their lives from failure to fame.

Case 1:

Case 2:

Case 3:

Case 4

Moral of the story:

16.2

CLOSURE

Some of the most successful people were not all that great as children or teenagers. When you become strong emotionally, nothing can prevent you from making it in life. Never give up on yourself!

Maslow's Revised Hierarchy of Needs

OBJECTIVE

Students will be able to label the seven levels of emotional needs and list a couple of defense mechanisms and roles that people use when needs are not fully satisfied through a classroom discussion.

NATIONAL STANDARDS

- #7 Healthy Behaviors
- #5 Decision Making
- #4 Communication

INTRODUCTION

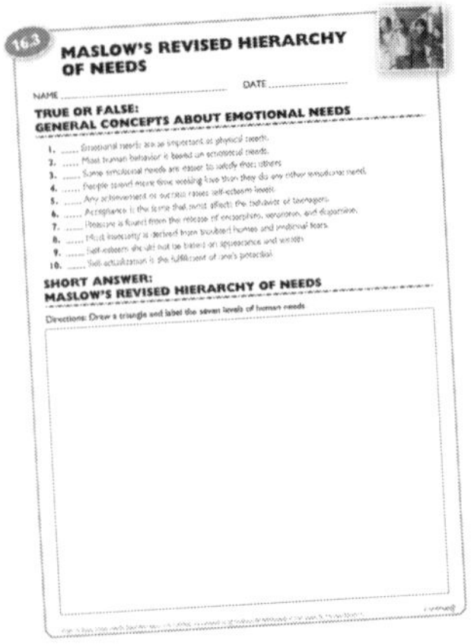
16.3 MASLOW'S REVISED HIERARCHY OF NEEDS

NAME DATE

TRUE OR FALSE: GENERAL CONCEPTS ABOUT EMOTIONAL NEEDS

SHORT ANSWER: MASLOW'S REVISED HIERARCHY OF NEEDS

Directions: Draw a triangle and label the seven levels of human needs.

16.3

Today we will discuss one theory on human emotional needs from the research of Abraham Maslow and other subsequent data.

HANDOUT 16.3

True or False: General Concepts About Emotional Needs

1. true
2. true
3. true
4. true
5. true
6. true
7. true
8. true
9. true
10. true

SHORT ANSWER: MASLOW'S REVISED HIERARCHY OF NEEDS

Emotional needs:

7. Self-actualization—the top emotional need, rarely reached in life
6. Self-esteem
5. Achievement
4. Love
3. Acceptance
2. Pleasure

Physical need:

1. Security

Puza, Roger F. 1980. The Effectiveness of an Emotional Health Unit on the Self-Esteem of Seventh Grade Students. Master's thesis, University of Wisconsin-LaCrosse.

Roles That People Play to Compensate for Unmet Emotional Needs

1. SE
2. L, A
3. A
4. AS
5. L, A
6. P
7. A
8. AS
9. SE
10. AS, SE
11. SE, S
12. P, S
13. SE, S
14. AS
15. S
16. S

HANDOUT 16.4

Emotional Health Discussion

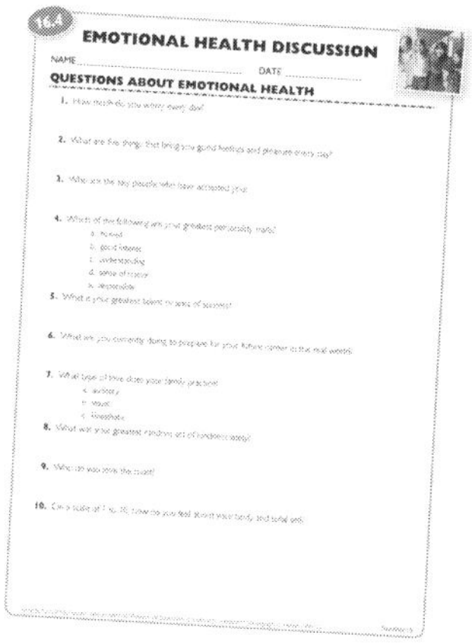

16.4

Have all students complete the questions about emotional health. The goal is then to go around the class and see how the students feel about the topic of emotional health. They will be in a circle. A student picks an interesting question and answers it. Then in turn others will answer the question while the rest of the students listen. There are no right or wrong answers. Students just say what they think at this time in their lives.

CLOSURE

Today was a great day to talk about the underlying factors that motivate all human behavior. Maslow's revised hierarchy is an interesting concept and makes a lot of sense. Many hospitals and psychologists use this data to deal with patients and understand their needs.

Self-Esteem Factors

OBJECTIVE

Students will be able to differentiate between people with high self-esteem and those who are emotionally immature following a group examination.

NATIONAL STANDARDS

- #1 Health Promotion
- #4 Communication

INTRODUCTION

In my examination of important aspects of healthy living over the years, one area stands above all others—self-esteem. Your self-respect and self-confidence are the core of who you are as a human being. Today we are going to examine the key factors to high self-esteem and some of the biggest mistakes that people make concerning their self-esteem.

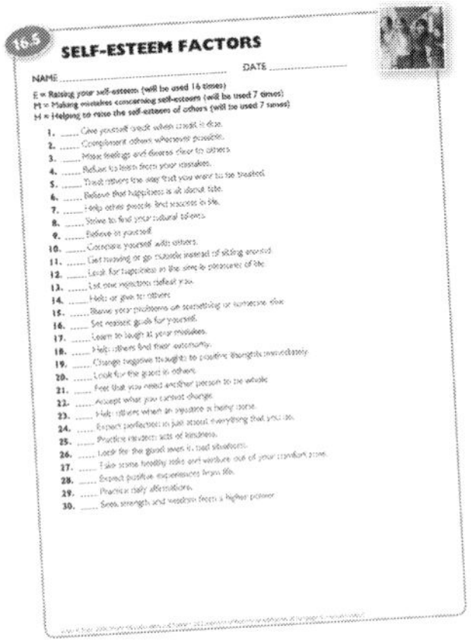
SELF-ESTEEM FACTORS

16.5

HANDOUT 16.5

Self-Esteem Factors

In the first activity you will examine the three major areas of self-esteem. There are 16 positive factors here. People make mistakes concerning their self-esteem, and 7 are noted here. The last factor is how people with high self-esteem can help others who are struggling emotionally. There are 7 of these techniques. See how many of these you can figure out on your own before we go over them.

1. E	**11.** E	**21.** M
2. H	**12.** E	**22.** E
3. E	**13.** M	**23.** H
4. M	**14.** H	**24.** M
5. E	**15.** M	**25.** H
6. M	**16.** E	**26.** E
7. H	**17.** E	**27.** E
8. E	**18.** H	**28.** E
9. E	**19.** E	**29.** E
10. M	**20.** H	**30.** E

SELF-ESTEEM ACTIVITY

HANDS IN HEART POSITION

16.6

HANDOUT 16.6

Self-Esteem Activity

Have students write positive things about each of their classmates on the handout with the human hands on it. This is a great activity!

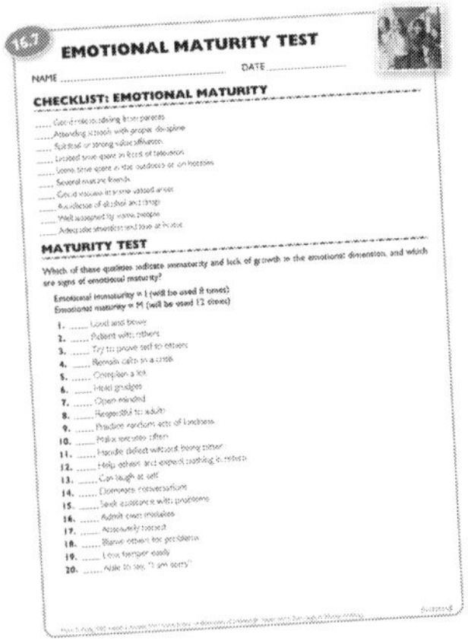
EMOTIONAL MATURITY TEST

CHECKLIST: EMOTIONAL MATURITY

MATURITY TEST

16.7

HANDOUT 16.7

Checklist: Emotional Maturity

How many do you have? Share with the class.

Maturity Test

See whether you can figure out which behaviors are immature (8 answers) and which are mature (12 answers).

1. I	**11.** M
2. M	**12.** M
3. I	**13.** M
4. M	**14.** I
5. I	**15.** M
6. I	**16.** M
7. M	**17.** M
8. M	**18.** I
9. M	**19.** I
10. I	**20.** M

Emotional Maturity: 10 Descriptive Words or Phrases

Here are some suitable answers. Go over this activity with the class. Have students generate the words or terms as you decide which ones are correct.

- patient
- open-minded
- helpful
- humble
- gracious
- honest
- even tempered
- responsible
- trustworthy
- forgiving
- admit mistakes
- accept others
- poised
- learn from defeats
- positive attitude
- sense of humor
- dependable
- kind

CLOSURE

Self-esteem and emotional maturity are key ingredients of a happy and meaningful life. Your emotional health governs all aspects of your life. Keeping a positive attitude and always believing in yourself are key factors to emotional well-being.

Satisfying Emotional Needs

OBJECTIVE

Students will be able to list several factors that will help people satisfy their basic emotional needs through a classroom examination activity.

NATIONAL STANDARDS

- #7 Healthy Behaviors
- #4 Communication

INTRODUCTION

All people have emotional needs, which are just as important as physical needs. If these needs are not met, people will do whatever they have to do to feel good about themselves emotionally. Unmet needs can outweigh other factors and interfere with learning and maintaining effective relationships. Satisfying emotional needs is vital to learning and being happy.

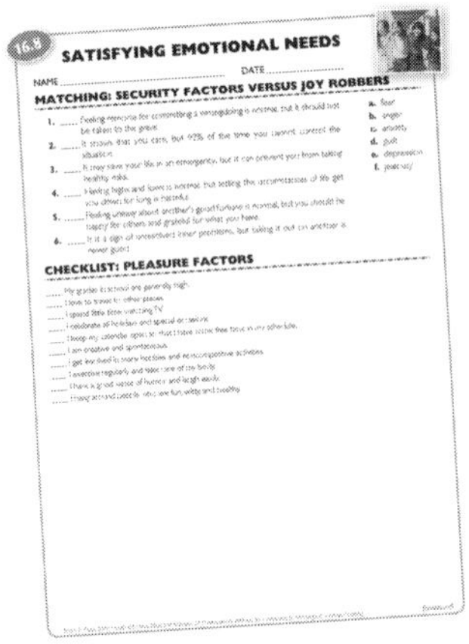

16.8

HANDOUT 16.8

Matching: Security Factors Versus Joy Robbers

1. d
2. c
3. a
4. e
5. f
6. b

Pleasure Factors

How many of the factors related to fun and pleasure did you check? The more items you checked, the more fun you will be having on a daily basis.

Acceptance Factors

Check to see whether you are making good first impressions and mastering the art of conversation. If not, you need to change now. Your personality is you. How many of these top personality traits are true of you?

Love Factors

How lovable you are is determined by your personal development in the five types of love:

Maternal love	___ 1 and 2
Narcissism	___ 3 and 4
Altruism	___ 5 and 6
Romantic	___ 7 and 8
Unconditional	___ 9 and 10

Achievement Factors

How many of these factors do you practice regularly? These are the key factors to success and achievement in life.

Self-Esteem Factors

Nothing is more important than your self-esteem. You can do many things to improve your confidence and respect for yourself. Go for it!

HANDOUT 16.9

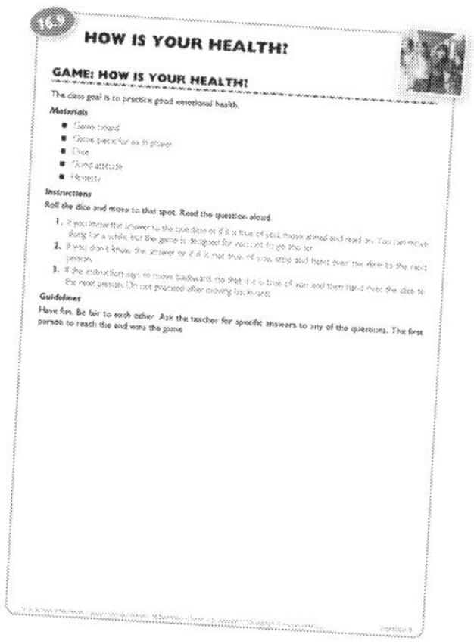
HOW IS YOUR HEALTH?

GAME: HOW IS YOUR HEALTH?

16.9

Game: How Is Your Health?

Students have always liked this interesting game based on emotional health and open communication. Divide the class into smaller groups and remind them to have fun and play fair. Follow the directions.

Here are answers to some board questions:

- If you are an internally controlled person (emotionally), move ahead 5. If you don't know what this is, move back 3.
  - Tip: An internally controlled person does not allow external forces to "get" to them.
- If you know what part of the body is enhanced by cross-laterals, inverted poses, and Baroque music, move ahead 3.
  - Tip: Brain performance is enhanced by cross-laterals, inverted poses, and Baroque music.
- If you know what this is:

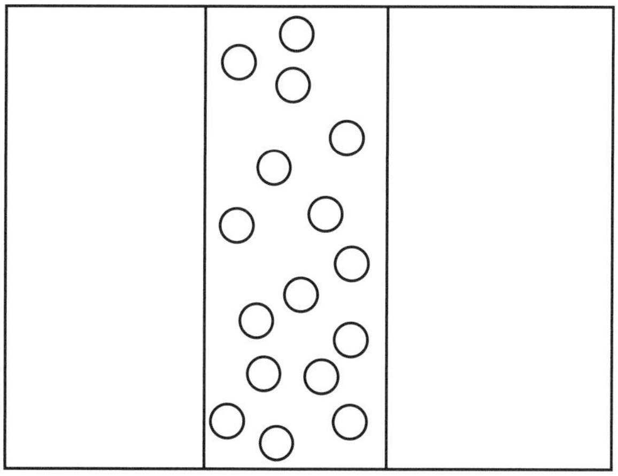

move ahead 3.
  - Tip: A giraffe walking by a window.
- If you do not know how to get out of a bad relationship, move back 3.
  - Tip: Seek assistance from others.
- If you know the top three aerobic exercises, move ahead 3. If you do not know what aerobic exercises are, move back 4.
  - Tip: Cross-country skiing, swimming, and jogging

- If you know what this is:

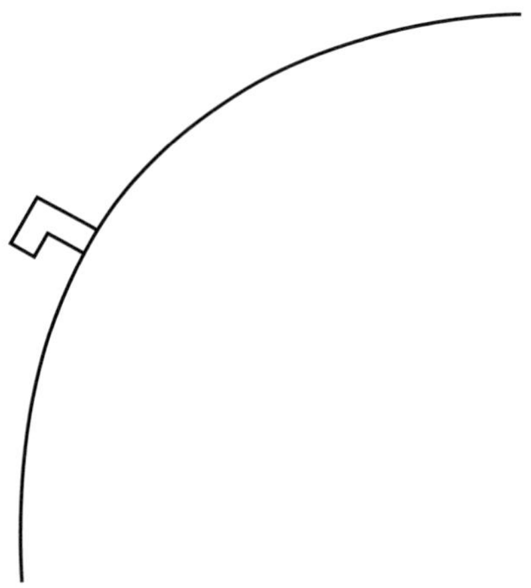

move ahead 2.

  - Tip: Submarine going over a waterfall.
- If you know how long it takes a person to get irreversible brain damage after their heart stops beating, move ahead 2.
  - Tip: Irreversible brain damage takes place 5 minutes after breathing stops.
- If you know the most important factor needed for successful relationships, move ahead 3.
  - Tip: Communication is the key factor in relationships.
- If you know what travels 40 mph, covers 70,000 miles, and pumps 8,000 gallons daily, move ahead 2.
  - Tip: The heart and blood vessels.
- If you know the five dimensions of life, move ahead 2.
  - Tip: The five dimensions are physical, emotional, social, intellectual, and spiritual.
- If you do not know the five different conflict resolution styles, move back 5.
  - Tip: The five conflict resolution styles are compromise, problem solving, avoidance, soothing helper, and aggressive.
- If you practice the golden rule of human relations, move ahead 3. If you do not know what this is, move back 6.
  - Tip: The golden rule is to treat others the way you want to be treated.
- If you know the difference between yoga, yote, and yogurt, move ahead 4.
  - Tip: Yoga is a type of stretching and meditation; yote is a game; and yogurt is a kind of food.
- If you can tell what the five key organs found right under the lungs (including one pair) are, move ahead 5.
  - Tip: The kidneys, pancreas, spleen, stomach, and liver are found right below the lungs.
- If you know what type of love is described by possessiveness, jealousy, and basic lust, move ahead 3.
  - Tip: Infatuation, or romantic love, is described by possessiveness, jealousy, and basic lust.
- If you know what the top three personality traits admired by others are, move ahead 2.
  - Tip: The top three personality traits are trust, sense of humor, and respect.

CLOSURE

Moral: Be nice to others and always be honest!

Random Acts of Kindness Assignment

OBJECTIVE

Students will practice random acts of kindness as an observation study to see how people respond to compliments and humanitarian acts.

NATIONAL STANDARDS

- #5 Decision Making
- #8 Advocacy

INTRODUCTION

In this assignment we are going to practice random acts of kindness. This activity will help us realize that all people need reinforcement in life. When you do these random acts of kindness, watch to see how people react to your help. The world would be a far better place if all people made an effort to help others on a daily basis.

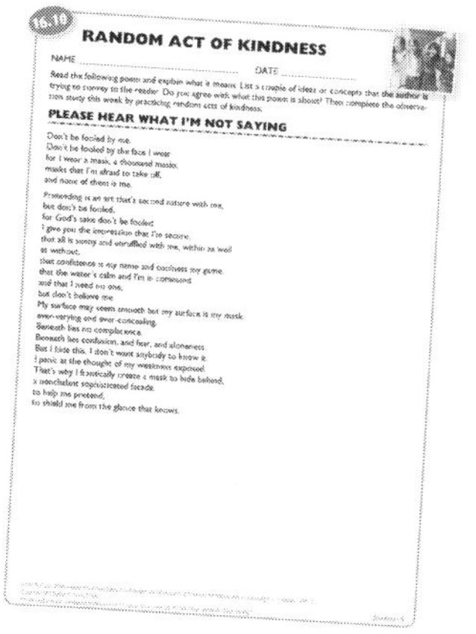
RANDOM ACT OF KINDNESS
PLEASE HEAR WHAT I'M NOT SAYING

16.10

HANDOUT 16.10

Random Acts of Kindness

Read the poem "Please Hear What I'm Not Saying."

List a couple of concepts that the author is trying to convey to the reader and give your personal feelings about the poem. One interpretation is that everyone carries a burden and needs someone to help lighten the load. Life is full of frustrations and problems. We should make an effort to help even if others act indifferently. Most people have little knowledge of what is going on in the lives of others.

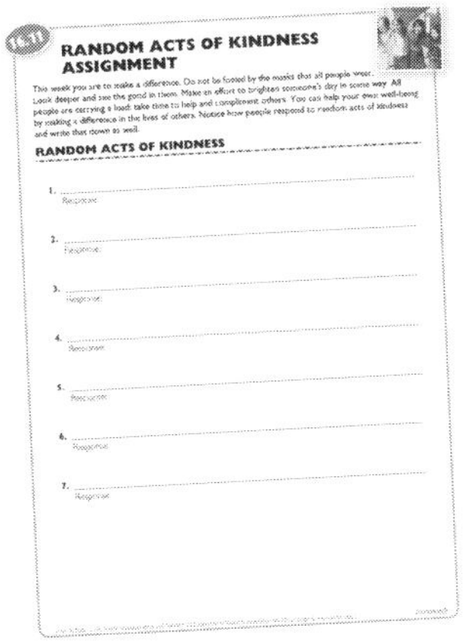
RANDOM ACTS OF KINDNESS ASSIGNMENT
RANDOM ACTS OF KINDNESS

16.11

HANDOUT 16.11

Random Acts of Kindness Assignment

You need to perform seven random acts of kindness this week—anything from helping someone out with a task to making life easier for your mother without her telling you to do so. You might want to reach out to a person who you know is struggling and needs a friend. Record how the people respond to your kindness. Do not tell anyone that you are doing this for an assignment. They are not to know.

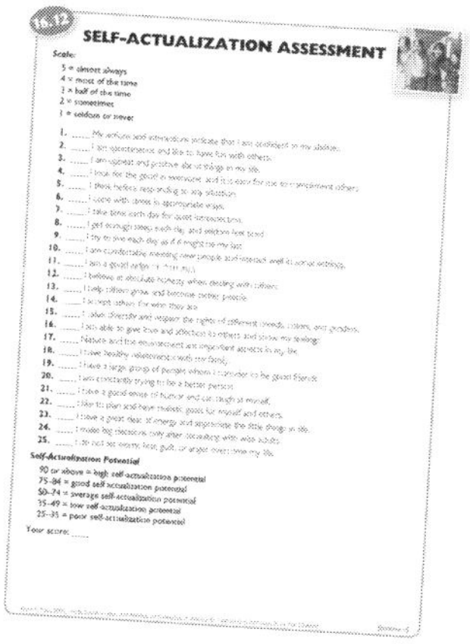
SELF-ACTUALIZATION ASSESSMENT

16.12

HANDOUT 16.12

Self-Actualization Assessment

Take this test to see how well you operate emotionally on a regular day. Emotional maturity is just living the random acts of kindness forever. What could you do to improve your emotional health?

What was your self-actualization score? ____

CLOSURE

Random acts of kindness are wonderful things to do. Helping others makes you feel good about yourself and encourages others to be kind.

Emotional Health Test Key

OBJECTIVE

Students will be able to pass a written test on emotional health after studying this unit.

NATIONAL STANDARDS

- #1 Health Promotion
- #7 Healthy Behaviors

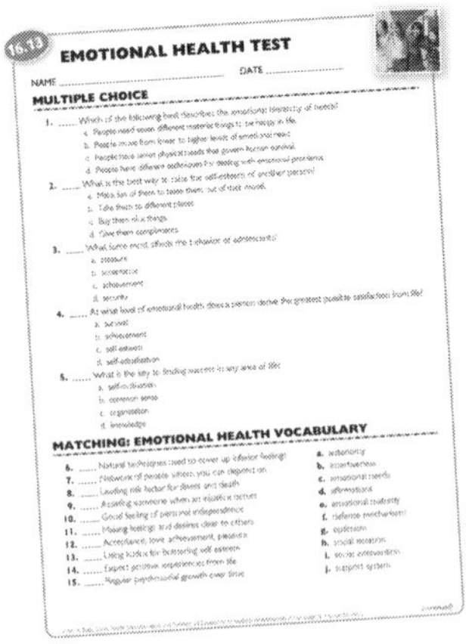
EMOTIONAL HEALTH TEST

MULTIPLE CHOICE

MATCHING: EMOTIONAL HEALTH VOCABULARY

16.13

INTRODUCTION

Hand your test back in as soon as you have finished it.

HANDOUT 16.13

Multiple Choice

1. b
2. d
3. b
4. d
5. a

Matching: Emotional Health Vocabulary

6. f	**11.** b
7. j	**12.** c
8. h	**13.** d
9. i	**14.** g
10. a	**15.** e

Matching: Common Defense Mechanisms

16. a
17. d
18. g
19. f
20. c
21. b
22. e

Matching: Hierarchy of Emotional Needs and Satisfaction Factors

23. a
24. f
25. g
26. c
27. b
28. e
29. d

Matching: Childhood Experiences and Solutions

30. d
31. f
32. a
33. e
34. c
35. b

Roles That People Play: What Emotional Need Is Lacking?

Answers will be used more than once.

36. f
37. e
38. c
39. f
40. a
41. a
42. f
43. f
44. d
45. b
46. d

Short Answer

Possible answers for questions 47–50.

- positive
- spontaneous
- helping
- energized
- sense of humor
- good relationships
- well adapted to stress
- peaceful
- environmentalist
- optimistic
- strives for self-improvement

CLOSURE

We will go over the answers during our next class period.

17

Mental Health Issues

THE MEASURE OF
MENTAL HEALTH IS
THE DISPOSITION
TO FIND GOOD
EVERYWHERE.

Ralph Waldo Emerson

Lesson Finder

Mental Health Facts

OBJECTIVE

Students will be able to examine some of the key factors and symptoms of the most common mental illnesses through a classroom discussion.

NATIONAL STANDARDS

- #1 Health Promotion
- #4 Communication

INTRODUCTION

In our country if you have a physical problem you get it examined by a doctor immediately. When you have a mental problem, however, you are supposed to cure it on your own. Many people struggle with mental illness, particularly depression. This section will examine mental health issues and treatment measures.

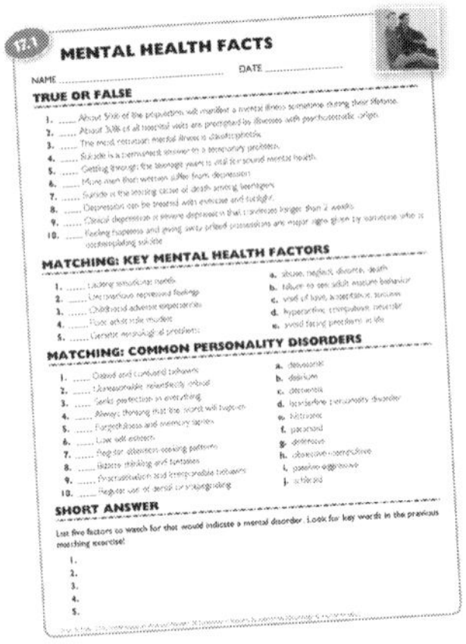
MENTAL HEALTH FACTS

TRUE OR FALSE

MATCHING: KEY MENTAL HEALTH FACTORS

MATCHING: COMMON PERSONALITY DISORDERS

SHORT ANSWER

17.1

HANDOUT 17.1

True or False

1. true
2. false—Closer to 65% of all hospital visits are related to psychosomatic origins.
3. false—Depression is the most common mental illness.
4. true
5. true
6. false—More women than men suffer from depression.
7. false—Accidents are the leading cause of death among teenagers.
8. true
9. true
10. true

Matching: Key Mental Health Factors

1. c
2. e
3. a
4. b
5. d

Matching: Common Personality Disorders

1. b
2. a
3. h
4. f
5. c
6. d
7. e
8. j
9. i
10. g

Short Answer

- confusion
- denial
- unreasonable
- memory lapses
- bizarre thinking
- thinking the worst
- perfectionism
- critical

CLOSURE

Mental illness is a big problem in our country and creates much sadness and frustration. We need to learn about common mental problems and, if necessary, seek proper medical assistance. I hope that this week will open your eyes to some of the mental health problems that we have in society.

Depression and Suicide

OBJECTIVE

Students will be able to understand the symptoms and key methods to help someone who is struggling with depression by discussing the topic.

NATIONAL STANDARDS

- #1 Health Promotion
- #4 Communication

INTRODUCTION

The most common mental illness in the United States is depression. Most people will suffer from depression at some point. For many, the battle lasts for years. Let us examine depression and its relationship to suicide as well.

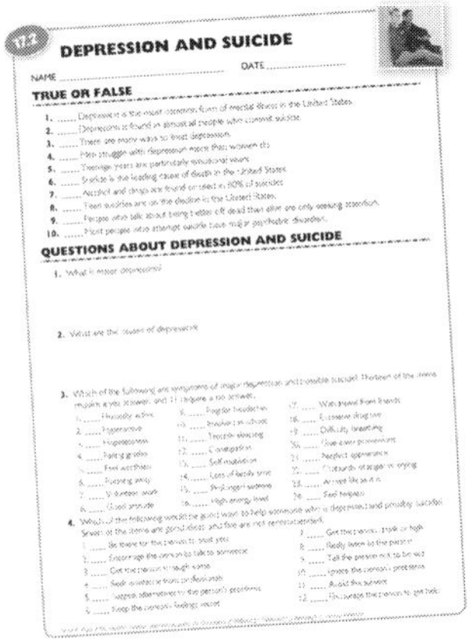
17.2 DEPRESSION AND SUICIDE
NAME DATE
TRUE OR FALSE
QUESTIONS ABOUT DEPRESSION AND SUICIDE

17.2

HANDOUT 17.2

True or False

1. true
2. true
3. true
4. false—More women than men struggle with depression.
5. true
6. false—Suicide is around the tenth most common cause of death.
7. true
8. false—Although it varies over the years, it is gradually increasing.
9. false—Verbal threats should be taken seriously.
10. true

Questions About Depression and Suicide

1. Depression is sadness and discouragement that continues for more than 2 weeks.
2. Causes of Depression
   1. Loss of loved one by breakup or death
   2. Focus on failure in life
   3. Feelings of hopelessness and worthlessness
   4. Imbalance in body chemistry
3. Symptoms of Major Depression

1. no	9. no	17. yes
2. no	10. no	18. yes
3. yes	11. yes	19. no
4. yes	12. no	20. yes
5. yes	13. yes	21. yes
6. yes	14. no	22. yes
7. no	15. yes	23. no
8. no	16. no	24. yes

4. Ways to Help a Depressed Person
   1. good
   2. good
   3. good
   4. good
   5. good
   6. not recommended
   7. not recommended
   8. good
   9. not recommended
   10. not recommended
   11. not recommended
   12. good

HANDOUT 17.3

Suicide Case Studies

Have students talk about each case study.

a. Have students talk about their high-risk behaviors, such as feelings of withdrawal, hopelessness, and worthlessness; self-neglect; or drug abuse.

b. List the warning signs together.

c. Have students talk about what they could do to help others.

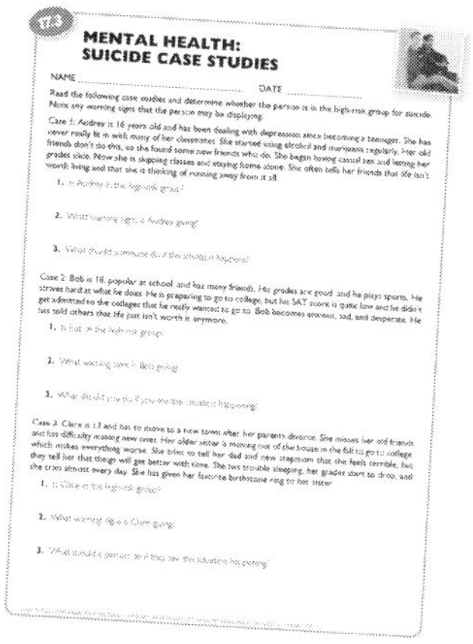
MENTAL HEALTH:
SUICIDE CASE STUDIES

NAME .... DATE ....

Read the following case studies and determine whether the person is in the high-risk group for suicide. Note any warning signs that the person may be displaying.

17.3

CLOSURE

Depression and suicide are major mental health problems that have solutions. The more we learn about life, changes, and problems, the better off we will be. This area of mental health is important to living well and having great relationships.

Treating Depression

OBJECTIVE

Students will be able to practice techniques that would help a person overcome depression.

NATIONAL STANDARDS

- #7 Healthy Behaviors
- #5 Decision Making
- #8 Advocacy

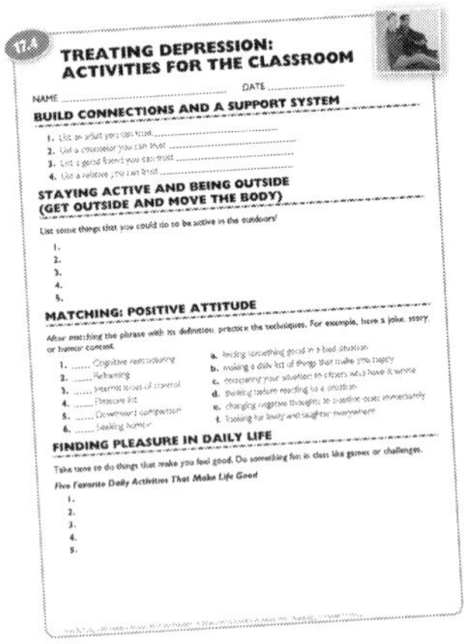
TREATING DEPRESSION: ACTIVITIES FOR THE CLASSROOM

BUILD CONNECTIONS AND A SUPPORT SYSTEM

STAYING ACTIVE AND BEING OUTSIDE (GET OUTSIDE AND MOVE THE BODY)

MATCHING: POSITIVE ATTITUDE

FINDING PLEASURE IN DAILY LIFE

17.4

INTRODUCTION

Today we are going to learn about ways to alleviate depression without using medication. We can choose from five activities that can change how we feel and think. We should always try to practice healthy behaviors that lead to contentment in life.

HANDOUT 17.4

Build Connections and a Support System

Do some trust or communication activities.

Staying Active and Being Outside

Take the class outside to play some fun games and move around in the sunlight.

Matching: Positive Attitude

Match the answers and then tell a few jokes.

1. e
2. a
3. d
4. b
5. c
6. f

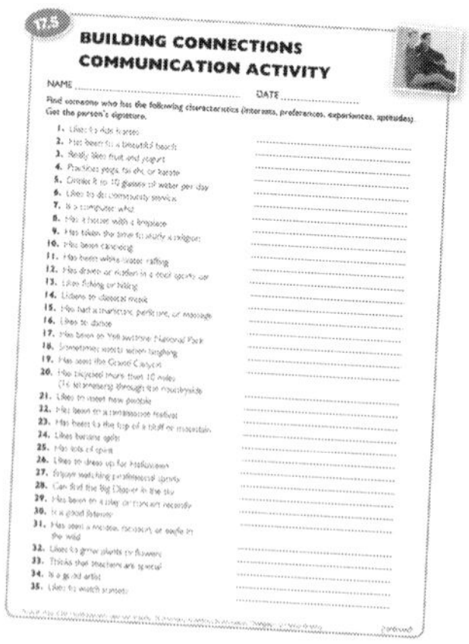
BUILDING CONNECTIONS COMMUNICATION ACTIVITY

17.5

Finding Pleasure in Daily Life

Do some games or puzzles that would be interesting and fun for the class.

HANDOUT 17.5

CLOSURE

This day was meant to be fun and uplifting. Depression is not fun, so we have learned about methods that can improve the quality of your life and the health of your mind. Take time to make each day special.

Mental Health Practical Exam

OBJECTIVE

Students will be able to assess their knowledge of mental illness by taking a practical exam in which classmates portray common mental illnesses.

NATIONAL STANDARDS

- #1 Health Promotion
- #5 Decision Making

INTRODUCTION

Today we are doing a practical exam about common mental disorders in the United States. Ten of your colleagues will be manifesting disorders. Your job is to guess what disorder each of them has.

HANDOUT 17.6

Mental Disorders Practical Exam

Give students time to look over the facts and data on the handout titled "Mental Disorders." Make it clear that the acting required for this activity must not be done in a mocking way. The students acting the roles should take the demonstration seriously and try to imitate the symptoms clearly. Give the students who are acting out roles a number that represents their disease, which they should keep hidden at their stations or desks.

Eventually students must meander around and talk to, listen, and watch each of the 10 clients who has a mental illness. They should consult their sheets to help them figure out what illnesses the clients have.

At the end of the session, have the students with the manifested diseases share with the class what their disorders were. Ask the students to check their answers before you collect their exams for grading.

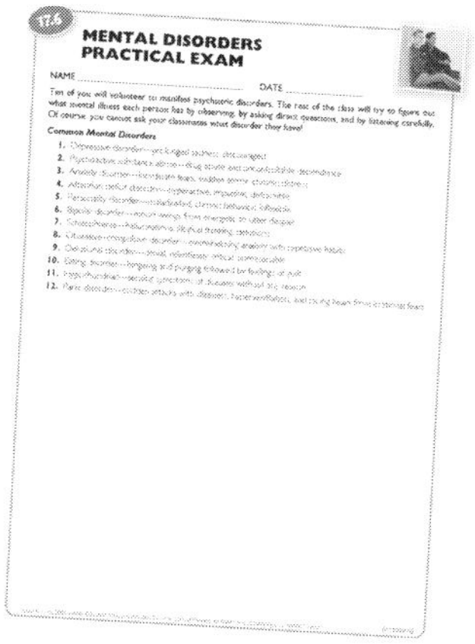
17.6
MENTAL DISORDERS
PRACTICAL EXAM
NAME DATE

17.6

CLOSURE

I hope that you learned more about some common mental disorders through this activity. This has been a successful lesson in other classes. Everyone did a good job today!

Mental Health Test Key

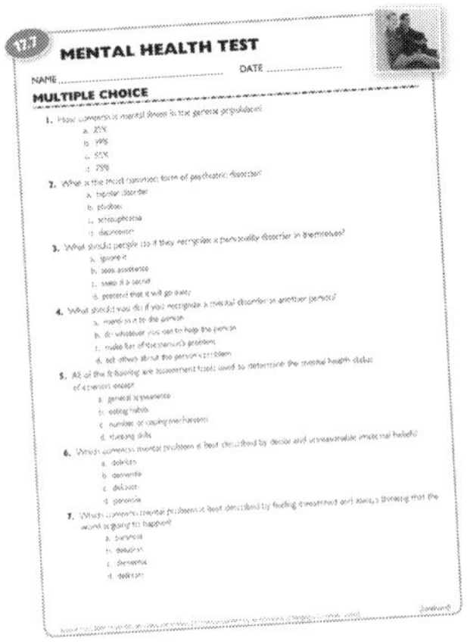
MENTAL HEALTH TEST

NAME DATE

MULTIPLE CHOICE

17.7

OBJECTIVE

Students will be able to pass a written test after studying depression and mental health issues.

NATIONAL STANDARDS

- #1 Health Promotion
- #7 Healthy Behaviors

INTRODUCTION

Complete this test to the best of your ability and hand it in to your instructor.

HANDOUT 17.7

Multiple Choice

1. c
2. d
3. b
4. b
5. b
6. c
7. a
8. a
9. d
10. d

True or False

11. true

12. false—Illnesses with psychosomatic origins prompt around 65% of all hospital visits.

13. false—Depression is the most common mental illness.

14. false—Suicide is a permanent solution to a temporary problem.

15. true

16. true

17. true

18. false—Exercise and sunlight can help treat depression.

19. true

20. true

Matching: 10 Most Common Personality Disorders

21. c
22. b
23. h
24. g
25. a
26. e
27. i
28. j
29. f
30. d

CLOSURE

We will go over the results of the test during the next class period.

18

Stress Management

IF ALL OUR MISFORTUNES WERE LAID IN ONE COMMON HEAP WHENCE EVERYONE MUST TAKE AN EQUAL PORTION, MOST PEOPLE WOULD BE CONTENTED TO TAKE THEIR OWN AND DEPART.

Socrates

Lesson Finder

Stress Management Facts

OBJECTIVE

Students will analyze many facts about stress and take a personal inventory to measure their own stress levels.

NATIONAL STANDARDS

- #1 Health Promotion
- #7 Healthy Behaviors

INTRODUCTION

A personal story is a good way to start any discussion. A friend told me this story:

> I remember walking out of the doctor's office at age 25 or so and being in shock. I had just found out that my blood pressure was that of a 50-year-old man. My doctor told me that it would take 20 years off my life if I didn't do something about it. That is when I began my regimen of high blood pressure medication. After a couple of years with a couple of different medications, I started to have some adverse side effects. Then I began to study stress and how to manage it better. Under my doctor's supervision, I eventually went off medication altogether and changed the way that I lived.

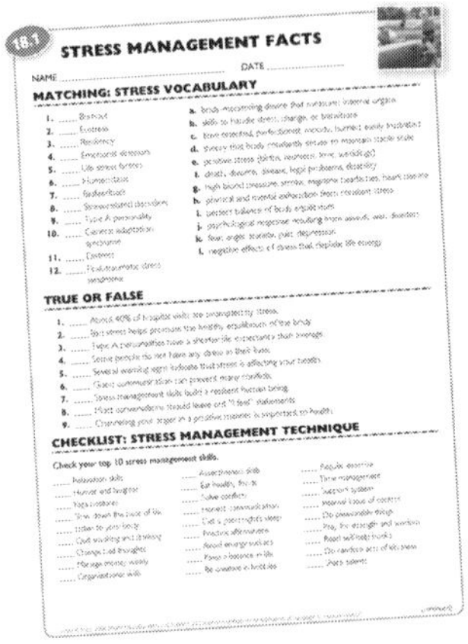
STRESS MANAGEMENT FACTS
NAME
DATE
MATCHING: STRESS VOCABULARY
TRUE OR FALSE
CHECKLIST: STRESS MANAGEMENT TECHNIQUE

18.1

How many of you are going to be in the same situation as my friend? Not many, I hope. You need to analyze the stress elements in your life and make changes now while you are young. This unit is about techniques that will help manage stress now and throughout your life.

HANDOUT 18.1

Matching: Stress Vocabulary

1. h	**7.** a
2. e	**8.** g
3. b	**9.** c
4. k	**10.** d
5. f	**11.** l
6. i	**12.** j

True or False

1. false—Stress prompts about 65% of hospital visits.
2. false—Bad stress causes an imbalance.
3. true
4. false—Everyone has some stress.
5. true
6. true
7. true
8. false—Most conversations should leave out "you" statements.
9. true

Checklist: Stress Management Techniques

This checklist will get you thinking about all the things that people can do to cut down on stress.

HANDOUT 18.2

Stress Symptom Assessment

Take the assessment to see how well you are currently handling stress. Write your score on the board when you are finished so that we can see how everyone is coping with stress.

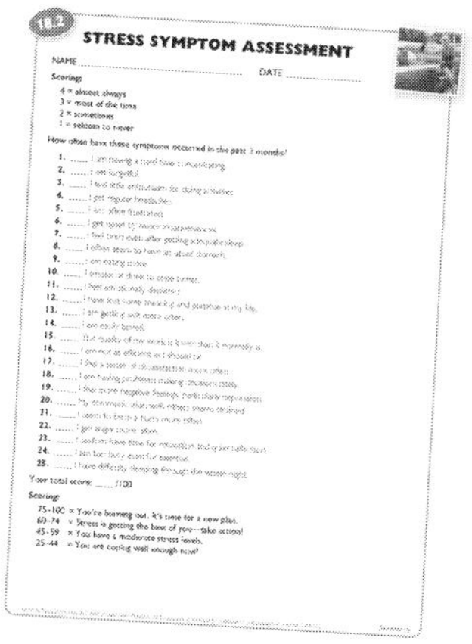
STRESS SYMPTOM ASSESSMENT

18.2

CLOSURE

Stress can make you sick, or even kill you. Stress is an underlying factor in most of the leading causes of death and can be related to cancer. Maybe we should start managing our lives better so that stress does not interfere with our enjoyment of life.

Instant Stress Relievers

OBJECTIVE

Students will be able to practice some instant stress relievers and rate their effectiveness during this week.

NATIONAL STANDARDS

- #7 Healthy Behaviors
- #5 Decision Making

INTRODUCTION

Today we are going to learn about instant stress relievers. We will practice them during this week. Sometimes we need to deal with all this stress business immediately, instead of letting it build up. What would happen if stress continued to build up in our bodies or veins? Yes, you are right: The pressure could damage our internal organs! Let us learn about some instant stress relievers that could come in handy.

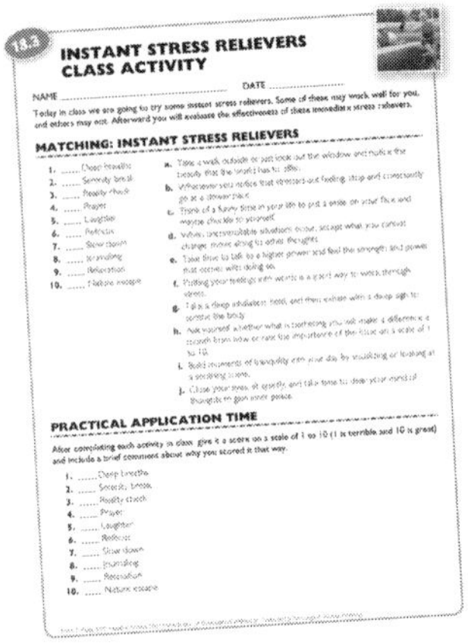
INSTANT STRESS RELIEVERS
CLASS ACTIVITY
MATCHING: INSTANT STRESS RELIEVERS
PRACTICAL APPLICATION TIME

18.3

HANDOUT 18.3

Matching: Instant Stress Relievers

1. g **6.** d
2. j **7.** b
3. h **8.** f
4. e **9.** i
5. c **10.** a

Perform some of the instant stress relievers each day. Some take only a minute, and others could require up to 5 minutes. We want to experience healthy behaviors and thoughts.

CLOSURE

Stress can be caught early before it builds up to a harmful level. These instant stress relievers are just the ticket when stress becomes apparent. Stress will affect your work performance. So let us learn some coping measures that lower stress levels immediately. Make sure that you record your score and feelings about each instant stress reliever.

OBJECTIVE

Students will be able to practice using the four key measures (the four Cs) for managing life better on a daily basis.

NATIONAL STANDARDS

- #7 Healthy Behaviors
- #5 Decision Making
- #4 Communication

INTRODUCTION

Anyone can learn these four skills and apply them to any situation. These four management techniques also can prevent most stress before it happens.

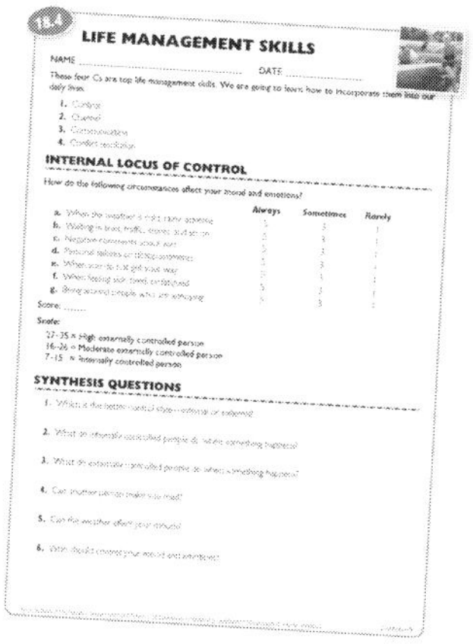

18.4

HANDOUT 18.4

Internal Locus of Control

You can be in control of your feeling and emotions. Take the locus of control assessment and then discuss the synthesis questions.

1. Internal is best.
2. Think and then decide how to act.
3. React and make rash decisions.
4. Only if you let them.
5. Not really, unless you are externally controlled.
6. You should think and then decide; be in control!

Channeling Techniques

How do you handle strong feelings when they occur? Here are some constructive techniques that you should be using.

1. D
2. C
3. C
4. C
5. D
6. D
7. C
8. C
9. D
10. D
11. D
12. D
13. D
14. C
15. C
16. D
17. C
18. C
19. C
20. D
21. C

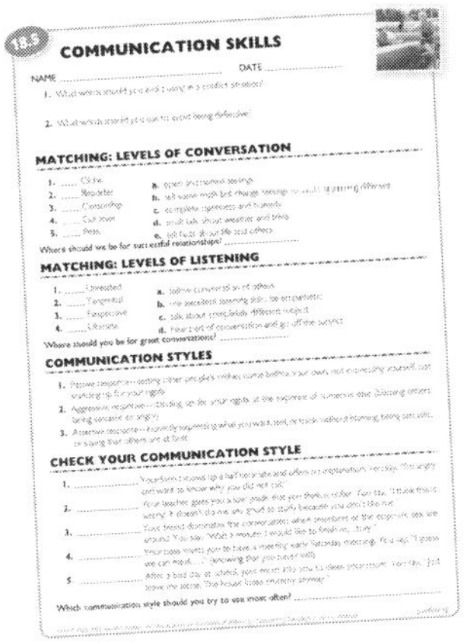

18.5

HANDOUT 18.5

Communication Skills

1. Avoid "you" statements.
2. Use "I feel" statements.

Matching: Levels of Conversation

1. d
2. e
3. b
4. a
5. c

Where should you be for a successful relationship? (Answer: at the gut level)

Matching: Levels of Listening

1. c
2. d
3. a
4. b

Where should you be for great conversation? (Answer: responsive listener)

Check Your Communication Styles

1. assertive
2. aggressive
3. assertive
4. passive
5. aggressive

Which one should you use the most? (Answer: assertive)

Communication Style Activity

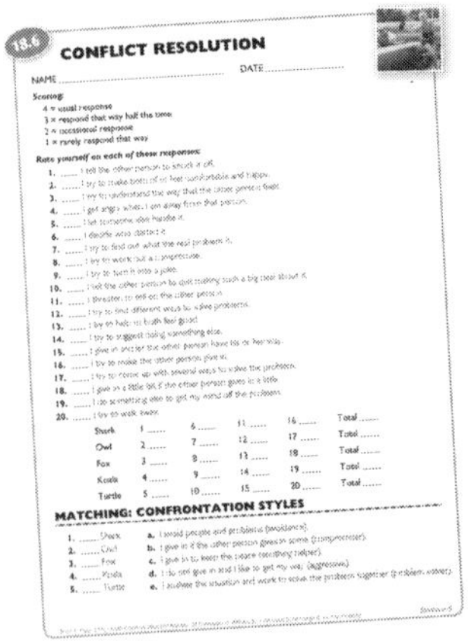
CONFLICT RESOLUTION

MATCHING: CONFRONTATION STYLES

18.6

This is an interesting activity to test general personality styles.

1. If a student lets the other push him or her or they both do nothing = passive.
2. If they start pushing each other = aggressive.
3. If they start to dance and just have fun = assertive.

HANDOUT 18.6

Conflict Resolution: Assessment for Style

Have students record on the board what animal they are after they figure it out and before they know what it means.

Matching: Confrontation Styles

1. d
2. e
3. b
4. c
5. a

What is the best technique? (Answer: the owl, the problem solver)
What is the worst technique? (Answer: the shark, the aggressive one)

CLOSURE

These are the best of the best. Practice them and see for yourself!

Time Management

OBJECTIVE

Students will be able to complete a time management program after a teacher-led discussion.

NATIONAL STANDARDS

- #7 Healthy Behaviors
- #5 Decision Making

INTRODUCTION

Have any of you ever done a time management activity before? Today is your chance. Time management is one of the best ways to make sure that you accomplish your top priorities. You have only so much time each day, and if you do not plan properly, you will not get important things done. Failing to accomplish things generally adds frustration to your life.

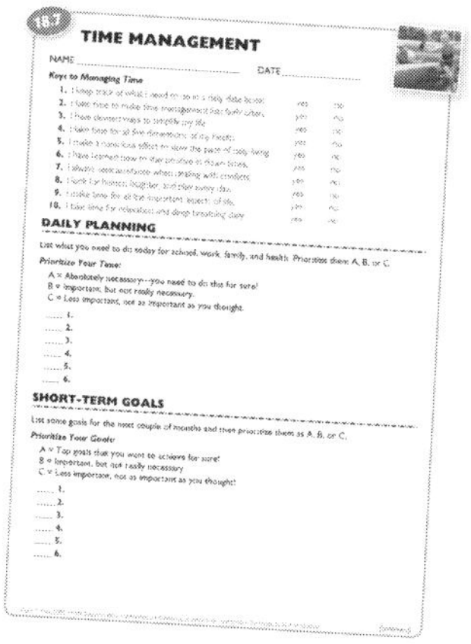

18.7

HANDOUT 18.7

Keys to Managing Time

Have students take the brief assessment to see whether they are currently doing any time management. Poll the class to see how many of the time management questions were true for them.

The time management activity has three parts:

1. Daily planner
2. Short-term goals
3. Long-term goals

Have the students list some goals for each of the three areas. After they have written some goals, they prioritize them by writing an A, B, or C next to each goal based on its importance to them.

Tell students that most people spend the majority of their time working toward low-level goals because they are easier to complete. Unfortunately, they do not accomplish their A goals. They then become frustrated and fail at the important things in life. Students should do time management every couple of months to guide them in the direction that they want to be going.

Last, students should take their top long-term goal and break it down into workable parts.

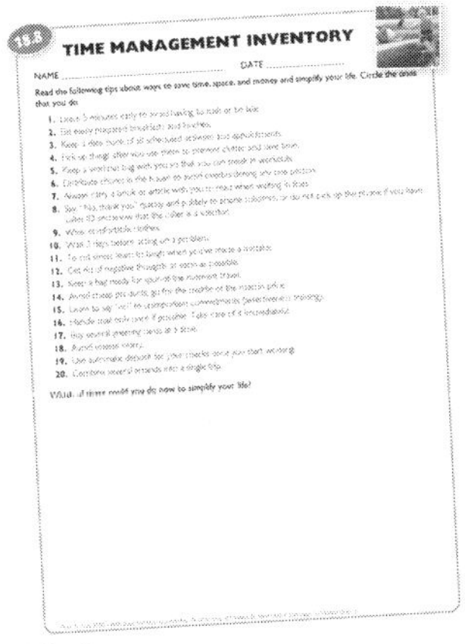

18.8

HANDOUT 18.8

Time Management Inventory

Read the guidelines and identify some tips that may help you save time.

CLOSURE

Time management is necessary if you want to succeed. Many people devote only 20% of their time to A goals. You want to spend 80% of your time on A goals.

Key Stress Relievers for Me Project

OBJECTIVE

Students will examine many different ways to manage stress and keep life in perspective as they make a little collage depicting their top 25 life management techniques.

NATIONAL STANDARDS

- #1 Health Promotion
- #5 Decision Making
- #7 Healthy Behaviors

INTRODUCTION

Spend some time today examining all the different ways to manage stress in your life. Then put together a collage depicting the best 25 techniques in your opinion. This assignment will be fun and interesting.

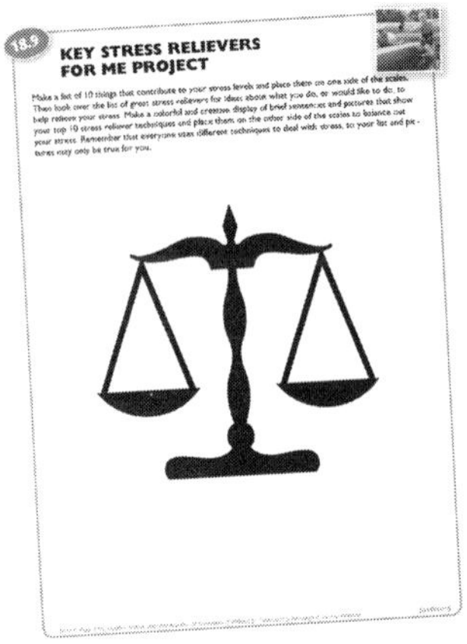

18.9

HANDOUT 18.9

SUGGESTED PROJECT MATERIALS

- magazines
- stencils
- word processor
- glue
- scissors
- colored pencils
- crayons

CLOSURE

This assignment should have helped you to find many good techniques that will help you manage stress for years to come.

Stress Management Test Key

OBJECTIVE

Students will pass a written test on stress management after studying all the facts and data.

NATIONAL STANDARDS

- #1 Health Promotion
- #7 Healthy Behaviors

INTRODUCTION

Complete this test on stress management and return it to the instructor when you are finished.

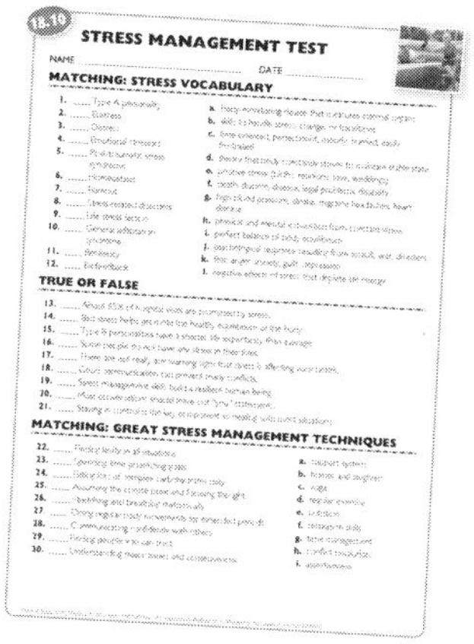

18.10

HANDOUT 18.10

Matching: Stress Vocabulary

1. c
2. e
3. l
4. k
5. j
6. i
7. h
8. g
9. f
10. d
11. b
12. a

True or False

13. true
14. false—Bad stress ruins the equilibrium of the body.
15. false—Type A personalities have a shorter life expectancy.
16. false—Everyone has some stress in their lives.
17. false—There are many warning signs.
18. true
19. true
20. true
21. true

Matching: Great Stress Management Techniques

22. b
23. g
24. e
25. f
26. c
27. d
28. i
29. a
30. h

CLOSURE

We will go over the test during the next class period.

19

Humor and Laughter

A CLOWN ARRIVING
TO TOWN IS MORE
BENEFICIAL THAN
10 MULES LADEN
WITH DRUGS.

Patch Adams

Lesson Finder

Humor and Laughter Facts

OBJECTIVE

Students will be able to write down 10 reasons why humor and laughter are vital to healing, learning, and relationships.

NATIONAL STANDARDS

- #1 Health Promotion
- #4 Communication

INTRODUCTION

Dr. Norman Cousins, professor at the School of Medicine at UCLA, wrote about how laughter changed his life before the scientific world began to take humor seriously. Dr. Cousins used laughter, vitamin C, and tenacity to overcome a crippling disease known as ankylosing spondylitis. Laughter helped alleviate symptoms of an illness that was previously described as progressive and incurable. Laughter makes it possible for good things to happen, according to Dr. Cousins. Let us learn how to incorporate healing humor into our lives, so that we may live with more joy.

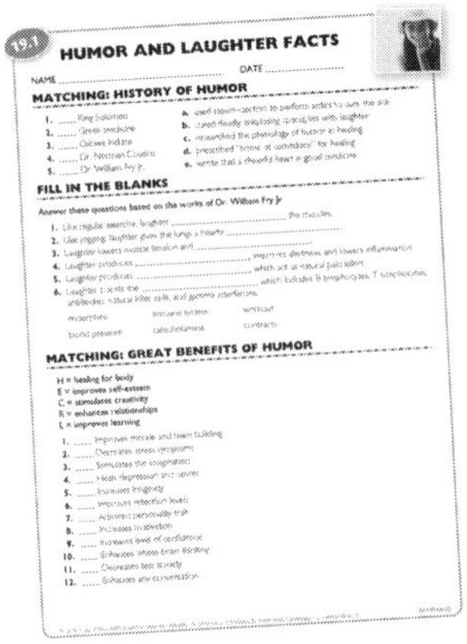
HUMOR AND LAUGHTER FACTS

MATCHING: HISTORY OF HUMOR

FILL IN THE BLANKS

MATCHING: GREAT BENEFITS OF HUMOR

19.1

HANDOUT 19.1

Matching: History of Humor

1. e
2. d
3. a
4. b
5. c

Fill in the Blanks: *Humor for Healing Medicine* by Dr. William Fry Jr.

1. contracts
2. workout
3. blood pressure
4. catecholamine
5. endorphins
6. immune system

Matching: Great Benefits of Humor

1. R
2. H
3. C
4. H
5. H
6. L
7. R
8. L
9. E
10. C
11. L
12. R

True or False

1. true
2. true
3. false—You should laugh with others, never at others.
4. true
5. false—Humor should not be used to correct a big behavior problem.
6. true
7. false—Ethnic and teasing humor are generally not acceptable.
8. true
9. true
10. true
11. false—The highest degree of laughter occurs when you laugh until you wet your pants.
12. true

CLOSURE

Humor is wonderful for healing. It enhances any relationship and makes life fun. You have to be creative and smart to use humor. It improves any learning situation and builds your self-confidence. Humor is one of the great natural human wonders.

Healing and Harmful Humor

OBJECTIVE

Students will be able to determine through a discussion which kinds of humor are for healing and which ones are harmful.

NATIONAL STANDARDS

- #1 Health Promotion
- #7 Healthy Behaviors
- #4 Communication

INTRODUCTION

Remember that not all humor is healing. Using humor at the expense of another is a poor choice. You are to laugh with others, not at others. Sarcasm, ridicule, put-downs, and cynicism are examples of harmful humor.

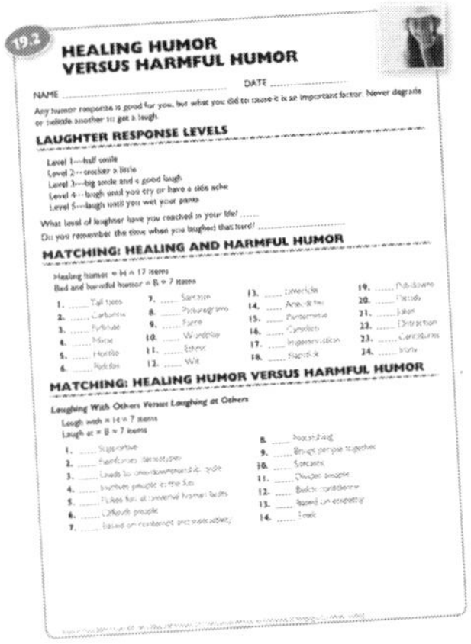
HEALING HUMOR VERSUS HARMFUL HUMOR

LAUGHTER RESPONSE LEVELS

MATCHING: HEALING AND HARMFUL HUMOR

MATCHING: HEALING HUMOR VERSUS HARMFUL HUMOR

19.2

HANDOUT 19.2

Laughter Response Levels

Allow yourself to laugh more and louder. It's OK to laugh.

Matching: Healing and Harmful Humor

1. H
2. H
3. B
4. H
5. B
6. H
7. B
8. H
9. H
10. H
11. B
12. H
13. H
14. H
15. H
16. B
17. H, but can become harmful if it is taken too far, if it impersonates a quality that is touchy for that person, or if it is done in a mocking manner.
18. H
19. B
20. H
21. H

22. B
23. H
24. H

Matching: Healing Humor Versus Harmful Humor

1. H
2. B
3. B
4. H
5. H
6. B
7. B
8. H
9. H
10. B
11. B
12. H
13. H
14. B

HANDOUT 19.3

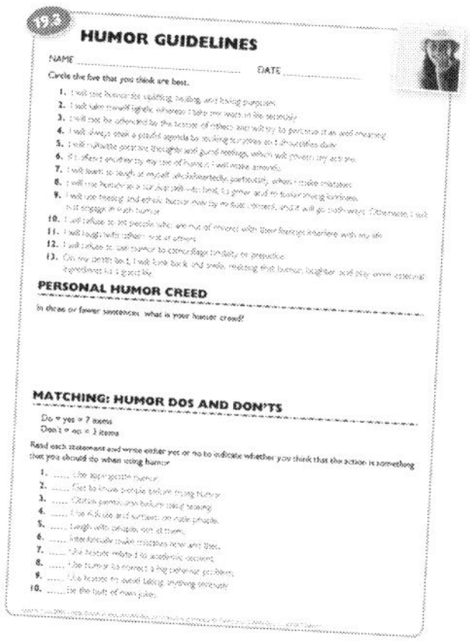
HUMOR GUIDELINES

PERSONAL HUMOR CREED

MATCHING: HUMOR DOS AND DON'TS

19.3

Personal Humor Creed

Have the students read the humor guidelines and then summarize them into their own personal humor creed.

Matching: Humor Dos and Don'ts

1. yes
2. yes
3. yes
4. no
5. yes
6. yes
7. yes
8. no
9. no
10. yes

CLOSURE

We must recognize that not all humor is healthy. Unfortunately, some people use humor to be mean and sarcastic. Humor can be a powerful tool in relationships, learning, and your personal health; use it to make a positive difference in the lives of others.

Humor Potential

OBJECTIVE

Students will be able to realize that each person has great humor potential and that in seeking humor they will find it.

NATIONAL STANDARD

#7 Healthy Behaviors

INTRODUCTION

Today we are going to discover your real humor potential. Some people think that they cannot be funny or witty. They say that they cannot remember jokes. Well, we should realize that all people can be funny in their own way. Or at least they can smile and laugh a lot. Laughter is one of the greatest healers. It is time for you to incorporate some fun and humor into your life. Seek and you will find.

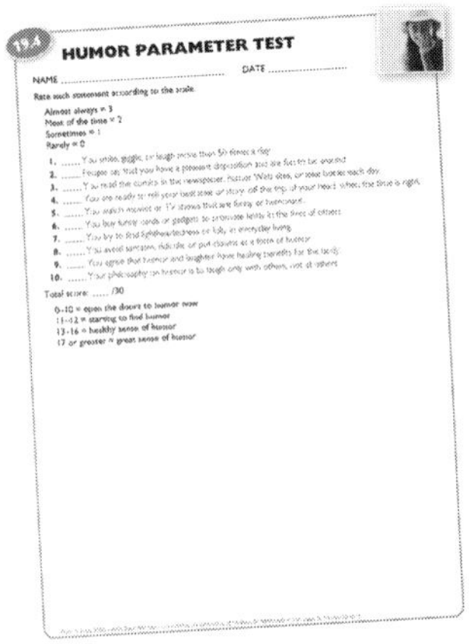
19.4 HUMOR PARAMETER TEST

NAME .... DATE ....

Rate each statement according to the scale.

Almost always = 3
Most of the time = 2
Sometimes = 1
Rarely = 0

Total score: ...... /30

0-10 = open the doors to humor now
11-12 = starting to find humor
13-16 = healthy sense of humor
17 or greater = great sense of humor

19.4

HANDOUT 19.4

Humor Parameter Test

Have students take the test and score it. Record their scores on the board. Tell them that opening their parameters wider will allow humor to come in and tickle their funny bones. This humor parameter test is meant to teach them to find humor in all aspects of life.

CLOSURE

Everyone has the potential to laugh and have a good time. Incorporating humor into your life takes time, but doing so is well worth it. Try to remember some funny stories or jokes that you can use from time to time. You can add humor to your life in lots of ways. Humor is something to be serious about!

Humor Incorporation

OBJECTIVE

Students will be able to evaluate several forms of humor and learn about how to incorporate humor into their lives.

NATIONAL STANDARD

#7 Healthy Behaviors

INTRODUCTION

You can incorporate humor into your daily life in many ways. Today we are going to evaluate several types of humor. I will also ask you to be involved in some fun activities. The goal is to enjoy and learn to incorporate all different types of humor (funny assessments, jokes, fun activities, humor bag, and so on). Remember: Try to have a sense of humor and have fun.

HANDOUT 19.5

Creative and Cooperative Fun

Have the class pick one of these to do this week.

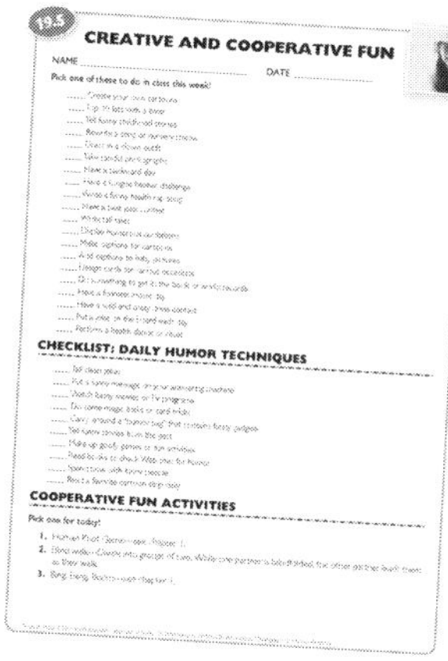

19.5

HANDOUT 19.6

Bumper Stickers and Zingers

Have students choose the best items on this sheet.

19.6

HANDOUT 19.7

Animal Jokes

Have students rate the jokes on this sheet for the best humor.

HANDOUT 19.8

Educational Jokes

Have students rate the jokes on this sheet as well.

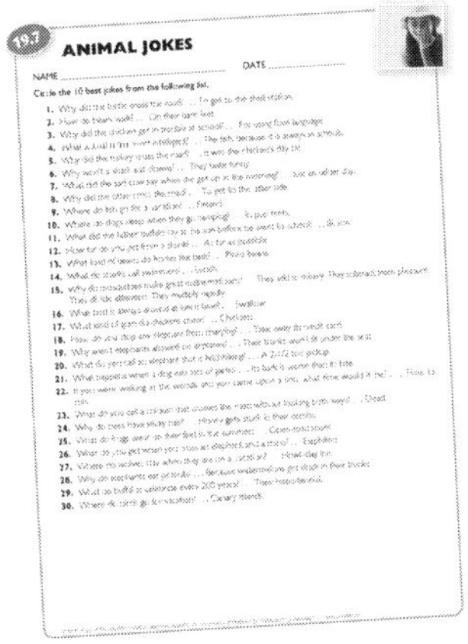

19.7

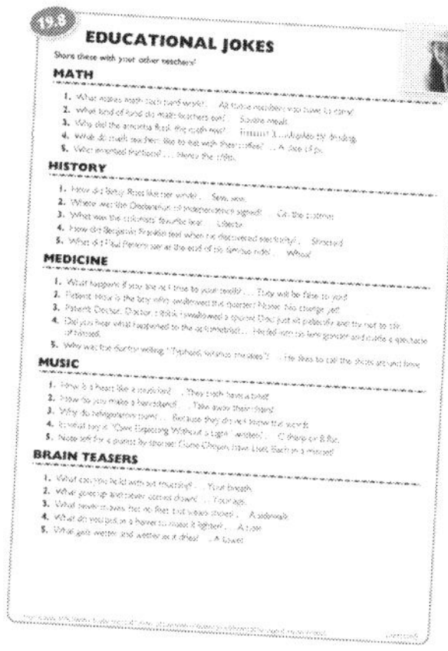

19.8

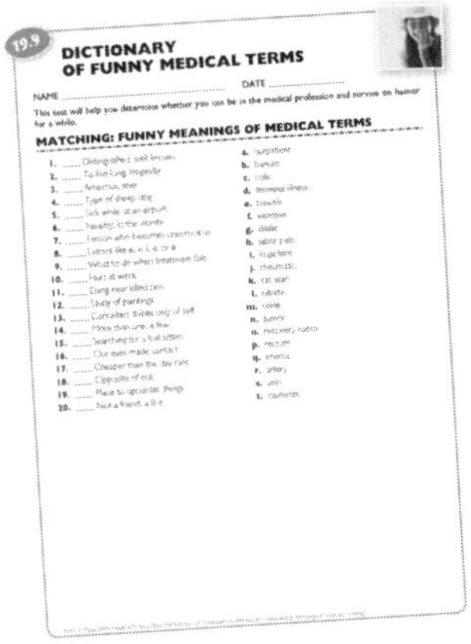

19.9

HANDOUT 19.9

Dictionary of Funny Medical Terms

Have the students rate the humor in the definitions in this section. They may not know some of the words, so you can help them understand if necessary.

Matching: Funny Meanings of Medical Terms

1. i	**6.** f	**11.** p	**16.** t
2. g	**7.** a	**12.** r	**17.** l
3. j	**8.** e	**13.** s	**18.** m
4. c	**9.** b	**14.** n	**19.** o
5. d	**10.** h	**15.** k	**20.** q

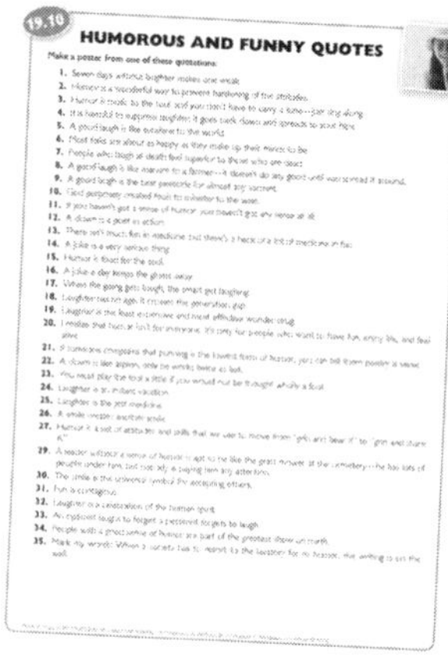

19.10

HANDOUT 19.10

Humorous and Funny Quotes

Have students work with partners to make posters with one of these quotations about humor and laughter. The project can be due at the end of the week.

HANDOUT 19.11

Picturegrams

Ask the class if they can figure out the picturegrams.

1. Eskimo apartment complex
2. Submarine going over a waterfall
3. Giraffe walking by a window
4. Diaper for a baby porcupine

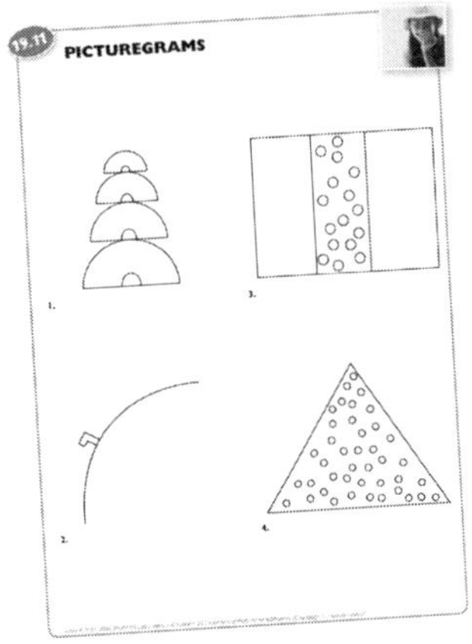

19.11

HANDOUT 19.12

In each category, students add others to the list. They can make them up or find them somewhere.

CLOSURE

Humor is a great part of life. Don't miss out on all the fun.

SEEK AND YOU WILL FIND.
FIND AND YOU WILL LAUGH.
LAUGH AND YOU WILL HEAL.
WHY DON'T YOU HAVE HUMOR FOR EVERY MEAL.

Roger Puza

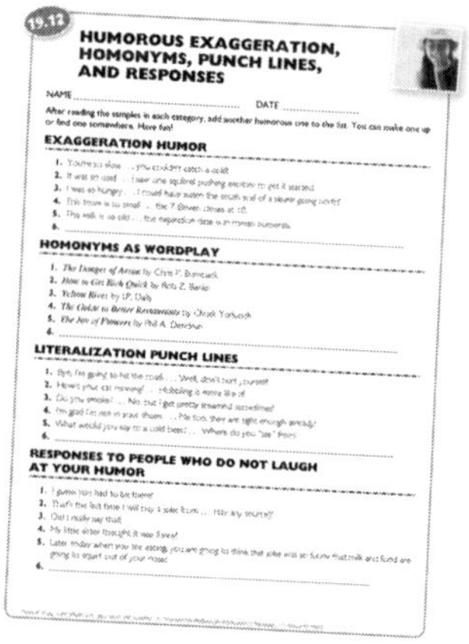

19.12

OBJECTIVE

Students will be able teach their classmates some humorous activities as part of a group project.

NATIONAL STANDARDS

- #1 Health Promotion
- #4 Communication
- #7 Healthy Behaviors
- #8 Advocacy

INTRODUCTION

As part of the grade in this unit you are going to come up with some funny activities, jokes, skits, stories, or other funny presentations as a group project. You will be randomly assigned to a group of three or four students. You will be graded on four criteria:

1. Communication skills
2. Organization
3. Laughter or fun element
4. Creativity

HANDOUT 19.13

Humor Project

Go over the humor options. After reading through the directions as a class, divide students randomly into groups of three or four and tell them when they will be presenting.

Give the students time to strategize what they will present to the class. Go around the room to each group to answer questions and note their general themes.

Remind students that each group member should have a part in the presentation.

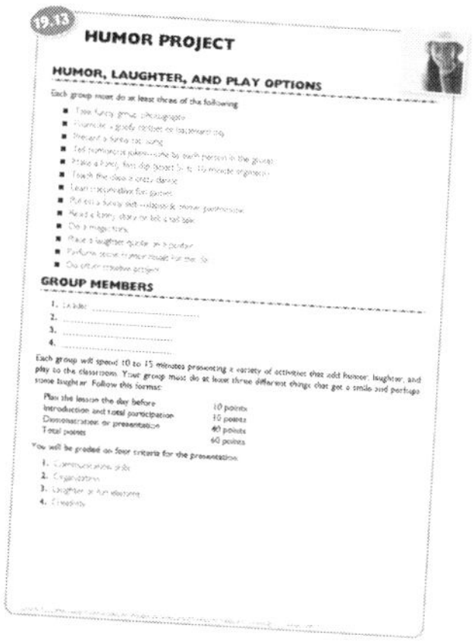
HUMOR PROJECT

HUMOR, LAUGHTER, AND PLAY OPTIONS

GROUP MEMBERS

19.13

CLOSURE

Each day during this unit, we will enjoy seeing your presentations about humor. The last day will be a makeup day for those who are absent on the day assigned for their presentation. Remember to keep the presentations fun for all and in good taste.

Humor and Laughter Test Key

OBJECTIVE

Students will pass a written test on humor, laughter, and play after a unit discussing these matters.

NATIONAL STANDARDS

- #1 Health Promotion
- #7 Healthy Behaviors

INTRODUCTION

Here is a nice test on humor, laughter, and play. Have fun and hand it in when you are finished.

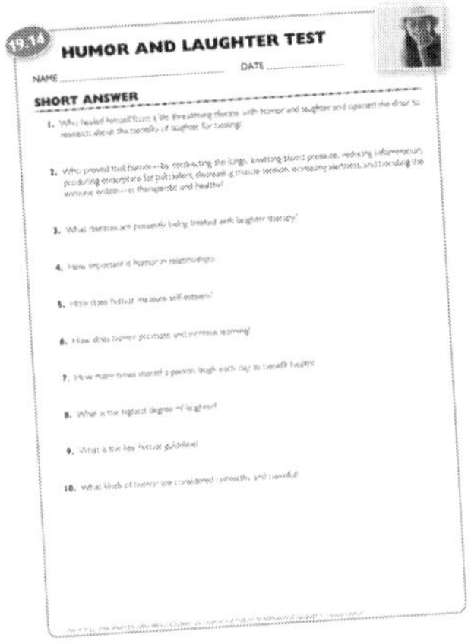
19.14 HUMOR AND LAUGHTER TEST
NAME DATE
SHORT ANSWER

19.14

HANDOUT 19.14

Short Answer

1. Dr. Norman Cousins
2. Dr. William Fry Jr.
3. depression, headaches, high blood pressure, cancer
4. rated as the number two personality trait admired, important for morale
5. by laughing at your own mistakes and gaining confidence by being funny
6. reduces stress, stimulates creativity, improves retention, increases motivation, decreases test anxiety
7. 400 times a day for children, 15 times a day for adults, 100 times a day for teenagers
8. laugh until you wet your pants
9. laugh with people, not at them
10. sarcasm, ridicule, ethnic, cynicism, put-downs, hostile, distraction

CLOSURE

We will go over the test during the next class period.

20

Tobacco, Alcohol, and Other Drug Abuse

ALCOHOL
AND DRUGS IS A
DEAD-END STREET.
JAIL, REHAB,
OR DEATH IS ALL
YOU'LL MEET.

Roger F. Puza

Lesson Finder

Drug Abuse Facts

OBJECTIVE

Students will analyze the major drugs abused in America and the rationale behind drug abuse through an open discussion.

NATIONAL STANDARDS

- #1 Health Promotion
- #7 Healthy Behaviors

INTRODUCTION

A major health concern for teenagers in America is drug abuse. This health issue causes many illnesses and deaths.

1. Question: So why do teenagers use drugs anyway?

Answer: They are seeking an altered state of mind because of boredom, peers are doing it, they want to escape personal problems, or drugs give them a feeling that they cannot find on their own naturally.

2. Question: What parts of the body are affected every time a person uses a toxic substance that alters neurochemistry?

Answer: brain, liver, kidneys, heart

3. Question: Why do health professionals want young people to stay drug free until at least 16 to 18 years of age?

Answer: The body is not fully developed before that age, and it is more susceptible to permanent damage as compared with the body of an adult.

4. Question: What drugs does the Food and Drug Administration consider unsafe for people of any age?

Answer: Marijuana, ecstasy, LSD, methamphetamine, cocaine, heroin, and many others. Possessing or using these drugs is against the law!

Today we are going to examine general facts concerning the most commonly used legal and illegal drugs in America.

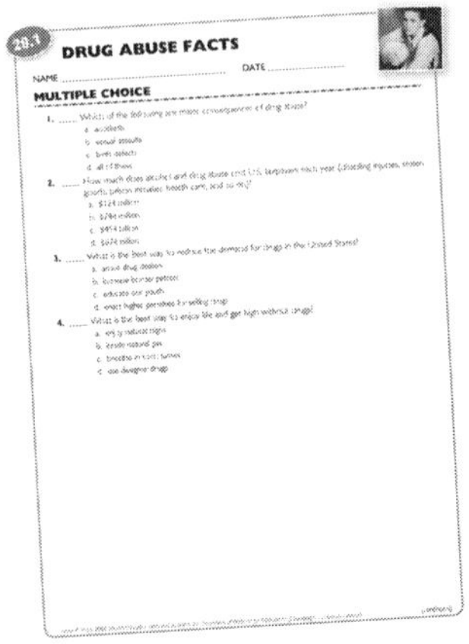

20.1

HANDOUT 20.1

DRUG ABUSE FACTS

Hand out the sheet titled "Drug Abuse Facts." Go through the sheet together and discuss the effects of tobacco, alcohol, and other drugs on society and personal well-being.

Multiple Choice

1. d
2. c
3. c
4. a

Matching: The Most Abused Drugs in America

1. b
2. g
3. k
4. a
5. d
6. j
7. c
8. e
9. h
10. f
11. i

HANDOUT 20.2

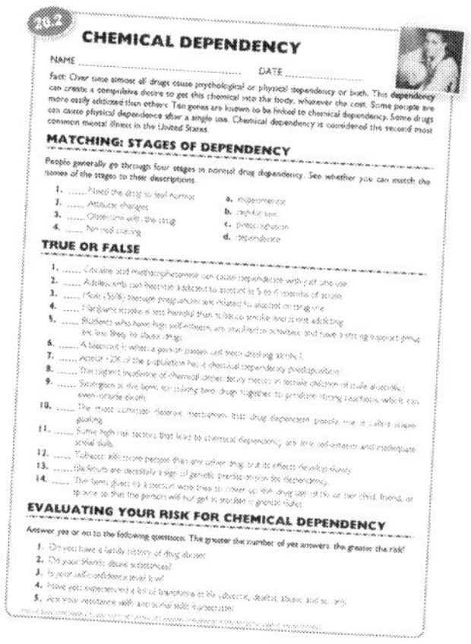

20.2

Chemical Dependency

Today we are going to examine the facts about chemical dependency. Some of you in class may be at high risk for chemical dependency.

Question: Does anyone in class know who is at the highest risk for chemical dependency?

Answer: Male children of male alcoholics.

Testimonial

Story of alcoholism or drug dependency, either personal or someone you know.

Matching: Stages of Dependency

1. d
2. b
3. c
4. a

True or False

1. true
2. true
3. true
4. false—Marijuana smoke is not less harmful and is addictive.
5. true
6. false—During a blackout, the person is awake, but has no recollection of events.
7. true
8. false—Male children of male alcoholics have the highest incidence of chemical dependency.
9. true
10. false—Denial is the most common defense mechanism used by drug dependent people.
11. true
12. true
13. true
14. false—Enablers are people who try to cover up the drug use of someone close to them.

CLOSURE

If you are at high risk for chemical dependency, be cautious! Chemical dependency is the second most common psychiatric disorder in America. Drug and alcohol dependence has caused more problems than any other single social issue. Do not let this happen to you!

Drug Consequences

OBJECTIVE

Students will enhance their awareness of drug problems by discussing statistics of community and personal problems from the abuse of alcohol and other drugs.

NATIONAL STANDARDS

- #7 Healthy Behaviors
- #5 Decision Making

INTRODUCTION

After looking at all the effects and consequences of drug abuse in our society, most people identify drug abuse as the number one problem in America. Drug abuse has a major effect on the economy and accounts for most of America's familial problems.

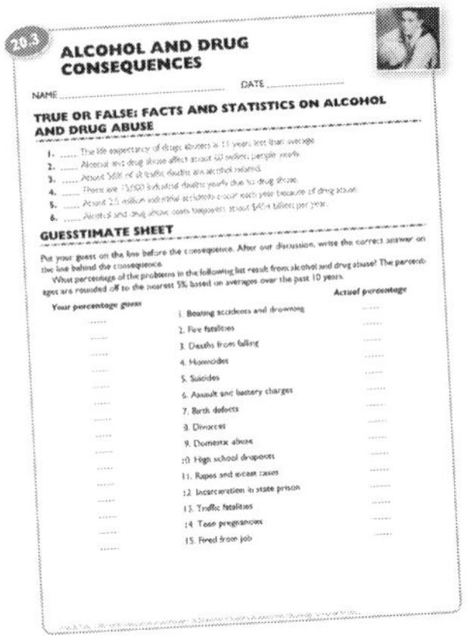
ALCOHOL AND DRUG CONSEQUENCES

TRUE OR FALSE: FACTS AND STATISTICS ON ALCOHOL AND DRUG ABUSE

GUESSTIMATE SHEET

20.3

HANDOUT 20.3

True or False: Facts and Statistics on Alcohol and Drug Abuse

1. true
2. true
3. true
4. true
5. true
6. true

Guesstimate Sheet

Tell the students that drug abuse contributes strongly to 15 major problems. The contribution of drug abuse ranges from a low of 15% to a high of 85%. For an incentive you may give an extra credit point or a small reward to anyone who guesses any percentage perfectly. This is a great activity!

1. 70
2. 65
3. 75
4. 60
5. 55
6. 80
7. 60
8. 20
9. 85
10. 80
11. 70
12. 70
13. 55
14. 60
15. 15

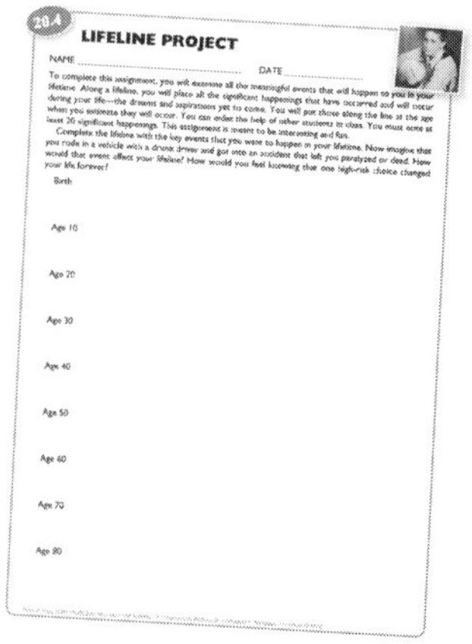
LIFELINE PROJECT

20.4

HANDOUT 20.4

Lifeline Project

Have students complete the lifeline project and then discuss their responses.

CLOSURE

Most people are not aware that alcohol and drug abuse contribute to many problems in society. Which statistic surprised you the most?

Drug Opinions

OBJECTIVE

Students will get a chance to express their opinion on a variety of drug-related questions by voting with their bodies.

NATIONAL STANDARD

#5 Decision Making

INTRODUCTION

Today you will vote with your body on a variety of drug-related questions. The questions do not have any right or wrong answers. Complete the sheet titled "Drug Opinions" by assigning a number to each statement. You will then walk to the sign that describes your opinion. Please complete the opinion survey now.

HANDOUT 20.5

Drug Opinions

You read the questions one at a time, and each student walks to the sign that best describes his or her opinion. This activity allows students to see what their classmates think about a variety of issues related to alcohol and drugs.

Some of the questions might lead to a discussion, or you might ask the one or several students whose answers are quite different from the majority to share the rationale behind their feelings. The best approach is to move rapidly through the questions and watch the results.

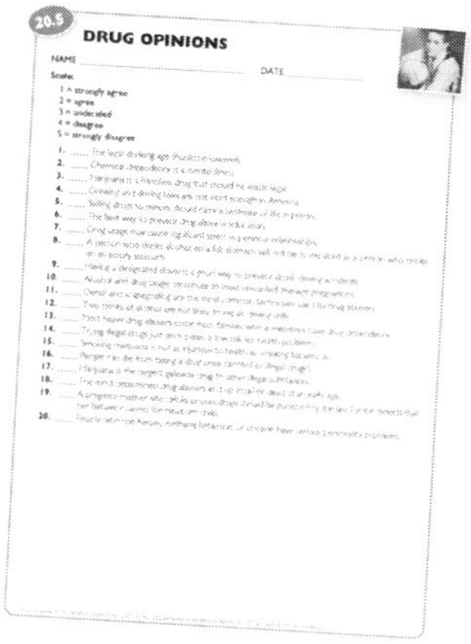
20.5
DRUG OPINIONS

20.5

CLOSURE

This activity gives you a good understanding of how your classmates feel on a variety of issues concerning drugs and society.

Tobacco Products

OBJECTIVE

Students will analyze the effects of tobacco smoke on their health and discuss its effect on all aspects of life by comparing it with alcohol and marijuana in a classroom discussion.

NATIONAL STANDARDS

- #1 Health Promotion
- #5 Decision Making
- #3 Information and Services

INTRODUCTION

Today we are going to talk about one of the leading causes of death and illness among Americans.

Question: Does anyone know what lifestyle habit contributes to over 400,000 deaths each year in the United States?

Answer: tobacco smoking

Question: How many of you have household members who use a tobacco product?

Anyone who can get another person to stop smoking or chewing tobacco for even one day will earn extra credit.

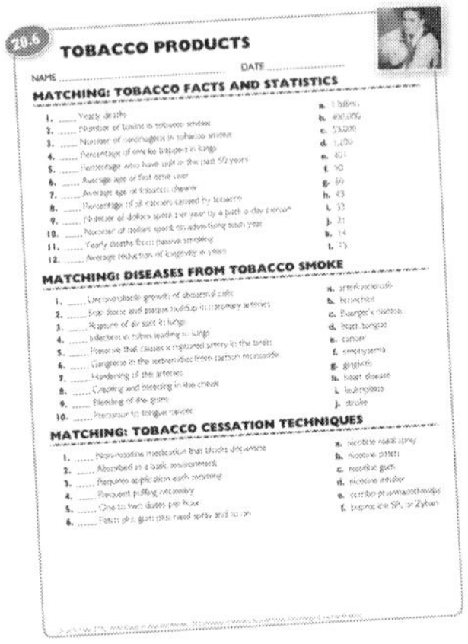
20.6 TOBACCO PRODUCTS
MATCHING: TOBACCO FACTS AND STATISTICS
MATCHING: DISEASES FROM TOBACCO SMOKE
MATCHING: TOBACCO CESSATION TECHNIQUES

20.6

HANDOUT 20.6

Matching: Tobacco Facts and Statistics

As a class, read the questions and go over the answers.

1. b	**7.** j
2. e	**8.** i
3. h	**9.** d
4. f	**10.** a
5. g	**11.** c
6. k	**12.** l

Matching: Diseases From Tobacco Smoke

1. e	**6.** c
2. h	**7.** a
3. f	**8.** i
4. b	**9.** g
5. j	**10.** d

Matching: Tobacco Cessation Techniques

1. f
2. c
3. b
4. d
5. a
6. e

Generate a short discussion about how tobacco companies attract lifelong customers. Then show some slides, pictures, or a video, or just brainstorm some of the health problems that smokers have. Talk about why two-thirds of smokers want to quit. Go over some of the successful smoking cessation techniques used today.

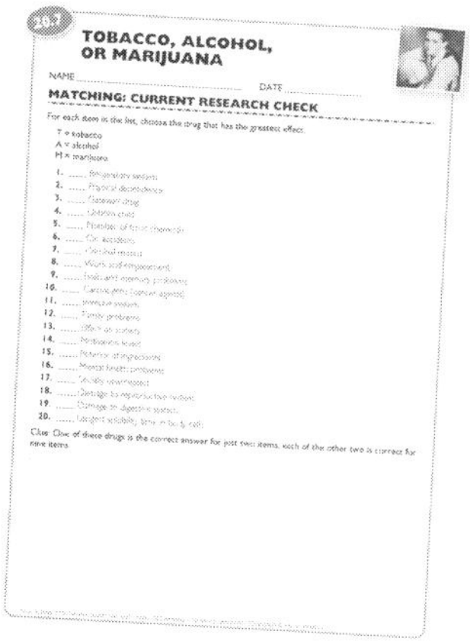
TOBACCO, ALCOHOL, OR MARIJUANA

MATCHING: CURRENT RESEARCH CHECK

20.7

HANDOUT 20.7

Tobacco, Alcohol, and Marijuana Assignment

Have a discussion about which of the big three—tobacco, alcohol, and marijuana—is worst based on these 20 areas. Then divide students into three teams and have a debate. Students use research data gathered on these 20 areas.

Matching: Current Research Check

Do this activity during the next class period to prove that although smoking is extremely harmful, these other drugs are even worse based on current research and data on societal problems.

1. M	**6.** A	**11.** M	**16.** A
2. T	**7.** A	**12.** A	**17.** M
3. M	**8.** A	**13.** A	**18.** M
4. A	**9.** A	**14.** M	**19.** A
5. M	**10.** M	**15.** T	**20.** M

CLOSURE

If you don't smoke, don't start! If you do smoke, try to quit now. If you know someone who is a smoker, be there to support him or her in trying to quit. No ifs, ands, or "butts"—cigarette smoking is dangerous to your health!

Drug Risks and Choices

OBJECTIVES

Students will be able to discuss risks and choices to make concerning drugs.

NATIONAL STANDARDS

- #7 Healthy Behaviors
- #5 Decision Making
- #4 Communication

INTRODUCTION

Life offers many choices. The average person makes about 2,000 choices every day. In making choices we should consider the degree of risk that each alternative presents for health problems, personal problems, legal problems, accidents, and injuries. Today we are going to examine some common risks that most of us will probably face someday.

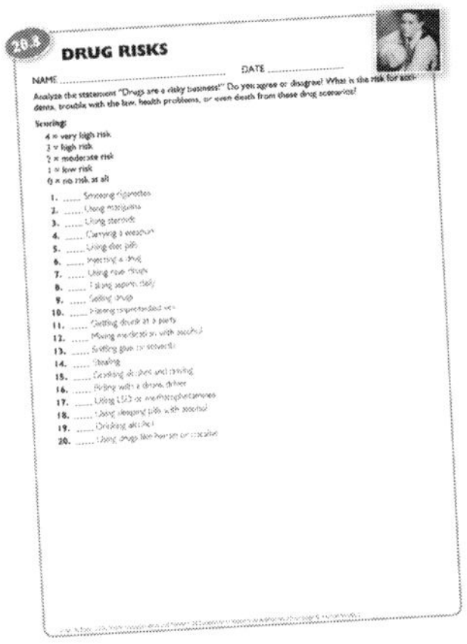
DRUG RISKS
NAME DATE

20.8

HANDOUT 20.8

Drug Risks

Have students rate the risk of the following scenarios. Then go through the list with the class to see how the students scored the situations. For each scenario, write a number that reflects the majority view of the situation. The numbers that follow are based on the view of medical experts. You may need to explain some of the answers.

1. 4	**6.** 4	**11.** 3	**16.** 4
2. 3	**7.** 4	**12.** 3	**17.** 4
3. 3	**8.** 2	**13.** 4	**18.** 4
4. 4	**9.** 4	**14.** 3	**19.** 3
5. 2	**10.** 4	**15.** 4	**20.** 4

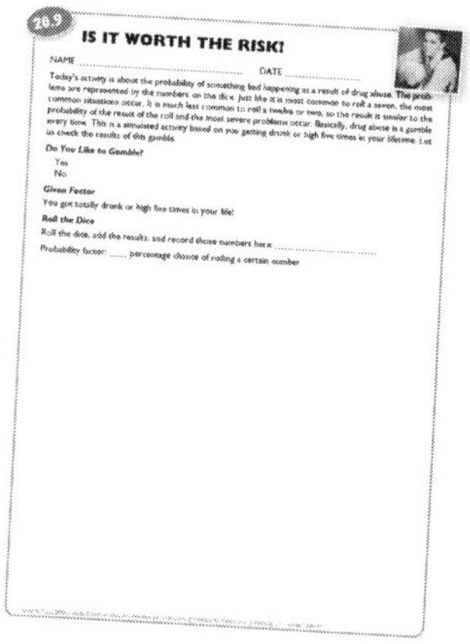
IS IT WORTH THE RISK?
NAME DATE

20.9

HANDOUT 20.9

Activity: Is It Worth the Risk?

Go through the five rolls and the results of the rolls. This activity helps students realize that some people are not lucky and that something bad can happen to them or someone they love. Most of these gambles are not worth the risk.

Record the five rolls of the dice: ____ ____ ____ ____ ____

Probability factor:

Roll 7 (the most common roll): Lucky you. Nothing at all bad happens!

Situation 1: Accidents (Driving, Falls, Choking, Other)

Roll 6: You have an accident, but it is not that serious!

Roll 5: You are injured in the accident!

Roll 3: You have a serious injury that requires hospital care!

Situation 2: Aggressive Behavior (You Become Mean)

Roll 9: You commit a crime (vandalism, stealing, or other crime).

Roll 10: You get in an argument and fight. You are arrested for battery.

Situation 3: Amorous Behavior (You Become Flirtatious and Uninhibited)

Roll 8: You act flirtatious and flaunt yourself.

Roll 12: You have unprotected sex.

Situation 4: Chemical Dependency (Bad Chemistry)

Roll 4: You are a high genetic risk for dependency.

Roll 2: You end up in jail, in a mental hospital, or dead!

Do these rolls of the dice represent your future?
Is it worth the risk? _______________

HANDOUT 20.10

MAKING HEALTHY CHOICES

20.10

Discussion Questions: Making Healthy Choices

Which of these reasons for not using drugs makes the most sense to you?

What natural highs do you participate in that bring great pleasure and personal satisfaction?

CLOSURE

Today we wanted you to examine the risks of each of your choices. The wrong decision can create many problems. Think about the choice and possible consequences before letting anyone talk you into anything. Life is a gamble, but some gambles are never worth the risk. Take time to find enjoyment in natural highs.

Freedom From Drug Dependence Project

OBJECTIVE

Students will be able to display their feelings and knowledge concerning drug abuse by producing a four-part project about being drug free.

NATIONAL STANDARDS

- #1 Health Promotion
- #2 Cultural Influence
- #3 Information and Services
- #5 Decision Making
- #7 Healthy Behaviors

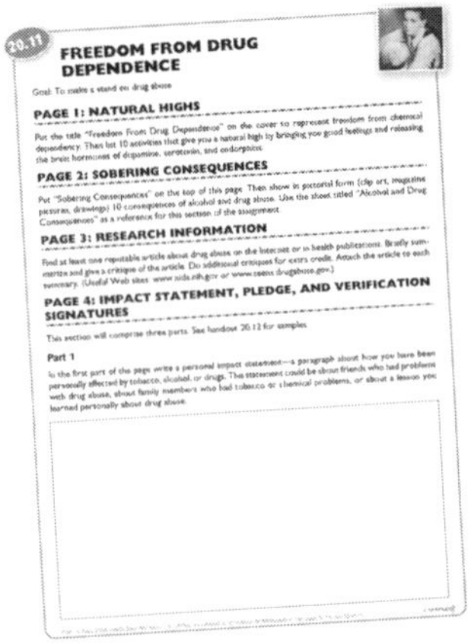

20.11

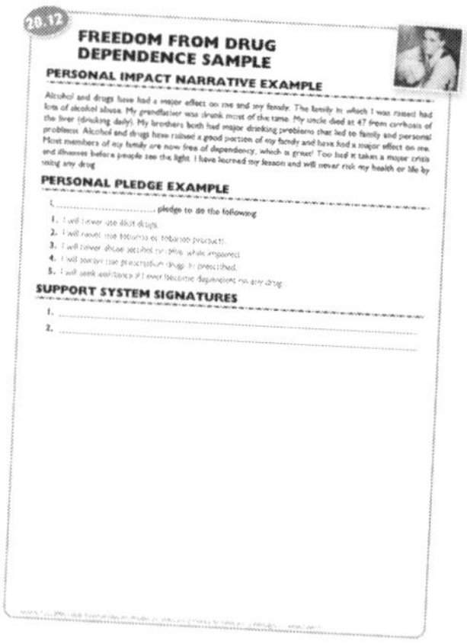

20.12

INTRODUCTION

This project will offer evidence that you understand the effects of drug abuse and are willing to make a stand concerning drug use. The project includes four parts:

1. Natural highs
2. Sobering consequences
3. Research information
4. Impact statement, pledge, and verification factor

HANDOUT 20.11

HANDOUT 20.12

Allow students time to work on the project each day of the unit or give them a whole day or two to work on it in class. Periodically check each student's progress so that no one falls behind. Help them with their projects and have a sample project for them to look at for general procedures.

CLOSURE

This project will help you learn about the effects of tobacco, alcohol, and drugs on our society and what you can do personally to be drug free. I hope that the project made you realize that drugs lead to a dead-end street. Why go there?

Drugs and the Law

OBJECTIVE

Students will examine the four types of crimes and be able to distinguish between a status offense, a misdemeanor, a violation, and a felony through a classroom discussion.

NATIONAL STANDARDS

- #1 Health Promotion
- #5 Decision Making
- #4 Communication

INTRODUCTION

Usually, the most serious immediate consequence of drug abuse is getting in trouble with the law. Today we are going to talk about what can happen to a juvenile who breaks the law.

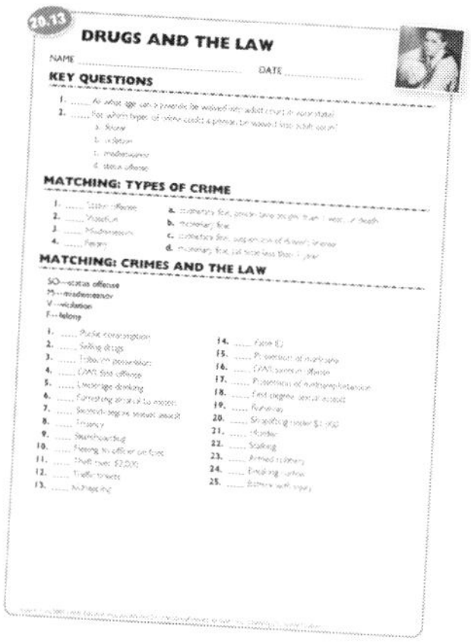
20.13
DRUGS AND THE LAW
KEY QUESTIONS
MATCHING: TYPES OF CRIME
MATCHING: CRIMES AND THE LAW

20.13

HANDOUT 20.13

A guest speaker on law enforcement is recommended.

Key Questions

1. The instructor will need to find out the answer for their state as the age varies from state to state.
2. a

Matching: Types of Crimes

1. c
2. b
3. d
4. a

Matching: Crimes and the Law

1. V	**6.** V	**11.** F	**16.** M	**21.** F
2. F	**7.** F	**12.** V	**17.** F	**22.** M, F
3. SO	**8.** SO	**13.** F	**18.** F	**23.** F
4. V	**9.** V	**14.** V	**19.** SO	**24.** SO
5. V	**10.** M	**15.** M	**20.** V, M	**25.** M

CLOSURE

We have many laws in our country. Laws are meant to keep order and allow for protection. Laws are also meant to deter people from making poor choices that lead to many problems.

Today we are checking your knowledge of laws so that you will know more about what might happen if you get caught. Breaking the law is not a good choice, and unlawful actions could put you behind bars for a long time. Jail takes away many of your rights and privileges as a human being. Think before you make decisions that will cause you to break the law.

Drinking and Driving Facts

OBJECTIVE

Students will be able to examine the facts about and consequences of drinking and driving.

NATIONAL STANDARDS

- #1 Health Promotion
- #5 Decision Making

INTRODUCTION

What is the number one cause of teenage death in the United States? Yes, you are right! Drinking and driving! If you are going to drive, you must not drink. Today we are going to check your knowledge of alcohol and its effect on your driving skills.

20.14
DRINKING AND DRIVING: ALCOHOL FACTS
MATCHING: STATISTICS ON DRINKING AND DRIVING
TRUE OR FALSE
DRINKING AND DRIVING CONSEQUENCES

20.14

HANDOUT 20.14

Guest speakers and videos are also recommended!

Matching: Statistics on Drinking and Driving

1. d
2. a
3. f
4. b
5. c
6. e

True or False

1. true
2. false—It is a depressant and causes the body to lose heat.
3. true
4. false—Only time, which allows liver oxidation, will sober up a person.
5. false—They are the result of a self-induced state.
6. true
7. true
8. false—The most common intoxication level is a .08 BAC level.
9. false—It is determined by body weight and the number of drinks.
10. true

Drinking and Driving Consequences

All these are either 4 or 5.

Brainstorming: Prevention Program

Possible responses:

- Stronger penalties
- Better education programs
- Designated drivers
- Bar responsibilities
- Bar fines

Penalties Around the World for Drunk Driving

1. Australia: The names of drunk drivers are sent to local newspapers, which print the names under the big heading "He's Drunk and in Jail."
2. Malaysia: The driver is jailed, and if married, his or her spouse is jailed as well.
3. South Africa: A 10-year sentence and a $10,000 fine.
4. Finland and Sweden: Automatic jail for 1 year of hard labor.
5. Russia: License revoked for life.
6. England: 1-year suspension, $250 fine, and 1 year in jail.
7. France: Loss of license for 3 years, 1 year in jail, and a $1,000 fine.
8. Bulgaria: A second conviction results in execution.
9. El Salvador: Execution by firing squad.
10. United States: Varies from state to state, but can include a fine, jail time, and license suspension.

CLOSURE

Civilized societies should not tolerate drinking and driving. Many innocent people die every year in accidents that could be almost totally prevented. Why are Americans not able to figure this out?

Drug Court

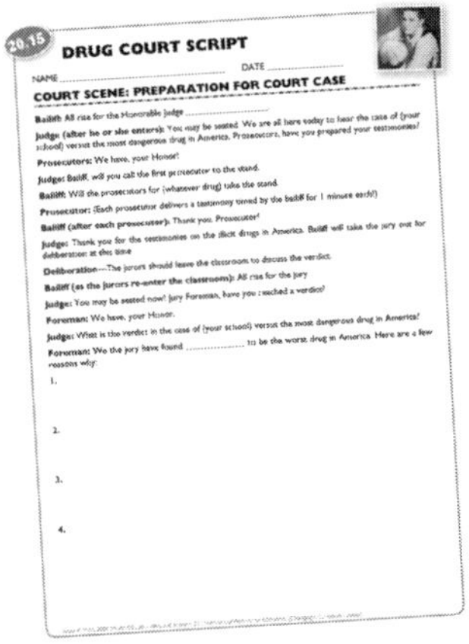

20.15 DRUG COURT SCRIPT

NAME ______ DATE ______

COURT SCENE: PREPARATION FOR COURT CASE

Bailiff: All rise for the Honorable Judge ______

Judge (after he or she enters): You may be seated. We are all here today to hear the case of (your school) versus the most dangerous drug in America. Prosecutors, have you prepared your testimonies?

Prosecutors: We have, your Honor!

Judge: Bailiff, will you call the first prosecutor to the stand.

Bailiff: Will the prosecutors for (whatever drug) take the stand.

Prosecutor: (Each prosecutor delivers a testimony timed by the bailiff for 1 minute each!)

Bailiff (after each prosecutor): Thank you, Prosecutor!

Judge: Thank you for the testimonies on the illicit drugs in America. Bailiff will take the jury out for deliberation at this time.

Deliberation—The jurors should leave the classroom to discuss the verdict.

Bailiff (as the jurors re-enter the classroom): All rise for the jury.

Judge: You may be seated now! Jury Foreman, have you reached a verdict?

Foreman: We have, your Honor.

Judge: What is the verdict in the case of (your school) versus the most dangerous drug in America?

Foreman: We the jury have found ______ to be the worst drug in America. Here are a few reasons why:

1.

2.

3.

4.

20.15

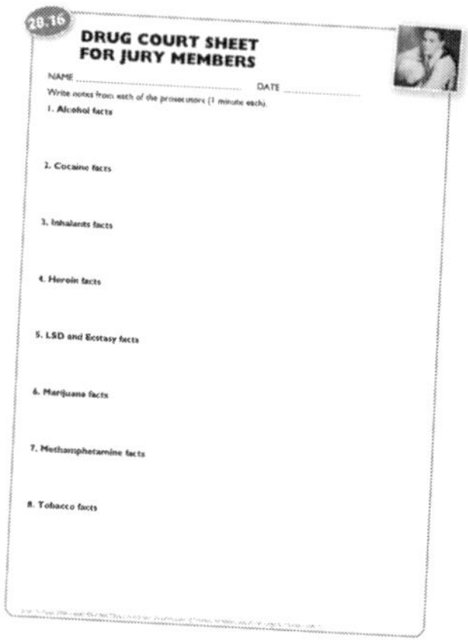

20.16 DRUG COURT SHEET FOR JURY MEMBERS

NAME ______ DATE ______

Write notes from each of the prosecutors (1 minute each).

1. Alcohol facts
2. Cocaine facts
3. Inhalants facts
4. Heroin facts
5. LSD and Ecstasy facts
6. Marijuana facts
7. Methamphetamine facts
8. Tobacco facts

20.16

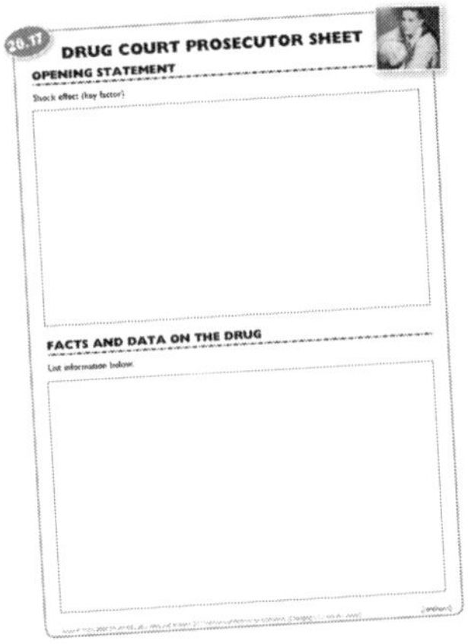

20.17 DRUG COURT PROSECUTOR SHEET

OPENING STATEMENT

Shock effect (hay factor)

FACTS AND DATA ON THE DRUG

List information below.

20.17

OBJECTIVE

Students will bring the absolute worst about all drugs to this courtlike atmosphere in which prosecutors present their researched data and the jury makes the decision.

NATIONAL STANDARDS

- #1 Health Promotion
- #5 Decision Making
- #3 Information and Services
- #4 Communication
- #8 Advocacy

INTRODUCTION

Today we are going to have a trial to determine the most dangerous drug in America. The prosecutors will present their cases, and the jury will listen to the information and try not to be biased. The judge will rule on the final decision. We will run this class today just as if we were in a courtroom.

HANDOUT 20.15
HANDOUT 20.16
HANDOUT 20.17

Drug Court

This is a great lesson! The teacher needs to prepare everyone.

Select the eight prosecutors the day before the activity. You can provide them some information from the National Institute on Drug Abuse, and they can find information themselves as well. Seek volunteers first and then pick some students who you know would do well. The class picks the judge, bailiff, and jury foreman by heads-down classroom voting. These students follow a script for the procedures. All other students are on the jury and must fill out their sheets as the prosecutors present their cases.

Compliment all the prosecutors and members of the court.

CLOSURE

Today we saw from the data presented that all the drugs being abused in America are harmful. We should surely realize that making healthy decisions about drugs is important to our lives.

Drug and Alcohol Test Key

OBJECTIVE

Students will be able to pass a written test on alcohol and drugs after a unit discussing the facts.

NATIONAL STANDARDS

- #1 Health Promotion
- #7 Healthy Behaviors

INTRODUCTION

Complete this test and turn it in as soon as you are finished.

HANDOUT 20.18

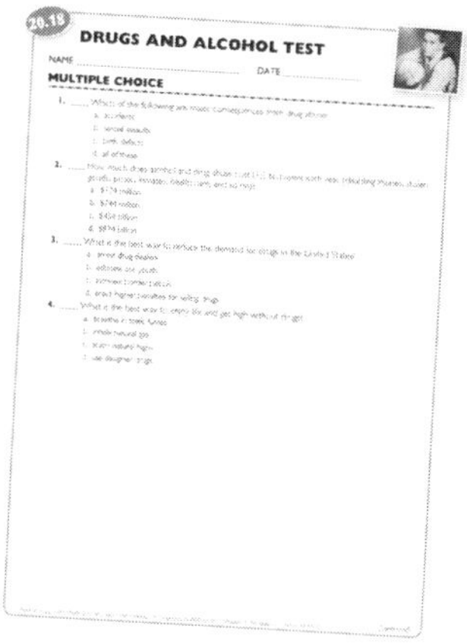
20.18 DRUGS AND ALCOHOL TEST
NAME DATE
MULTIPLE CHOICE

20.18

Multiple Choice

1. d
2. c
3. b
4. c

Matching: The Most Abused Drugs in America

5. d
6. a
7. f
8. g
9. b
10. i
11. c
12. e
13. h

Matching: Drug Dependence Stages

14. d
15. b
16. a
17. c

True or False: Chemical Dependency

18. true
19. true
20. false—About 55% are related to alcohol or drug use.
21. false—Marijuana smoke is not less harmful and is addictive.
22. false—They are less likely to abuse drugs.
23. false—Male children of male alcoholics have the highest incidence of chemical dependency.

24. false—Synergism is the word for mixing two drugs together.
25. true
26. true
27. true
28. true
29. true
30. true

True or False: Drinking and Driving

31. true
32. false—Around 50-55% are alcohol related.
33. false—It is .08 in most states.
34. true
35. false—It reaches the bloodstream in about 20 seconds.

Short Answer

36. cerebellum
37. nine
38. cirrhosis
39. one
40. body weight and number of drinks

CLOSURE

We will go over the test when we meet next time in class.

21

Human Relations

SO MANY GODS,
SO MANY CREEDS,
SO MANY PATHS
THAT WIND
AND WIND,
WHILE JUST THE ART
OF BEING KIND
IS ALL THE SAD
WORLD NEEDS.

Ella Wheeler Wilcox

Lesson Finder

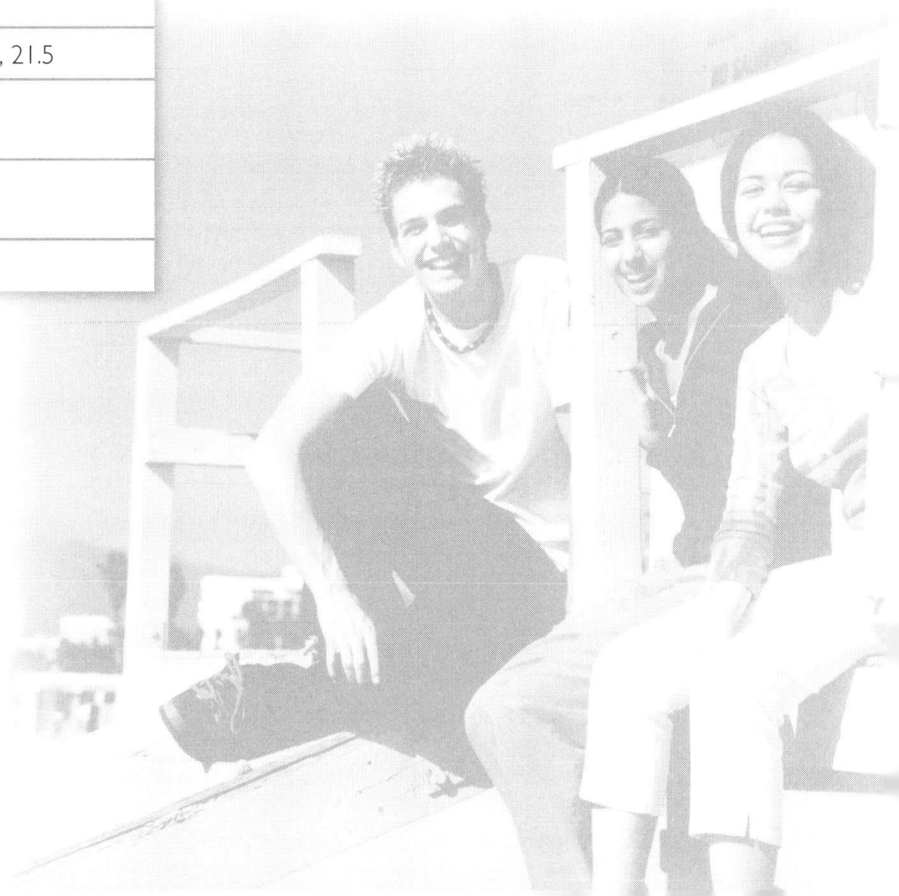

Human Relations Facts

OBJECTIVE

Students will be able to learn the key factors to getting along with people through a close analysis of human relations.

NATIONAL STANDARDS

- #1 Health Promotion
- #7 Healthy Behaviors
- #4 Communication

INTRODUCTION

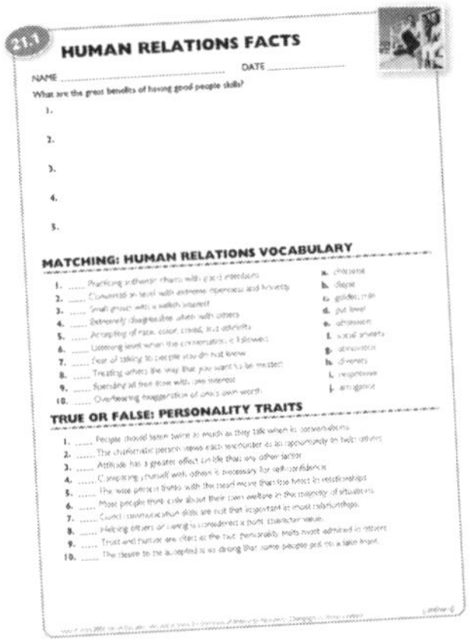
HUMAN RELATIONS FACTS

MATCHING: HUMAN RELATIONS VOCABULARY

TRUE OR FALSE: PERSONALITY TRAITS

21.1

Having good people skills is one of the greatest advantages that a person can have. Getting along with others is an art that can be learned. How well do you do with people? Do you create pleasant situations and have fun with others? Can you carry on a conversation with most any person? This unit is about what we can do to enhance our self-confidence with others.

HANDOUT 21.1

What are the great benefits of having good people skills?

1. Treated better by everyone
2. Helps get and keep job
3. Builds self-confidence
4. Improves leadership abilities
5. Helps build good family relations

Matching: Human Relations Vocabulary

1. a	**6.** i
2. d	**7.** f
3. b	**8.** c
4. g	**9.** e
5. h	**10.** j

True or False: Personality Traits

1. true
2. true
3. true
4. false—Comparisons are not good for self-confidence.
5. false—The wise person thinks more with their heart.
6. true
7. false—They are very important.
8. false—It is a good character value.
9. true
10. true

Short Answer: First Impressions

List the three best ways to make a good first impression. Possible responses:

- Smile
- Look people in the eye
- Shake hands
- Remember the person's name

Short Answer: Art of Conversation

List the three best ways to master the art of conversation. Possible responses:

- Ask questions
- Listen more than talk
- Be interesting and knowledgeable

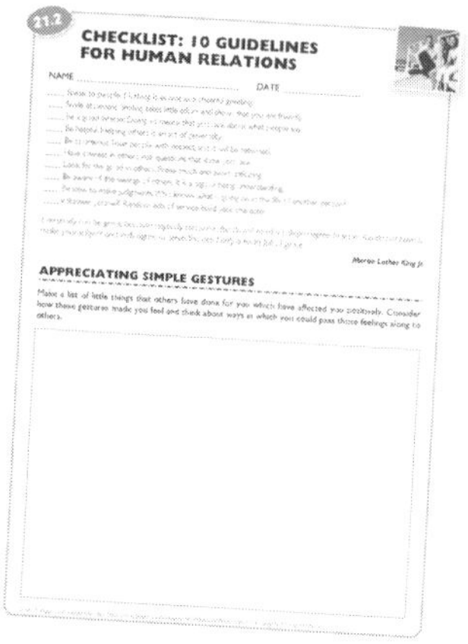
CHECKLIST: 10 GUIDELINES FOR HUMAN RELATIONS

APPRECIATING SIMPLE GESTURES

21.2

Matching

1. C	**6.** D
2. D	**7.** C
3. C	**8.** D
4. D	**9.** C
5. C	**10.** D

HANDOUT 21.2

Checklist: 10 Guidelines for Human Relations

How many of these are true of you?

Martin Luther King Jr. Quotation

Read aloud in class! Learn to serve! The highest level of human relations is reaching out to others instead of always focusing on oneself.

Appreciating Simple Gestures

After students have finished drawing up their list, lead a discussion about the importance of simple kindness.

CLOSURE

Developing your people skills is one of the best things that you can do for yourself. Take time to build bridges to others, not walls!

Human Relations Values and Opinions

OBJECTIVE

Students will vote with their feet on a variety of questions concerning relationships, sexuality, marriage, and families.

NATIONAL STANDARDS

- #5 Decision Making
- #4 Communication

INTRODUCTION

People have different thoughts and opinions concerning dating, relationships, sexuality, marriage, and families in general. Today we are going to see how each of you votes on the 30 scenarios listed on the handout. Try to avoid putting undecided for any of the questions. Go to the station that best describes your current feelings and values. If you go to a station that no one else in the class chooses, we may ask you to explain the rationale behind your choice.

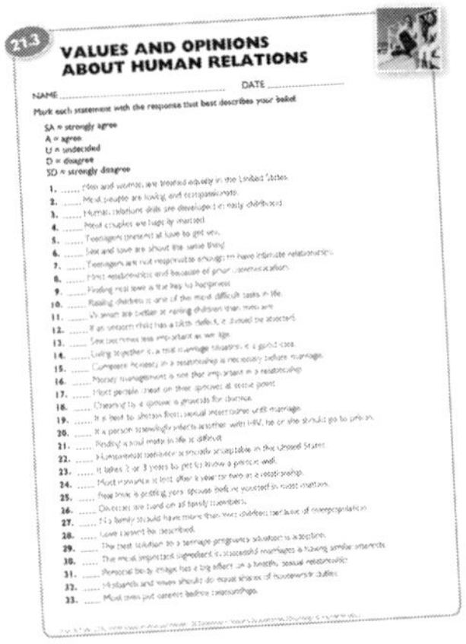
VALUES AND OPINIONS ABOUT HUMAN RELATIONS

21.3

HANDOUT 21.3

Tape five signs on the walls in various parts of the room (strongly agree, agree, undecided, disagree, and strongly disagree). Have the students complete the handout "Values and Opinions About Human Relations" on their own. Explain that there are no right or wrong answers. They should respond to the statements by what they believe at this time in their lives.

After the students have finished filling out the handout, ask them to take their sheets with them and proceed to the station that describes their beliefs as you go through the questions one by one. Each student should go to the station that reveals his or her belief, even if no one else chooses that response. Their thoughts may encourage others to see another side of the situation. From time to time you may wish to ask students to share their thoughts behind their choices.

CLOSURE

All of us should have opinions and values on life issues. Having opinions shows that you have analyzed matters concerning human relations. Hearing the facts and opinions of others will broaden your knowledge and help you understand why others think the way they do. This unit will help you learn about the skills necessary to get along well with others, no matter what their race, creed, religion, or age.

Personal Interviews

OBJECTIVE

Students will be able to learn about life and develop people skills by interviewing family members and friends of different ages and generations.

NATIONAL STANDARDS

- #5 Decision Making
- #4 Communication

INTRODUCTION

The best way to improve interpersonal skills is to become involved with people of all ages. Today you will interview a classmate, who in turn will interview you. The second part of the assignment is to interview three older people. One is to be between 18 and 25 years old, one is to be your parent's age, and one is to be the age of your grandparents or great-grandparents. This assignment will be a great learning experience for all of you.

Have students identify and interview someone in class they do not know well. They will ask the questions on the classmate interview sheet. After students have interviewed their partners, the partners will interview them. Then have students decide which three people they will interview for the second part of the assignments.

HANDOUT 21.4

HANDOUT 21.5

CLOSURE

This activity is a great way to learn about people and about what it takes to be a good listener. Learning about the lives of people in other generations should be interesting and fun. These interviews are due at the end of the unit.

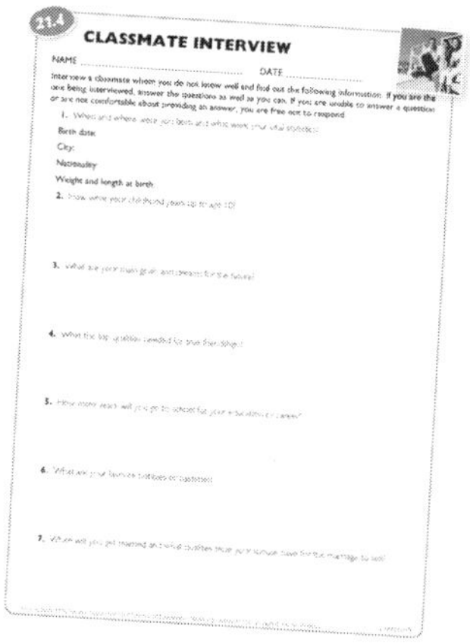

21.4

CLASSMATE INTERVIEW

NAME .... DATE ....

Interview a classmate whom you do not know well and find out the following information. If you are the one being interviewed, answer the questions as well as you can. If you are unable to answer a question or are not comfortable about providing an answer, you are free not to respond.

Birth date:

City:

Nationality:

Weight and length at birth:

21.4

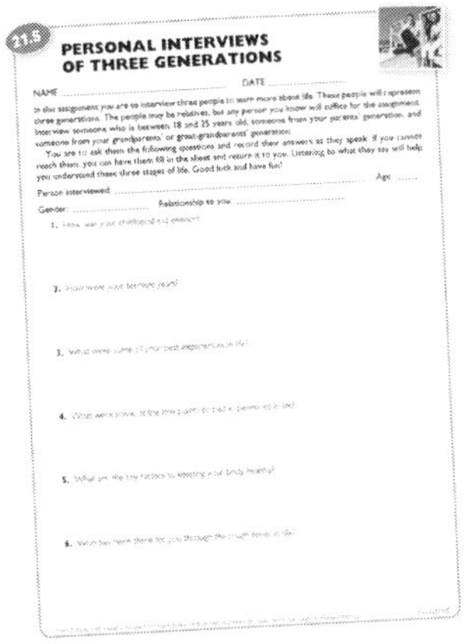

21.5

PERSONAL INTERVIEWS OF THREE GENERATIONS

NAME .... DATE ....

In this assignment you are to interview three people to learn more about life. These people will represent three generations. The people may be relatives, but any person you know will suffice for the assignment. Interview someone who is between 18 and 25 years old, someone from your parents' generation, and someone from your grandparents' or great-grandparents' generation.

You are to ask them the following questions and record their answers as they speak. If you cannot reach them, you can have them fill in the sheet and return it to you. Listening to what they say will help you understand these three stages of life. Good luck and have fun!

Person interviewed: .... Age ....

Gender: .... Relationship to you: ....

21.5

Communication and Problem Solving

OBJECTIVE

Students will be able to put together a puzzle by solving problems as a group and using communication and listening skills in the process.

NATIONAL STANDARDS

- #5 Decision Making
- #4 Communication
- #8 Advocacy

INTRODUCTION

Today is about improving your group problem-solving skills and practicing your communication and listening skills.

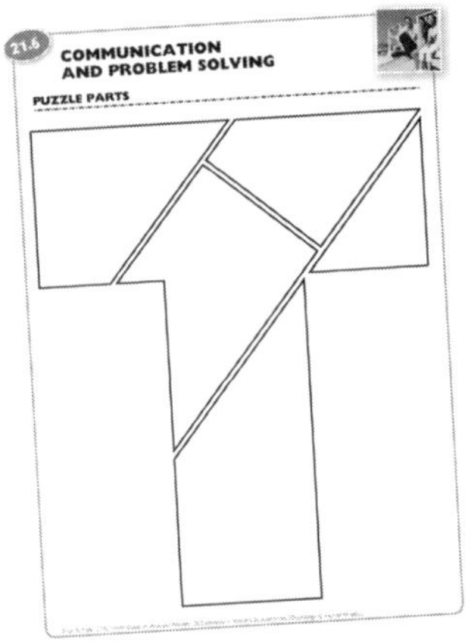

21.6

HANDOUT 21.6

Divide the students into small groups and provide each group with the pieces of the *T* puzzle. Be sure to cut the puzzle apart first so that the solution is not given away!

Explain to the students that each group will use all five pieces of the puzzle and assemble them to form the capital letter *T*. As the groups complete the puzzle, they should see if any of the other groups would like help. If so, they should explain to the other group how to put the puzzle together without allowing them to see their completed puzzle. Students will make use of their communication skills by giving clear directions or listening carefully and following directions.

If the groups seem to be struggling, help one group figure out the puzzle so that they are then able to assist the other groups. Once all the groups have completed the puzzle, compliment them on completing a difficult task.

CLOSURE

This is a great activity for developing group problem-solving skills and communication skills. Thank you for working well together. Does anybody know what the letter *T* stands for? The word I am thinking of is the most important personality trait for good relationships. Yes, the *T* is for *trust*!

Personal Transformation Concepts

OBJECTIVE

Students will analyze maladjustment in our society and the key concepts for change in our character values.

NATIONAL STANDARDS

- #7 Healthy Behaviors
- #5 Decision Making
- #4 Communication

INTRODUCTION

Social maladjustment is common in our society and in other parts of the world. Here is a checklist that you can use to see how you are doing. But our real task today is to learn about the transformation process. Dr. Martin Luther King Jr. practiced nonviolence in the wake of prejudice and injustice in our country. Listed here are the 10 guidelines for the change process. Our job today is to interpret these guidelines so that we can understand and remember the principles.

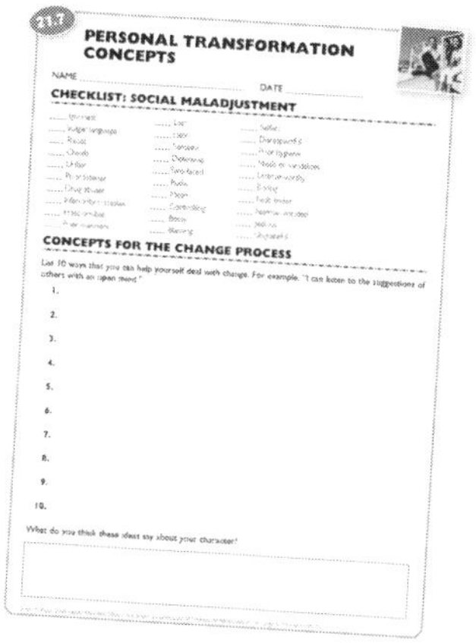
PERSONAL TRANSFORMATION CONCEPTS

CHECKLIST: SOCIAL MALADJUSTMENT

CONCEPTS FOR THE CHANGE PROCESS

21.7

HANDOUT 21.7

Checklist: Social Maladjustment

Have the students check to see how they are doing with these poor adjustment traits.

Concepts for the Change Process

Have the students create a list of 10 things they can do to help themselves deal with change in their lives. In a group discussion, have the students discuss their ideas.

CLOSURE

Examining your character values is always beneficial. To improve relations with people, at times we may need to change our ways in dealing with them. Personal transformation is a process developed by Martin Luther King Jr. to improve situations with people. See whether you can change your weak personal traits into skills for building human relationships.

Human Relations Test Key

21.8

OBJECTIVE

Students will be able to pass a written test on human relations after an extensive unit.

NATIONAL STANDARDS

- #1 Health Promotion
- #7 Healthy Behaviors

INTRODUCTION

Complete this test and turn it in when you are finished.

HANDOUT 21.8

True or False: Benefits of Good People Skills

1. false—They can prevent you from being fired and keep you employed.
2. true
3. true
4. false—It improves self-confidence.
5. false—It can help solve family conflicts.
6. true

Short Answer: Key Concepts of Personal Transformation

Possible responses (questions 7–10):

- patience
- carefree
- pride
- understanding
- expect change
- security
- sense of humor
- self-control
- open-minded
- kindness

Matching: Human Relations Vocabulary

11. b	**16.** c
12. i	**17.** f
13. d	**18.** e
14. g	**19.** h
15. a	**20.** j

True or False

21. true

22. true

23. true

24. false—Comparisons are bad for self-confidence.

25. false—The wise person thinks more with the heart,

Short Answer: Art of Conversation

Possible responses (questions 26–27):

- Ask questions
- Listen more than talk
- Be interesting

Short Answer: First Impressions

Possible responses (questions 28–30):

- Smile
- Shake hands
- Make eye contact
- Remember the person's name

CLOSURE

During the next class period, we will go over the results of the test.

22

Human Sexuality

LOVE AND SEX ARE NOT THE SAME, BUT THE WISE LEARN HOW TO COMBINE THEM FOR A DEEP BONDING RELATIONSHIP.

Puza

Lesson Finder

Human Sexuality Issues

OBJECTIVE

Students will be able to examine the major public health issues concerning sexuality in our society through a classroom discussion.

NATIONAL STANDARDS

- #1 Health Promotion
- #5 Decision Making
- #4 Communication

INTRODUCTION

Human sexuality is a big issue in the United States. Our teenagers lead the western world in the incidence of STIs, unplanned pregnancies, sexual assaults, and birth defects. This is not a proud statistic for a country that likes to consider itself the most advanced country in the world. This week we will study these major teenage issues.

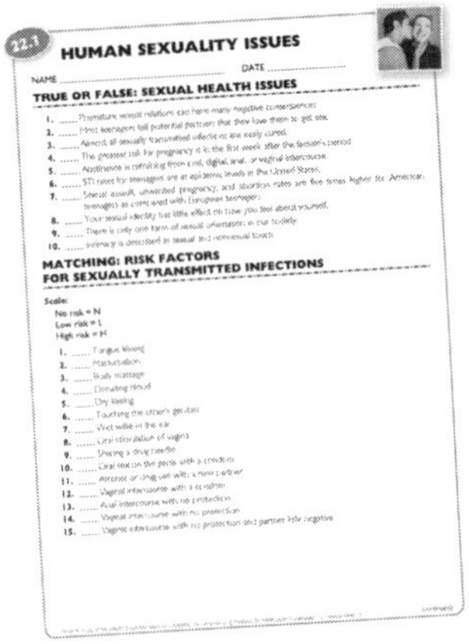
HUMAN SEXUALITY ISSUES

TRUE OR FALSE: SEXUAL HEALTH ISSUES

MATCHING: RISK FACTORS FOR SEXUALLY TRANSMITTED INFECTIONS

22.1

HANDOUT 22.1

True or False: Sexual Issues

1. true
2. true
3. false—Some have no cure.
4. false—The greatest risk for pregnancy is 14 days from the end of the cycle.
5. true
6. true
7. true
8. false—It is important.
9. false—There are many kinds of orientation.
10. true

Matching: Risk Factors for Sexually Transmitted Infections

1. L	**6.** L	**11.** H
2. N	**7.** N	**12.** L
3. N	**8.** H	**13.** H
4. N	**9.** H	**14.** H
5. N	**10.** L	**15.** H

Sex Talk: What Do You Think?

This activity can lead to some positive peer pressure. Just listen as a teacher and encourage the students to speak and share.

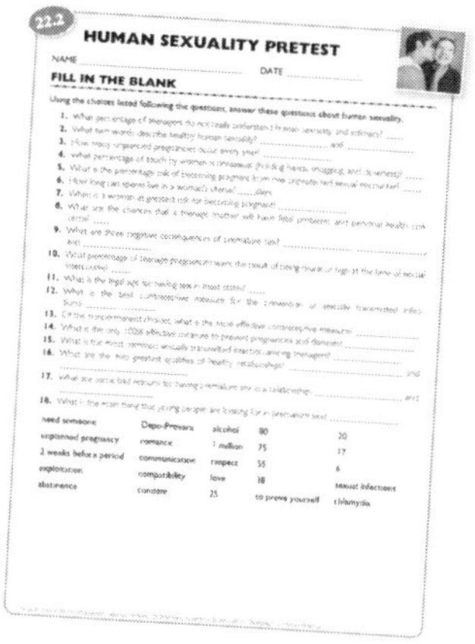
HUMAN SEXUALITY PRETEST

FILL IN THE BLANK

22.2

HANDOUT 22.2

Human Sexuality Pretest Answers

1. 75%
2. romance; respect
3. 1 million
4. 80%
5. 20%
6. 6
7. 2 weeks before period
8. 38%
9. sexual infections; unplanned pregnancy; exploitation
10. 55%
11. 17 (although the age may be higher or lower in your state)
12. condom
13. Depo-Provera
14. abstinence
15. chlamydia
16. communication; compatibility
17. need someone; to prove yourself
18. love

CLOSURE

Being sexually active brings with it a lot of responsibility and consequences. I am not sure that people your age are ready for all that. Do not ever let people talk you into something that you may regret for the rest of your life. Always protect yourself. Remember that each choice you make may affect you for a long time to come.

Sexually Transmitted Infections

OBJECTIVE

Students will analyze an epidemic that affects teenagers in the United States (STIs) through a classroom presentation from a guest speaker from the health department.

NATIONAL STANDARD

#1 Health Promotion

INTRODUCTION

For this lesson I usually introduce a guest speaker from the health department who gives a PowerPoint® presentation on eight common sexually transmitted infections. I tell the students that the handout on sexually transmitted infections can serve as their notes. They should answer as many questions as they can from the speaker's presentation. Go over the sheet later for further discussion.

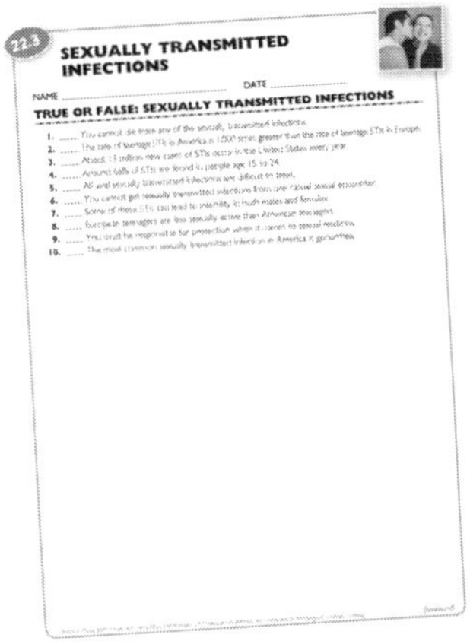

22.3

HANDOUT 22.3

Invite a guest speaker from your local health department to give a presentation about sexually transmitted infections.

True or False: Sexually Transmitted Infections

1. false—AIDS and syphilis can cause death.
2. true
3. true
4. true
5. true
6. false—Yes, you can.
7. true
8. false—No, but they tend to use better sexual health practices.
9. true
10. false—Chlamydia is the most common STI in America.

Matching: Common Sexually Transmitted Infections

1. V	**6.** A	**11.** A	**16.** B
2. W	**7.** C, G	**12.** W	**17.** W
3. W	**8.** C	**13.** S	**18.** H
4. B	**9.** A	**14.** G	**19.** V
5. B	**10.** C, G	**15.** H	**20.** W

Short Answer

1. abstinence
2. safe sex
3. monogamy
4. avoid drug abuse

CLOSURE

Sexually transmitted infections are occurring in epidemic proportions in the United States, and people do not realize what it is like until they have one. Be cautious! Do not use drugs! Be choosey about whom you spend time with! Be safe! Having sex is not worth dying for or suffering with a disease for a lifetime.

Sexual Assault

OBJECTIVE

Students will be able to determine when a crime is committed after a general discussion on sexual assault by a guest speaker.

NATIONAL STANDARDS

- #1 Health Promotion
- #5 Decision Making

INTRODUCTION

Sexual assault is a horrific and extremely personal felony crime that sends many people to prison every year. The victims are often left confused and with emotional issues that they must try to overcome. Do you know what acts are considered sexual assault and what the penalties are for that crime? You will after today.

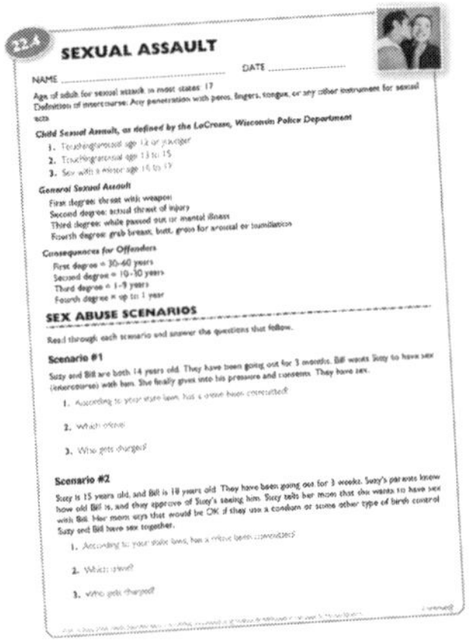

22.4

HANDOUT 22.4

Try to arrange for a guest speaker from your local police department to give a presentation on sexual assault. Discuss the difference between child sexual assault and general sexual assault. Have the students evaluate the three following scenarios and discuss their responses. (Although the age of an adult for sexual assault is 17 in most states, the age varies from state to state. You should learn the age for your state.)

Sex Abuse Scenarios

Scenario #1

1. yes
2. second-degree sexual assault of a minor
3. both

Scenario #2

1. yes
2. second-degree sexual assault of a minor
3. Bill

Scenario #3

1. yes
2. second-degree general assault
3. Bill

CLOSURE

The law recognizes that young people are not capable of making adult decisions, so the penalty for having sex with a child is the most severe in the books. Forcing someone to have sex or taking advantage of a person because of age or condition is clearly wrong. Sexual assault can affect a person mentally and physically for the rest of his or her life. It can ruin the person's chances of ever having an intimate adult relationship. Make sure that you know the law.

Teenage Pregnancy Choices

OBJECTIVE

Students will become aware of the seriousness of an unplanned pregnancy by doing a problem-solving strategy situation.

NATIONAL STANDARDS

- #1 Health Promotion
- #5 Decision Making

INTRODUCTION

Every year around 1 million teenagers become pregnant out of wedlock. This situation is a tragedy for an educated society and poses many problems for the teenagers and the future of the baby. Raising children is difficult for all parents, especially if the parents are themselves children. Today we will examine the effect of an unplanned pregnancy and the problems that can result from this bad choice.

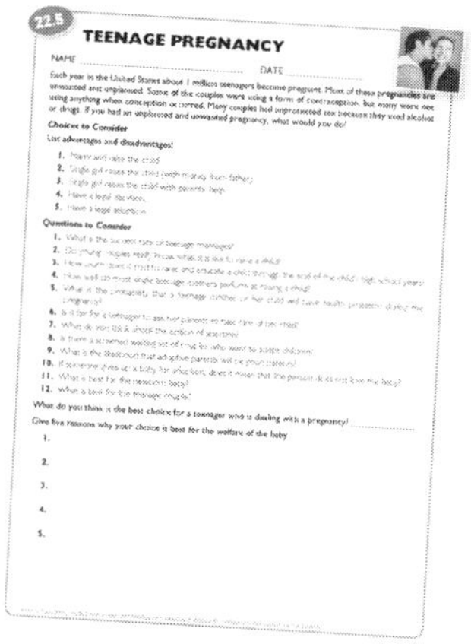

22.5

HANDOUT 22.5

Teenage Pregnancy

Help the students get a feeling for what an unplanned pregnancy would be like for them.

Questions to Consider

1. Very low (less than 10%).
2. Most do not.
3. Average $200,000 through high school.
4. They struggle with no income.
5. The risk for a young teenager increases 38%.
6. No, it is not—they already raised their kids.
7. Carefully monitor this open discussion. Allow all viewpoints. You may not want to discuss this issue in your classroom.
8. Yes. The waiting list is now up to 10 years for a healthy child and 1 month for an unhealthy child.
9. They have the same success rate as other families.
10. You are doing what is best for your child, a choice that shows great love!
11. The adoption process is often best.
12. They should make that decision only after considering all the factors!

Have the students choose an option, write it down, and list the five best reasons for making that choice about pregnancy. Tally the scores from a show of hands.

National Statistics: Teenage Pregnancy Choices

Share the following statistics with your class. Out of 100 pregnancies:

50 gave birth (most kept the child),

34 had abortions, and

16 had miscarriages.

CLOSURE

It is interesting that most teenage mothers choose to keep the baby. Raising a child is a formidable task, even for an adult. Some teenagers think that having a baby is the most important thing in life and do not want to give the baby up because they fear that no one else will ever really love them. This is an unfortunate scenario. Terminating a baby because of your mistake does not seem right either. Almost all choices have serious consequences. Maybe you will think before you have unprotected sex!

Contraceptive Techniques

OBJECTIVE

Students will be able to examine the latest contraceptive measures after hearing a guest speaker on the subject.

NATIONAL STANDARDS

- #1 Health Promotion
- #5 Decision Making

INTRODUCTION

In the United States today about 50% of all teenagers are having sexual intercourse by age 16, which is before the age of consent according to the law in many states. Regardless, at some point in your life you will likely be having a loving relationship that involves sex. Almost all couples choose a method of preventing pregnancies for a variety of reasons. Look at the list and see how many of these reasons are good reasons for limiting or spacing children.

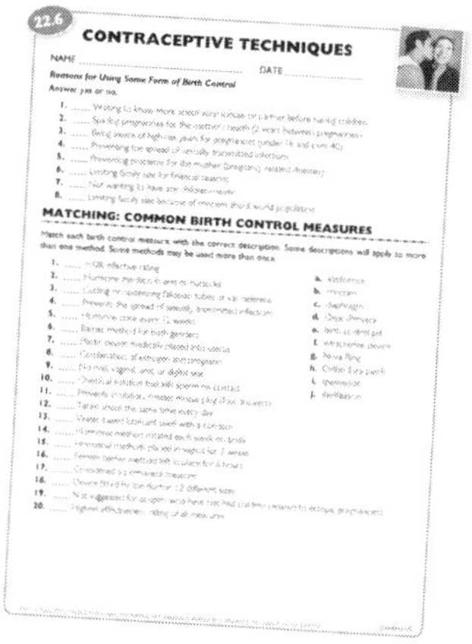

22.6

HANDOUT 22.6

Introduce the guest speaker.

Contraceptive Techniques

Go over the list of contraceptive techniques and discuss the reasons for using birth control.

Matching: Common Birth Control Measures

Go over the material on the handout about birth control measures. A PowerPoint® presentation or a film with discussion is a good way to cover this information.

1. a	**6.** b	**11.** d, e, g, h	**16.** c
2. d	**7.** f	**12.** e	**17.** j
3. j	**8.** e	**13.** i	**18.** c
4. b	**9.** a	**14.** h	**19.** f
5. d	**10.** i	**15.** g	**20.** d

Contraceptive Questions

1. abstinence
2. Depo-Provera, birth control pill, Ortho Evra Patch
3. birth control pill
4. condom and spermicides
5. class vote to determine most common choice

CLOSURE

Some day all of us will be making educated choices about contraception. I hope that you will weigh the pros and cons of each measure and that you and your partner will make a good choice as a couple. At your age, however, if it all seems confusing and complicated, the choice is easy—be abstinent until you are emotionally ready to have a loving sexual relationship.

Conception Care Versus Birth Defects

OBJECTIVE

Students will be able to list the 10 major environmental factors that cause birth defects in the United States after a PowerPoint® presentation and discussion.

NATIONAL STANDARDS

- #1 Health Promotion
- #5 Decision Making

INTRODUCTION

True health care for a child begins at conception. Because that is the case, we need to analyze what people can do to help ensure that their baby will be physically and mentally healthy. We need to study two major factors: genetics and environmental factors. Let us see how much you really know about having healthy children.

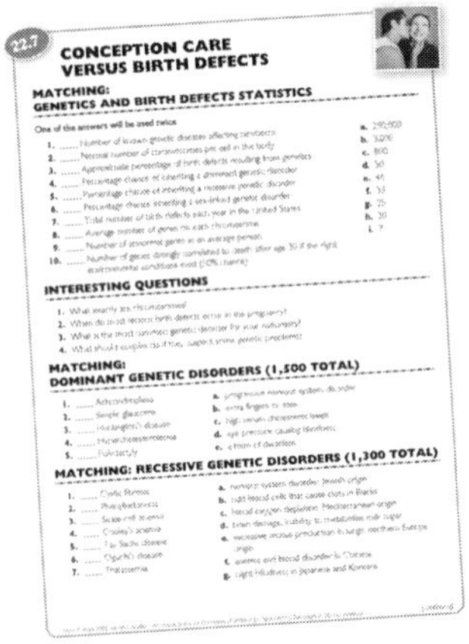

22.7

HANDOUT 22.7

Matching: Genetics and Birth Defects Statistics

1. b	**6.** d
2. e	**7.** a
3. f	**8.** c
4. d	**9.** h
5. g	**10.** i

Interesting Questions

1. blueprint of parents in a strand of DNA and protein in the nucleus of cells

2. first trimester (first 40 days)

3. see following section on recessive disorders

4. seek genetic counseling

Matching: Dominant Genetic Disorders

1. e
2. d
3. a
4. c
5. b

Matching: Recessive Genetic Disorders

1. e
2. d
3. b
4. c
5. a
6. g
7. f

Matching: X-Linked Disorders

1. d
2. e
3. a
4. b
5. c

Matching: Environmental Factors and Birth Defects

1. a
2. b
3. c
4. d
5. e
6. f
7. g
8. h
9. i
10. j

Matching: Birth Defects Vocabulary

1. k
2. a
3. f
4. j
5. c
6. i
7. g
8. d
9. b
10. h
11. e

Questions About Pregnancy

1. the first trimester (first 40 days)
2. not for almost a month—pretty late
3. alcohol
4. saunas, hot tubs, high fever over 102 °F (39 °C)
5. Say, "How important is a healthy child to you? Avoid high-risk behaviors!"
6. methylmercury, lead, and PCBs (fish); carbon monoxide and hydrocarbons (pollution)
7. syphilis, gonorrhea, herpes, german measles, toxoplasmosis, CMV, AIDS
8. vital and necessary
9. 25 to 30 years old
10. protein, folic acid, B-complex vitamins, vitamin A
11. at least 25 pounds (11 kilograms)
12. mother younger than 18 or older than 40

CLOSURE

What is more important to a couple than having a healthy baby? "Nothing" is what I hope you would say. Everyone should have a fair chance in this world. A child who starts out in life with a mental deficiency or physical abnormality is at a tremendous disadvantage. Give your child a healthy start by practicing healthy living from the time of conception.

Human Sexuality Test Key

HUMAN SEXUALITY TEST

TRUE OR FALSE: SEXUAL HEALTH ISSUES

MATCHING: COMMON SEXUALLY TRANSMITTED INFECTIONS

22.8

OBJECTIVE

Students will be able to pass a written test on sexual health care after the classroom unit.

NATIONAL STANDARDS

- #1 Health Promotion
- #7 Healthy Behaviors

INTRODUCTION

Complete this test and turn your answers in when you are finished.

HANDOUT 22.8

True or False: Sexual Health Issues

1. false—tend to have more negative consequences
2. true
3. false—Most STIs are either difficult to cure or incurable.
4. true
5. false—Abstinence is refraining from oral, digital, anal, or vaginal intercourse.
6. true
7. false—They are just the opposite.
8. false—It does affect how you feel about yourself.
9. true
10. true

Matching: Common Sexually Transmitted Infections

11. V
12. W
13. B
14. C, G
15. A
16. C, G
17. A
18. W
19. S
20. G
21. H
22. W
23. H
24. C

Short Answer: Sexual Assault Scenario

25. yes
26. second-degree sexual assault of a minor
27. Bill
28. yes
29. second-degree general assault
30. Bill

Matching: Environmental Factors and Birth Defects

31. d
32. b
33. a
34. c
35. e
36. e
37. d
38. c
39. b
40. a

Matching: Birth Defects Vocabulary

41. a
42. e
43. f
44. b
45. i
46. c
47. g
48. h
49. j
50. d

Short Answer

51. 17 (in most states; may be different in your state)
52. 55%
53. 13 million
54. abstinence
55. respect, responsibility, romance

CLOSURE

We will go over the test the next time we meet.

23

Love and Compassion

LOVE ALONE IS CAPABLE OF UNITING LIVING BEINGS IN SUCH A WAY AS TO COMPLETE AND FULFILL THEM BY JOINING THEM IN WHAT IS DEEPEST IN THEMSELVES.

Anonymous

Lesson Finder

Love Facts

OBJECTIVE

Students will analyze the progressions, stages, languages, and criteria for loving relationships.

NATIONAL STANDARDS

- #1 Health Promotion
- #4 Communication

INTRODUCTION

What do most people consider the single most important aspect of life and overall happiness? You are right—it is having loving relationships! This is one area that many people do not really understand. What is love?

1. The most mysterious of all feelings
2. The most difficult emotion to understand
3. An emotion impossible to control
4. A fragile emotion, yet the most powerful one
5. An emotion that one cannot live without

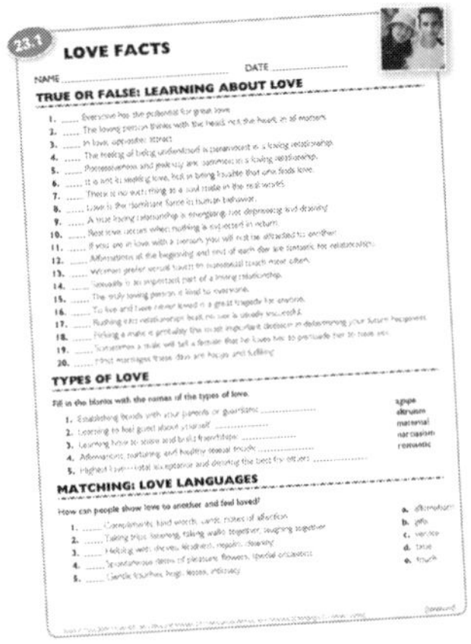

23.1

HANDOUT 23.1

True or False: Learning About Love

1. true
2. false—The loving person thinks with both heart and head.
3. false—Generally, this is not so true anymore.
4. true
5. false—They are common in infatuation.
6. true
7. false—There could be many soul mates for you.
8. true
9. true
10. true
11. false—People could still be attracted to some degree.
12. true
13. false—Women prefer nonsexual touch.
14. true
15. true
16. true
17. false—These relationships usually have a low success rate.
18. true
19. true
20. false—Approximately 50% of marriages end in divorce.

Types of Love

1. maternal
2. narcissism
3. altruism
4. romantic
5. agape

Matching: Love Languages

1. a
2. d
3. c
4. b
5. e

Matching: Happy and Successful Relationships

1. a
2. b
3. d
4. c
5. e

Pain in Relationships

1. Find what you do not want
2. Using flirting to avoid major commitment and the risk of pain
3. Hitting, drugs, negative attitude, fighting
4. Fear, hurt, lack of money, will not find anyone
5. 1 hour
6. Loss of focus and seeing only negative traits
7. Thinking with the heart; being kind, positive, thoughtful, and loving
8. Unconditional
9. Yes

CLOSURE

Love is the most wonderful aspect of life—feel it in your heart!

Love Languages

OBJECTIVE

Students will be able to determine their primary love language by completing the 10-question assessment.

NATIONAL STANDARD

#7 Healthy Behaviors

INTRODUCTION

There are innumerable ways to show people that you love them. These methods can be broken down into five general ways to show people that you love them. Today you will discover your primary love language.

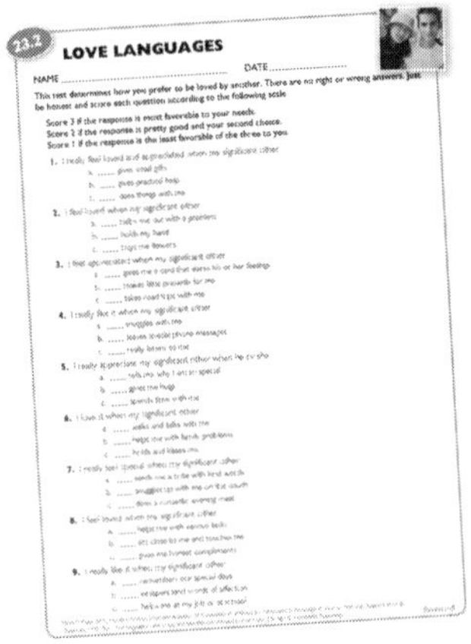
LOVE LANGUAGES

23.2

HANDOUT 23.2

Love Languages Test

Read the directions aloud and do the first one together. Then have the students complete the rest of the assessment. When they are done they must tally their scores in the grid. Have them indicate their primary love language and their least important love language on the board. By having them do this, you know when they are done and the entire class can see where they stand.

Questions to Ponder

In order to be loving, students must ascertain the love language of their significant other. Then they must try to use the love language that means the most to that person.

CLOSURE

Discovering your primary love language will give you an idea of what you believe is really important. Remember that each person has his or her own priorities when it comes to being loved. Learn to practice all five love languages and see which ones work best for you.

Love Definition and Insights

OBJECTIVE

Students will be able to write their own definition of love after reading some definitions and studying some great insights into true love.

NATIONAL STANDARD

#5 Decision Making

INTRODUCTION

Today you are going to take time to read some thoughts about love, written by people who have dreamed about this need over the years. This activity is meant to inspire you to write a poem or definition of love in your own words. Your poem or essay must be at least 10 sentences in length. Write it only after you have read the five definitions of love.

HANDOUT 23.3

Give the students time to read the definitions and come up with some phrases and sentences that they would like to use in their own poems or definitions.

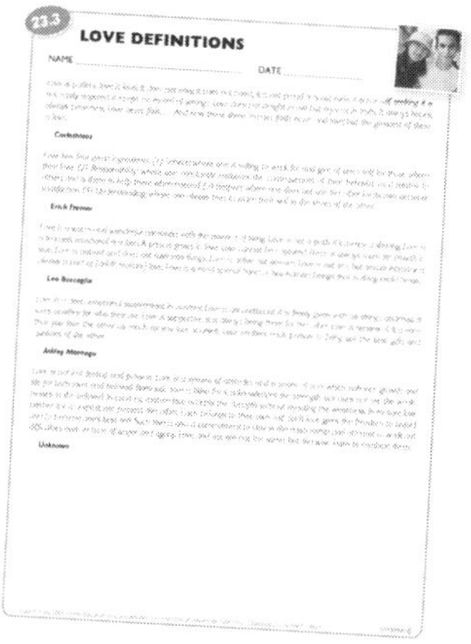
23.3 LOVE DEFINITIONS
NAME DATE

23.3

HANDOUT 23.4

Students can create a poster from the handout "Love Insights" to earn extra credit.

23.4 LOVE INSIGHTS
NAME DATE

23.4

CLOSURE

Defining love is difficult, but you should try to come up with a working definition for your life. The study of love is both interesting and challenging!

Love and Romance Talk

OBJECTIVE

Students will be able to have an open discussion about love in their life and list some great romancing ideas.

NATIONAL STANDARDS

- #1 Health Promotion
- #4 Communication

INTRODUCTION

Today is a good day to talk about love. I am curious about what you know and what you think.

This activity has no right or wrong answers. We are going to ask your thoughts and opinions at this time in your life. I am sure that some of you have thought a lot about love and romance. Love is a big deal. Finding love is probably the most wonderful experience in this world.

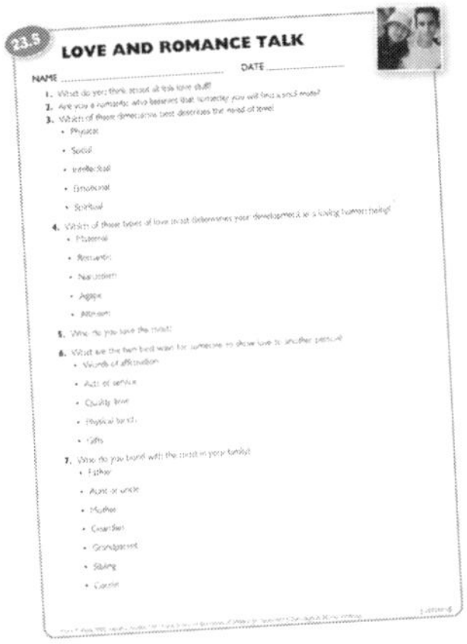
23.5
LOVE AND ROMANCE TALK
NAME
DATE

23.5

HANDOUT 23.5

Break the class into groups of about 10. Mix up the groups with males and females. In each group, have a student leader pick a question and answer it. Then, in a clockwise manner, every student answers that question. When all have responded to that question, the person next to the leader picks a question and answers it. The others then answer it. The process moves around the circle so that a different person starts every time. You can move around and spend time in each group.

Students can choose the questions in any order. They should pick interesting ones because they may not finish all the questions in one day.

CLOSURE

I hope that you all learned a lot from each other. Yes, love is a difficult topic, but by talking about it and learning about it you greatly increase your chances of finding it.

Happy and Successful Relationships

OBJECTIVE

Students will be able to list the key ingredients needed in a significant other in order to have a happy and successful relationship.

NATIONAL STANDARDS

- #1 Health Promotion
- #5 Decision Making

INTRODUCTION

Would you like to know the key factors to having happy and successful relationships? That is what today's class is all about.

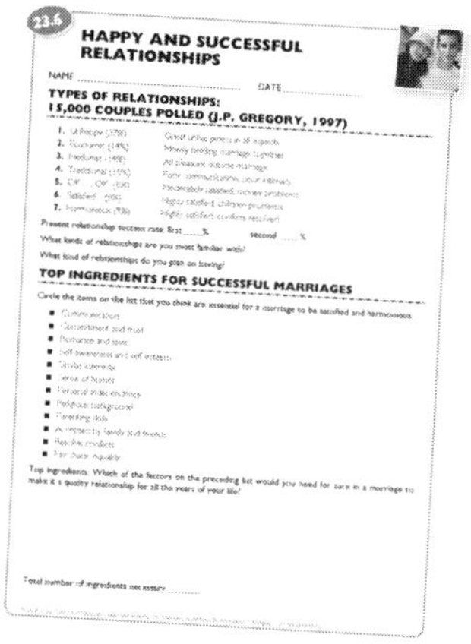
HAPPY AND SUCCESSFUL RELATIONSHIPS

TYPES OF RELATIONSHIPS: 15,000 COUPLES POLLED (J.P. GREGORY, 1997)

TOP INGREDIENTS FOR SUCCESSFUL MARRIAGES

23.6

HANDOUT 23.6

Types of Relationships

1. First marriages: 50%
   Second marriages: 35%
2. Discuss the types of relationships that they are most familiar with.
3. What do they want?
   Have an open discussion.

Top Ingredients for Successful Marriages

All students must share with the class the total number of qualities that they would need from the list for their marriage to succeed. A discussion should follow.

CLOSURE

You should know what you need in another person to have a happy and harmonious relationship. The list that you compiled is specific to you. Knowing what you need can increase your chances of having a great relationship someday.

Love Project

OBJECTIVE

Students will be able to make a love project that depicts their understanding of love at this point in their lives.

NATIONAL STANDARDS

- #5 Decision Making
- #3 Information and Services
- #8 Advocacy

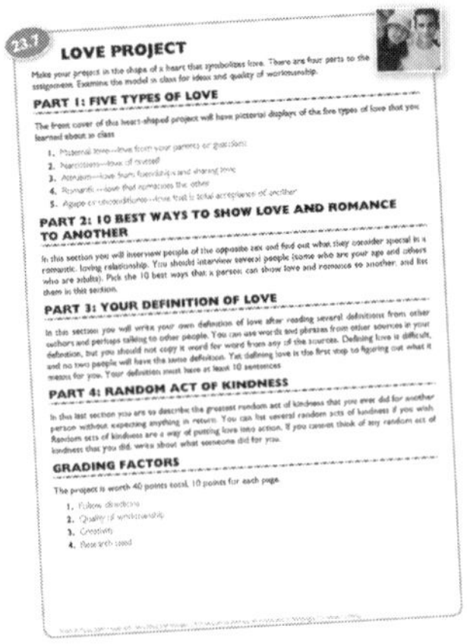

23.7

INTRODUCTION

Students over the years have really enjoyed doing this project. It is about the most important aspect of life: love. I hope that you find the project interesting and that you learn a lot by doing it. The classroom lessons should have prepared you for completing this project.

HANDOUT 23.7

Make a sample product for the students to study. Then go over the directions for how they should do the project. Give them some time in class to work on the project. You can then ensure that everyone gets started and makes progress each day.

CLOSURE

This assignment is worth a lot of points and is meant to be interesting and fun. Good luck and do a great job!

Love Test Key

OBJECTIVE

Students will be able to pass a written test on love and relationships after a unit of studying these.

NATIONAL STANDARDS

- #1 Health Promotion
- #7 Healthy Behaviors

INTRODUCTION

Complete this test on love and hand it in when you are finished.

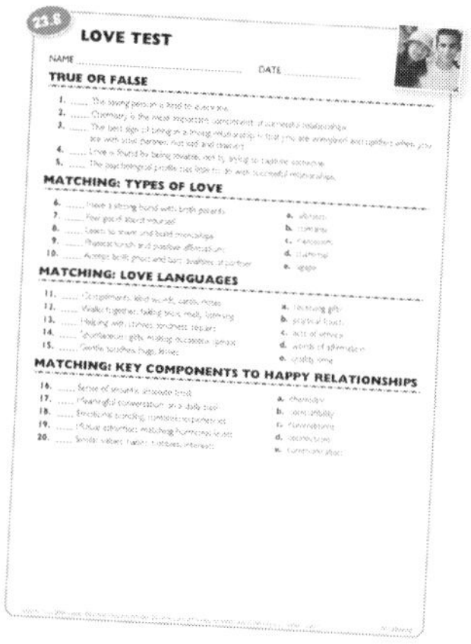
LOVE TEST
NAME
DATE
TRUE OR FALSE
MATCHING: TYPES OF LOVE
MATCHING: LOVE LANGUAGES
MATCHING: KEY COMPONENTS TO HAPPY RELATIONSHIPS

23.8

HANDOUT 23.8

True or False

1. true
2. false—Commitment and communication are the most important components.
3. true
4. true
5. false—You do need to have similar beliefs, ideas, and values.

Matching: Types of Love

6. d
7. c
8. a
9. b
10. e

Matching: Love Languages

11. d
12. e
13. c
14. a
15. b

Matching: Key Components to Happy Relationships

16. c
17. e
18. d
19. a
20. b

Short Answer

21. seek assistance
22. children, money, fear, hurt, will not find better relationship
23. 1 hour
24. unconditional

CLOSURE

We will go over the test during the next class meeting.

24

Aging and Death

> THERE IS A LAST CHAPTER IN LIFE, AND IT IS ONLY IN UNDERSTANDING DEATH THAT WE CAN FULLY UNDERSTAND LIFE. IT IS IN THE WINTER OF OUR LIVES THAT OUR EYES AND HEART WILL OPEN TO FIND MEANING AND PURPOSE, THUS LIVING LIFE TO OUR FULLEST POTENTIAL.
>
> **R.F. Puza**

Lesson Finder

Aging and Death Facts

OBJECTIVE

Students will be able realize from a multifaceted teacher-led discussion that aging and death are important aspects of life that they should understand.

NATIONAL STANDARDS

- #1 Health Promotion
- #5 Decision Making
- #4 Communication

INTRODUCTION

Most people fear the important final chapter of life. The process of aging and the prospect of dying scare most people. After we discuss the facts, you may have a better understanding of aging and death. It is said, "You will not understand life, until you understand death."

AGING AND DEATH FACTS
TRUE OR FALSE: GERIATRICS AND THANATOLOGY
MATCHING: DEATH VOCABULARY

24.1

HANDOUT 24.1

True or False: Geriatrics and Thanatology

1. false—It is the study of death.
2. true
3. false—Funerals are for the living.
4. true
5. true
6. true
7. false—They can be valuable assets.
8. false—It depends on how you prepare for retirement and your general health.

Matching: Death Vocabulary

1. n	**7.** d	**13.** p
2. q	**8.** b	**14.** k
3. o	**9.** e	**15.** r
4. f	**10.** h	**16.** i
5. l	**11.** c	**17.** a
6. j	**12.** m	**18.** g

Matching: Psychological Stages of Dying

1. d
2. a
3. c
4. e
5. b

Matching: Stages of Death

1. d
2. e
3. c
4. a
5. b

Matching: Body Disposal

1. c
2. a
3. b
4. d
5. e

Matching: Teenage Deaths

1. a
2. c
3. e
4. b
5. d

Matching: Acceptance of Death

1. e
2. d
3. c
4. a
5. b

Functions of the Funeral

a. recognition by family and friends of the person's death; finality and closure
b. time for grieving and sorrow
c. support for family of deceased

Have students write four things that they want people to say about them after their death. Then have students write their own epitaph—their last words about life.

CLOSURE

We have gone over lots of information about the process of aging and death. I hope that the discussion today helped you understand this last process of life. Remember: If you don't understand death, you will not understand life.

Basic Concepts of Aging

OBJECTIVE

Students will be able to list the major concepts of aging following a classroom discussion.

NATIONAL STANDARDS

- #1 Health Promotion
- #5 Decision Making

INTRODUCTION

A large part of the population today is made up of baby boomers, those who were born in the years following World War II. These people are now nearing retirement age. What is the best approach to understanding and dealing with the elderly in society? First, we need to analyze the facts concerning aging.

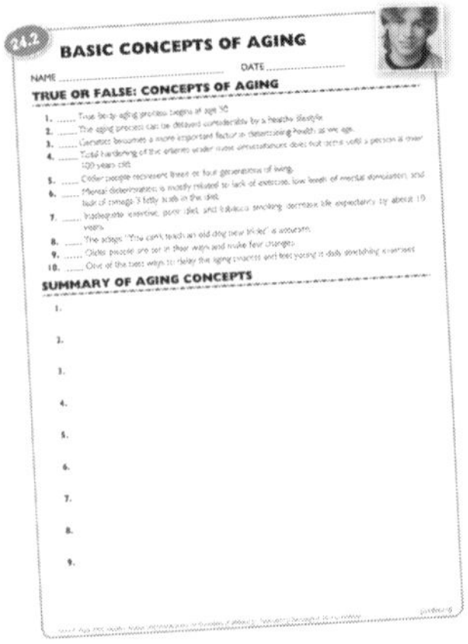
24.2 BASIC CONCEPTS OF AGING

TRUE OR FALSE: CONCEPTS OF AGING

SUMMARY OF AGING CONCEPTS

24.2

HANDOUT 24.2

True or False: Concepts of Aging

1. false—Cell growth begins to slow at age 30.
2. true
3. true
4. false—It usually occurs between ages 80 and 90.
5. true
6. true
7. false—They decrease it by closer to 20 years.
8. false—Older people can and do learn things, just not as fast
9. false—There are a great many changes that older people have to deal with.
10. true

Summary of Aging Concepts

Complete the summary section on aging together. What are the true concepts of aging?

1. Aging is reality and begins around age 30 when cell growth begins to slow.
2. Aging varies as people age at different rates due to lifestyle and other factors.
3. Genetics affects us.
4. Elderly are valuable.
5. Maximum 120, although the record for oldest person is age 126.
6. Represent all generations.
7. Use it or lose it.
8. Lifestyle is key.
9. Elderly can learn.
10. Many changes occur.
11. Golden is good.
12. Acceptance is necessary.

Checklist: Golden Years

How many of the items on the checklist are your parents or guardians doing in their lives? _____

How many of these are your grandparents doing currently? _____

Extra Credit: Senior Citizen Interview

Have students interview senior citizens and share their responses with the class.

CLOSURE

The aging process varies for each person, but people can do some things to make those golden years the best years of their lives. What are your elderly years going to be like?

Aging and Death Discussion

OBJECTIVE

Students will be able to share their thoughts and feelings on the topics of aging, dying, and death in a roundtable discussion.

NATIONAL STANDARDS

- #5 Decision Making
- #4 Communication

INTRODUCTION

Talking about aging and death is important because most people are afraid of those topics. But only by understanding aging and death can we live life to its highest potential. I learn a lot by hearing what you young folks think about aging and death. We can all learn from this discussion.

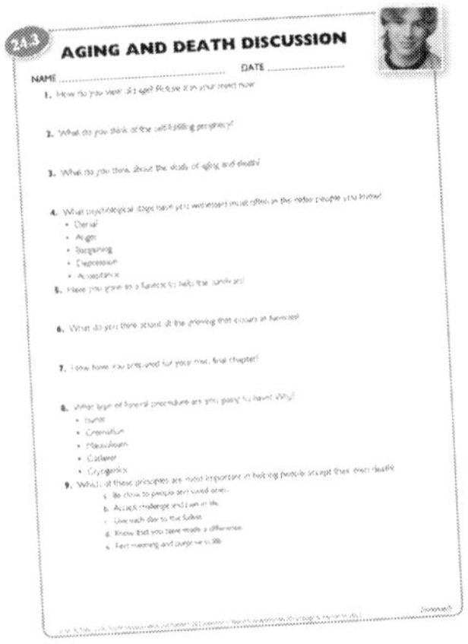

24.3

HANDOUT 24.3

Aging and Death Discussion

Break the class into two groups of about 15 each. Mix the students so that the discussion goes well. One student starts by picking any question and reading it aloud. The student answers that question, and afterward so will everyone else in the circle (going around clockwise). You should go from group to group and set the tempo for the activity.

CLOSURE

I hope that you all had interesting discussions. Most people avoid the topic of aging, dying, and death. We should try to understand this issue, not avoid it. Thank you for being so open and honest today.

Dealing With Death: *Tuesdays With Morrie*

OBJECTIVE

Students will be able to talk about life and death after watching *Tuesdays With Morrie*, a movie based on a true story about a college professor who was dying.

NATIONAL STANDARDS

- #1 Health Promotion
- #5 Decision Making

INTRODUCTION

A good movie that discusses the topic of aging and death is *Tuesdays With Morrie*, a film about a college professor who is dying from amyotrophic lateral sclerosis (ALS), also known as Lou Gehrig's disease. ALS is the most common motor neuron disease that causes muscle atrophy—over 30,000 Americans now have the disease. The book *Tuesdays With Morrie* was a bestseller for several years, and the movie came out later. I like to discuss the movie each day, answering questions as the movie goes along.

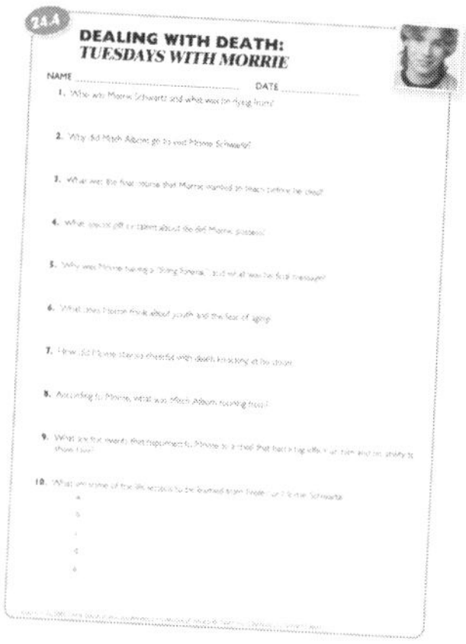
24.4
DEALING WITH DEATH: TUESDAYS WITH MORRIE
NAME DATE

24.4

HANDOUT 24.4

1. Morrie Schwartz was a college professor who was dying from Lou Gehrig's disease.
2. Morrie was dying. Mitch, once a student of Morrie's, had promised earlier to keep in touch. Janine, Mitch's girlfriend, helped.
3. Morrie wanted to teach Human Text, a course about living.
4. Morrie could understand life with incredible clarity.
5. He wanted to teach people to express their feelings to others before it becomes too late.
6. He thought it reflects on those who have not matured or found meaning in life.
7. He accepted his own finality.
8. Mitch was running from fear of commitment and fear of problems that come with relationships, such as divorce.
9. Morrie's mother died. His father wouldn't talk about her. His stepmother taught him love.
10. Life lessons:
    - Love is the only rational act. Let it come in.
    - Dying is bad. So is living unhappily.
    - If you know how to die, you know how to live.
    - We must love one another or die.
    - Touch people while alive. Make a difference.
    - Forgive everybody for everything.
    - Are you living the life that you really want to live?

CLOSURE

Although this unit marks the end of class, it is not the end of health or life. We have many lessons to learn. Get your life in order. Make sure to get your priorities straight. Live well, laugh often, love much, and learn daily.

Aging and Death Test Key

OBJECTIVE

Students will be able to pass a written test on aging and death after a unit of study.

NATIONAL STANDARDS

- #1 Health Promotion
- #7 Healthy Behaviors

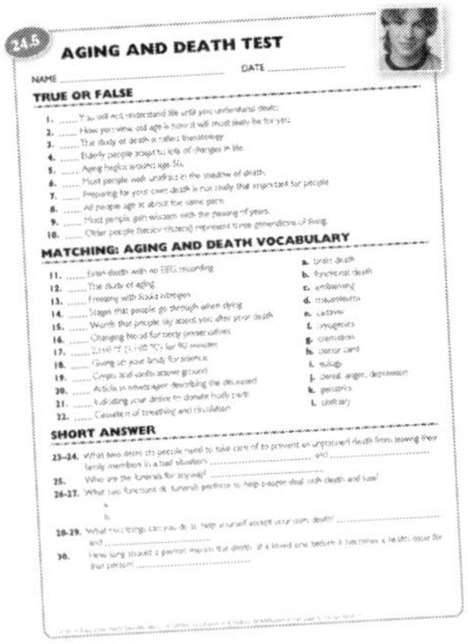
AGING AND DEATH TEST
TRUE OR FALSE
MATCHING: AGING AND DEATH VOCABULARY
SHORT ANSWER

24.5

INTRODUCTION

Take your time and hand in the test once you have finished answering the questions.

HANDOUT 24.5

True or False

1. true
2. true
3. true
4. true
5. false—Aging begins around age 30.
6. false—Many people are afraid of death.
7. false—It is very important.
8. false—The rate of aging can depend on various factors, such as lifestyle.
9. true
10. true

Matching: Aging and Death Vocabulary

11. a
12. k
13. f
14. j
15. i
16. c
17. g
18. e
19. d
20. l
21. h
22. b

Short Answer

23–24. life insurance; will
25. living relatives
26–27. grieving and closure; support family
28–29. find meaning and purpose and be close to people; make a difference and live life fully
30. 2 years maximum

CLOSURE

We will go over this test when we meet together next class time.

References and Resources

Adams, Patch. 1998. *Gesundheit*. Rochester, VT: Healing Arts Press.

Aero, Rita, and Elliot Weiner. 1983. *The Brain Game*. New York: William Morrow.

Bickel, Bruce, and Stan Jantz. 2002. *God Is in the Small Stuff*. Uhrichsville, OH: Barbour.

Blanchard, Bob, and Melinda Blanchard. 2005. *Live What You Love*. New York: Sterling.

Blyth, Laureli. 2002. *Brain Power*. New York: Barnes and Noble.

Bottom Line Personal. 2004. *Total Health and Wellness*. Stamford, CT: Boardroom.

Bowman, Sharon. 1999. *Shake, Rattle and Roll*. Glenbrook, NV: Bowperson.

Brantley, Jeffery, and Wendy Millstine. 2005. *Five Good Minutes: 100 Morning Practices for Calm and Focus*. Oakland, CA: New Harbinger.

Brewer, Sarah. 2000. *Simply Relax*. Berkeley, CA: Ulysses Press.

Burgess, Ron. 2000. *Laughing Lessons*. Minneapolis: Free Spirit.

Buscaglia, Leo. 1994. *Born for Love*. New York: Ballantine Books.

Carlson, R. and K. Carlson. 1999. *Don't Sweat the Small Stuff in Love*. New York: Hyperion.

Chapman, Gary. 1995. *The Five Love Languages: How to Express Heartfelt Commitment to Your Mate*. Chicago: Northfield Publishing.

Clark, Carolyn Chambers. 1997. *Creating a Climate for Power Learning*. Duluth, MN: Whole Person Associates.

Courage Books. 2002. *Secrets of Serenity*. Philadelphia: Running Press Book.

Craze, Richard. 2001. *Chillout: 100 Creative Ways to Relax*. Naperville, IL: Sourcebooks.

Duncan, K., and A. Akers. 1996. *Amusing Grace: Humor to Heal*. Knoxville, TN: Seven Worlds.

Eliopoulous, Charlotte. 2004. *Invitation to Holistic Health: A Guide to Living a Balanced Life*. Sudbury, MA: Jones and Bartlett.

Fahlman, Clyde. 1997. *Laughing Nine to Five*. Portland, OR: Steelhead Press.

Fine Communications. 1994. *More Random Acts of Kindness*. New York: MFJ Books.

Fraser, Tara. 2001. *Total Yoga*. London: Thorson.

Friedman, Scott. 1997. *Using Humor for a Change*. Saratoga Springs, NY: Humor Project.

George, Mike. 1998. *Learn to Relax*. San Francisco: Chronicle Books.

Godek, Gregory J.P. 1997. *Love: The Course They Forgot to Teach You in School*. Naperville, IL: Casablanca Press.

Goodman, Joel. 1995. *Laffirmations*. Deerfield Beach, FL: Health Communications.

Graimes, Nicola. 2004. *Healing Foods*. Bath, UK: Parragon.

Hales, Diane. 2003. *An Invitation to Health*. Belmont, CA: Wadsworth/Thomson Learning.

Hallmark Cards. 2002. *50 Things That Really Matter*. Emmaus, PA: Rodale.

Hensrud, Donald. 2006. *The Mayo Clinic Plan: 10 Essential Steps to a Better Body and Healthier Life*. New York: Time.

Hirschi, Gertrud. 2000. *Mudras: Yoga in Your Hands*. York Beach, ME: Samuel Weiser, Inc.

Hodgin, Michael. 1994. *1001 Humorous Illustrations for Public Speaking*. Grand Rapids, MI: Zondervan.

Horn, Sam. 1996. *Tongue Fu!* New York: St. Martin's Press.

Iyengar, B.K.S. 1990. *Yoga: The Iyengar Way*. New York: Dorling Kindersley Books.

Jaye, Aye. 1998. *The Golden Rule of Schmoozing*. Naperville, IL: Sourcebooks.

Kasl, Charlotte Davis. 1999. *Finding Joy*. New York: HarperCollins.

Kingma, Daphine Rose. 1991. *True Love*. York Beach, ME: Conari Press.

Klein, Alan. 1989. *The Healing Power of Humor*. New York: Penguin Putnam.

Kostick, Anne, Charles Fosgrover, and Michael Pellowski. 1998. *3650 Jokes, Puns, and Riddles*. New York: Black Dog and Leventhal.

Kroehnert, Gary. 1991. *100 Training Games*. Sydney: McGraw-Hill.

Kubler-Ross, Elisabeth. 1984. *On Death and Dying*. New York: Scribner's.

Lenehan, Arthur F. 1994. *The Best of Bits and Pieces*. Fairfield, NJ: Economics Press.

Love, Patricia. 2001. *The Truth About Love*. New York: Simon and Schuster.

MacHale, Des. 2005. *Lovers' Wit*. London: Prion.

Maniatis, Amy, Elizabeth Weil, and Natasha Bondy. 2006. *Love Notes*. San Francisco: Chronicle Books.

Martinet, Jeanne. 1992. *The Art of Mingling*. New York: St. Martin's Press.

McGraw, Phillip C. 1999. *Life Strategies*. New York: Hyperion.

Morley, Carol, and Liz Wilde. 2001. *Detox: 100 Ways to Cleanse and Purify*. London: MQ Publications Ltd.

Morreall, John. 1997. *Humor Works*. Amherst, MA: HRD Press.

Nelson, Bob. 1994. *1001 Ways to Reward Employees*. New York: Workman.

Oliver, Joan Duncan. 2005. *Happiness: How to Find It and Keep It*. London: Duncan Baird.

Peck, M. Scott. 2003. *Abounding Happiness: A Treasury of Wisdom*. Kansas City, MO: Andrews & McMeel.

Paull, Candy. 2006. *The Art of Abundance*. New York: Stewart, Tabori, and Chang.

Phillips, Bob. 1992. *Encyclopedia of Good Clean Jokes*. Eugene, OR: Harvest House.

Powell, John. 1990. *Happiness Is an Inside Job*. Allen, TX: Tabor.

Pratt, Steven, and Kathy Matthews. 2003. *Super Foods: 14 Foods That Will Change Your Life*. New York: HarperCollins.

Puza, Roger F. 1980. The Effectiveness of an Emotional Health Unit on the Self-Esteem of Seventh Grade Students. Master's thesis, University of Wisconsin-LaCrosse.

Reader's Digest. 1997. *Laughter, The Best Medicine*. Pleasantville, NY: Reader's Digest Association.

Rechtschaffen, Stephan, and Marc Cohen. 1999. *Vitality and Wellness*. New York: Dell.

Resnick, Stella. 1997. *The Pleasure Zone*. Berkeley, CA: Conari Press.

Rose, Ed. 1998. *Presenting and Training with Magic*. New York: McGraw-Hill.

Ryan, M.J. 2000. *365 Health and Happiness Boosters*. Berkeley, CA: Conari Press.

Samara, Cal, and Rose Samara. 1997. *Holy Humor*. Nashville, TN: Nelson.

Savant, Marilyn vos, and Leonore Fleischer. 1991. *Brain Building in Just 12 Weeks*. New York: Bantam Books.

Schueneman, Martha. 2004. *The Calorie, Carbohydrate, and Cholesterol Directory*. Edison, NJ: Chartwell Books.

Schwartz, Andrew E. 1995. *Guided Imagery for Groups*. Duluth, MN: Whole Person Associates.

Serebriankoff, Victor. 1998. *How Intelligent Are You?* New York: Barnes and Noble.

Shanahan, John M. 1999. *The Most Brilliant Quotes of All Time*. New York: HarperCollins.

Sivananda Yoga Vedanta Center. 1998. *Yoga: Mind and Body*. New York: DK Books.

Shade, Richard A. 1996. *License to Laugh*. Englewood, CO: Teachers Ideas Press.

Shaw, Beth. 2001. *YogaFit*. Champaign, IL: Human Kinetics.

Smollin, Anne Bryan. 1999. *Tickle Your Soul*. Notre Dame, IN: Sorin Books.

St. James, Elaine. 2001. *Simplify Your Life*. New York: MJF Books.

Streiker, Lowell D. 1998. *An Encyclopedia of Humor*. Peabody, MA: Hendrickson.

Time Life Books Editors. 1993. *Mind and Brain*. Alexandria, VA: Time Life Books.

Urban, Hal. 2003. *Life's Greatest Lessons*. New York: Simon and Schuster.

Westheimer, Ruth K. 2004. *52 Lessons on Communicating Love*. Boulder, CO: Blue Mountain Press.

Worth, Yvonne. 2004. *60 Day Fitness Plan*. Bath, UK: Parragon.

About the Author

Roger Puza, MS, is a school consultant, curriculum writer, and university professor with more than 30 years of health education experience at the middle school, high school, and college levels. He was the health coordinator for the LaCrosse, Wisconsin, school district where he wrote the entire health curriculum. He also participated in writing state standards as a member of Wisconsin's Model Academic Task Force.

Mr. Puza earned his master's degree in health education from the University of Wisconsin at LaCrosse. He has been involved in AHPERD for many years as a presenter and leader. In 1996, he earned WAHPERD's Wisconsin Health Educator Award. Mr. Puza is a lifetime learner of health and a positive role model.

HOW TO USE THIS CD-ROM

SYSTEM REQUIREMENTS

You can use this CD-ROM on either a Windows®-based PC or a Macintosh computer.

Windows

- IBM PC compatible with Pentium® processor
- Windows® 98/2000/XP/Vista
- Adobe Reader® 8.0
- Microsoft® PowerPoint® Viewer 97 (included)
- 4x CD-ROM drive

Macintosh

- Power Mac® recommended
- System 10.4 or higher
- Adobe Reader®
- Microsoft® PowerPoint® Viewer OS9 or OS10 (included)
- 4x CD-ROM drive

USER INSTRUCTIONS

Windows

1. Insert the *Health Education Ideas and Activities: 24 Dimensions of Wellness for Adolescents* CD-ROM. (Note: The CD-ROM must be present in the drive at all times.)
2. Select the "My Computer" icon from the desktop.
3. Select the CD-ROM drive.
4. Open the "Start.pdf" file.

Macintosh

1. Insert the *Health Education Ideas and Activities: 24 Dimensions of Wellness for Adolescents* CD-ROM. (Note: The CD-ROM must be present in the drive at all times.)
2. Double-click the CD icon located on the desktop.
3. Open the "Start.pdf" file.

For customer support, contact Technical Support:

Phone: 217-351-5076 Monday through Friday (excluding holidays) between 7:00 a.m. and 7:00 p.m. (CST).

Fax: 217-351-2674

E-mail: support@hkusa.com